Becoming Simple and Wise

Becoming
Simple and Wise

Moral Discernment in Dietrich Bonhoeffer's
Vision of Christian Ethics

Joshua A. Kaiser

◥PICKWICK *Publications* • Eugene, Oregon

BECOMING SIMPLE AND WISE
Moral Discernment in Dietrich Bonhoeffer's Vision of Christian Ethics

Copyright © 2015 Joshua A. Kaiser. All rights reserved. Except for brief quotations in critical publications or reviews, no part of this book may be reproduced in any manner without prior written permission from the publisher. Write: Permissions. Wipf and Stock Publishers, 199 W. 8th Ave., Suite 3, Eugene, OR 97401.

Pickwick Publications
An Imprint of Wipf and Stock Publishers
199 W. 8th Ave., Suite 3
Eugene, OR 97401

www.wipfandstock.com

ISBN 13: 978-1-62032-741-8

Cataloguing-in-Publication Data

Kaiser, Joshua A.

    Becoming simple and wise : moral discernment in Dietrich Bonhoeffer's vision of Christian ethics / Joshua A. Kaiser.

    xiv + Y p. ; 23 cm. Includes bibliographical references and index(es).

    ISBN 13: 978-1-62032-741-8

    1. Bonhoeffer, Dietrich, 1906–1945. 2. Discernment (Christian theology). 3. Theology, Practical—Germany—History—20th century. I. Title.

BX4827.B57 K33 2015

Manufactured in the U.S.A.   04/13/2015

New Revised Standard Version Bible, copyright 1989, Division of Christian Education of the National Council of the Churches of Christ in the United States of America. Used by permission. All rights reserved.

For Becky, my steadfast companion

Contents

Preface | ix

Acknowledgments | xi

Abbreviations | xiii

1 Introduction | 1
2 The Problem of Moral Discernment | 20
3 The Christological Foundation of Discernment | 56
4 Christian Formation and the Practice of Discernment | 77
5 The Simplicity of Discernment | 120
6 The Penultimate Context of Discernment | 154
7 Conclusion | 181

Bibliography | 187

Index | 195

Preface

THIS BOOK IS A revision of my doctoral dissertation completed at the University of Edinburgh in 2011. At that time I believed my research on Bonhoeffer and moral discernment to be significant because no one had yet explored Bonhoeffer's understanding of discernment and because the practice of moral discernment had not received adequate attention within the field of theological ethics. In my mind this assessment remains accurate; thus, in revising the dissertation for publication, I have chosen not to radically alter the original study, but instead to reorganize and clarify certain elements of the text so that the current book exists as a clearer and more succinct presentation of the original research. It is my hope that the contents of the book will be valuable for those interested in Bonhoeffer and in moral discernment, although it will be left to the reader to determine both the merits and shortcomings of the book and to help discover new avenues for further exploration in the field of Bonhoeffer studies.

Joshua A. Kaiser

South Bend, Indiana
August 2014

Acknowledgments

DURING THE COURSE OF writing my doctoral dissertation and revising it into its present book form I received gracious assistance and encouragement from many people, both inside and outside the academic community. It turns out that completing a dissertation and transforming it into a book are not solitary exercises, but depend for their success on a large community of people.

My thanks go to Oliver O'Donovan, my primary academic supervisor at the University of Edinburgh, who helped me see my dissertation project through to the end, and in the process, helped me become a more capable and competent researcher. My thanks also go to my secondary supervisor, Paul Nimmo, who provided important insight, encouragement, and perspective at key moments during the dissertation process. Particular thanks go to Michael Northcott and Bernd Wannenwetsch, who acted as examiners at my *viva voce* and gave feedback that helped me revise the dissertation into a more accessible book, and to Lisa Dahill, Christiane Tietz, Stephen Plant, Tom Greggs, and Philip Ziegler, who each provided helpful feedback and answers to questions at various stages of my research. I am also indebted to Ian Clausen and Nigel Zimmermann, who read through my original dissertation before submission, and to Michael Mawson, who was kind enough to read through a draft of the book manuscript. I am extremely thankful to other friends at the University of Edinburgh—Ryan Gladwin, Richard Davis, Matthew Arbo, and Scott Manor—who provided the necessary camaraderie to help me persevere through my research. Finally, I am grateful to the University of Edinburgh, the Sir Richard Stapley Educational Trust, the Deutscher Akademischer Austausch Dienst, and

Acknowledgments

Reedwood Friends Church for financial support during the original research for this project.

No less important to the completion of this project were my parents, Rod and Joan Kaiser, my parents-in-law, Var and Dorothea Artinian, and special friends, Irv and Shirley Brendlinger. Their prayers, encouragement, good wishes, and "scholarship" assistance often came at just the right moment to provide a boost to my spirits. There is also the special group of people who attend St. Martin of Tours Scottish Episcopal Church in Edinburgh: many of them provided support to me in more ways than they know.

Lastly, there is my wife Becky Artinian-Kaiser, who provided regular support as both a gifted academic and a caring spouse. Becky shared with me her editorial expertise when I had questions and provided encouragement when I was frustrated with my progress. It is a special blessing to have her as a life partner.

Abbreviations

DBWE   Bonhoeffer, Dietrich. *Dietrich Bonhoeffer Works*. 17 vols. Minneapolis: Fortress, 1996–2014. Cited by volume number and page number: e.g., DBWE 6:301.

DBW   Bonhoeffer, Dietrich. *Dietrich Bonhoeffer Werke*. 17 vols. Munich/Gütersloh: Chr. Kaiser/Gütersloher, 1986–99. Cited by volume number and page number: e.g., DBW 6:301.

CD   Barth, Karl. *Church Dogmatics*. 13 part vols. Edinburgh: T. & T. Clark, 1969–80. Cited by volume number and page number: e.g., CD 2/2:3.

1

Introduction

WHAT DOES IT MEAN for a Christian to discern God's will? Such a question implies that one does not simply know God's will, but must come to know it through a mental process of discriminating one option from another and determining the correct path amidst false alternatives and temptations. This practice of perception and discrimination describes what we mean when we speak of "discernment" in its most general sense. And taken in this most general sense, we can say that the question of discernment occupied the mind of Dietrich Bonhoeffer throughout a large portion of his adult life. He pursued it from the time of his first lecture on Christian ethics in 1929 until his death in 1945, often framing it in terms of how to hear God's commandment, how to perceive the form of Christ in the world, or how to recognize what Jesus wants to say to us today.[1] In *Ethics*, the collection of manuscripts offering the best window into his mature ethical thinking, he focuses this general line of inquiry on the simple question: what is the will of God?[2] For him, answering this question was central to the Christian life and required a process of moral discernment. It was not enough to rely on a depository of moral knowledge gained through universal ethical principles or static orders of creation; instead, one had to carefully discern God's will afresh on every new occasion in order to act faithfully. Thus, discernment was both spiritual and theological for Bonhoeffer, but also intensely practi-

---

1. For examples of Bonhoeffer's statements about hearing God's commandment, perceiving the form of Christ in the world, and considering what Jesus wants to say to us today, see DBWE 11:362–65; DBWE 6:99; DBWE 4:37.

2. DBWE 6:47, 75, 320–26.

cal, for it helped to facilitate everyday decisions and actions. In fact, as I will demonstrate in what follows, discernment lies at the heart of his vision of Christian ethics and illustrates its hidden unity.

The *concept* of discernment, however, is not present throughout his corpus, but emerges only at a late stage in his writing. He offers no systematic engagement with the concept, and his aversion to anything resembling "method" in Christian ethics makes him hesitant to speak in detail about the precise process of discernment. Moreover, running throughout his corpus is a strong emphasis on simple, unreflective obedience to Christ, which seems to pose challenges for any sort of mental process of discrimination whereby one comes to determine God's will. Perhaps the question "what is the will of God?" does *not* suggest any kind of rational deliberation after all. Could it be that the only answer to the question of discernment is simple faith in the immediate lucidity of God's direction, which demands either obedience or disobedience with no room for reflection in between? A closer reading of Bonhoeffer, however, suggests more complexity. There is a contrasting emphasis in his work on the importance of reason, wisdom, experience, and an accurate perception of reality. Thus, while he advocates a simple, unreflective approach to God's will, he also indicates the need for a rational, reflective moral deliberation that makes use of the best of human ability and recognizes its embedded place within the reality of the world. I will investigate this tension in his account during the course of this book and argue that the two contrasting emphases are not mutually exclusive. In fact, I will contend that his theology contains the necessary resources to incorporate, on Christological grounds, both simplicity and reflective moral deliberation into his concept of moral discernment. Furthermore, I will argue that this conceptual unity, premised on the relationship between Christ's two natures, becomes efficacious in the lives of Christians through a process of conformation to the form of Christ, which includes as an essential element the disciplined practice of spiritual exercises. Finally, I will demonstrate how simple obedience, while precluding self-centered moral reflection, nevertheless creates space for meditative reflection that understands reality through a Christological lens. In so doing, this meditative reflection finds its orientation in the natural, penultimate world, which serves as a crucial context and guide for those who want to discern God's will.

Introduction

Bonhoeffer as a Practitioner of Discernment

Throughout his life Bonhoeffer had many occasions, both common and extraordinary, to practice discernment. Early in his life he had to determine which career path he would pursue; later he had to decide whether a potential visit to Gandhi's ashram in India or a return to Germany to take charge of the Confessing Church seminary was more important; as war loomed over Europe in 1939, he had to make up his mind whether to remain in relative safety in the United States or to return to his homeland to be with his fellow Germans. As Lisa Dahill puts it:

> Bonhoeffer models a Christian life centered in ongoing, clear-sighted discernment in the midst of complex and ambiguous historical circumstances. His witness therefore demonstrates the tremendous power for good which can flow through a life well skilled in Christian discernment—as well as the risky courage in faithfulness into which its sustained practice draws a person.[3]

Discernment was far more than a theological concept for Bonhoeffer; it was a concrete practice central to his life as a Christian. It follows that his reflections on moral discernment throughout his writings, but particularly in *Ethics*, are not merely a product of theological curiosity, but a result of a deep conviction about the practical necessity of discernment within the Christian experience.

But here one must exercise caution because determining the precise relationship between Bonhoeffer's life and thought is one of the primary interpretive challenges for studies dealing with his theology. There are some scholars who believe a "biographical or narrative approach" to Bonhoeffer is indispensible.[4] If one does not understand Bonhoeffer's life experience or recognize the "autobiographical dimension" in his writing, a full understanding of his theology is impossible and one falls prey to what Thomas Day describes as the "common mistake of theologians . . . to suppose that the biographer has shown the contexts so that we [the theologians] may now zero in on texts."[5] Other scholars, however, advise caution when employing Bonhoeffer's life story too heavily as an interpretive aid, lest his

---

3. Dahill, "Probing the Will of God," 43.

4. De Gruchy, "Reception of Bonhoeffer's Theology," 97; Green, *Theology of Sociality*, 3.

5. Day, *Christian Community*, 109; cf. Green, *Theology of Sociality*, 3.

"enduring significance" be reduced to his "remarkable biography alone."[6] Worse, there exists the danger of committing a causal fallacy by interpreting Bonhoeffer's theological formulations as the direct result of specific life experiences or historical events.[7]

While in the present book I am careful to avoid an overreliance on Bonhoeffer's life story as an interpretive key to his theology, I also recognize the utility of drawing upon his biography in a limited and responsible manner to illustrate and explain some of his thoughts about moral discernment. Thus, it is fitting to offer a brief biographical sketch at the outset, with special emphasis on two important transitions in his life that have a direct bearing on the topic of discernment and to which I refer back at various points in the following chapters.[8] The first transition point occurs in late 1931 or early 1932, and changes the trajectory of his theological thinking regarding Christian discipleship, spiritual exercise, and obedience to God's commandment, and by extension, his thinking on discernment. The second transition takes place in 1939 and radically influences the course of his life from that point forward: it is particularly relevant because it offers special insight into his own process of discernment.

Bonhoeffer was born in 1906 and grew up in an upper middle class family, mostly in Berlin. He attended university first at Tübingen and then at Berlin where teachers such as Adolf von Harnack, Karl Holl, and Reinhold Seeberg stimulated his thinking.[9] This education did not, however, keep him from reading Karl Barth's theology, which had a greater influence

---

6. Floyd, "Bonhoeffer's Literary Legacy," 71.

7. Friesen makes such an error in his early study of Bonhoeffer's *Ethics* when he details how the events of 1940 provide direct insight into Bonhoeffer's manuscript "God's Love and the Disintegration of the World" (hereafter referred to as "God's Love"). Later research demonstrates that Bonhoeffer wrote "God's Love" in 1942 rather than 1940, suggesting that Friesen was too quick to interpret Bonhoeffer's theology through a biographical lens. See Friesen, "Comparative Analysis," 48ff. For evidence of the dating of Bonhoeffer's *Ethics* manuscripts, including "God's Love," see Tödt et al., "Editors' Afterword," 440–49; Tödt, "Appendix 2," 467–76.

8. For the best full-length account of Bonhoeffer's life, see Bethge's magisterial biography, *Dietrich Bonhoeffer*. For other insightful accounts of Bonhoeffer's life that serve as important supplements to Bethge's work, see Kelly and Nelson, *Moral Leadership*, 1–35; Marsh, *Strange Glory*; Schlingensiepen, *Dietrich Bonhoeffer*. Each of these works has informed the brief biographical sketch that follows.

9. For a good overview of the influence of Bonhoeffer's Berlin teachers, see Rumscheidt, "Significance," 201–24; Bethge, *Bonhoeffer*, 67–71.

INTRODUCTION

on his thought than that of his Berlin instructors.[10] During his time at university he established himself as a gifted academic as well as an independent and creative thinker, evidence of which one can see in his two doctoral dissertations, *Sanctorum Communio*, completed in 1927, and *Act and Being*, finished in 1930. In addition to his academic work, he also had his first taste of parish life in 1928-29 when he spent a year in Barcelona as an assistant pastor to a German-speaking congregation. This ministry experience confirmed his desire to pursue church work later on, although his academic ambitions nevertheless remained. After returning to Berlin for about a year and working as an academic assistant at the university, he left for a year of postdoctoral studies at Union Theological Seminary in New York in 1930-31, a move that would alter the course of his life.

While at Union, Bonhoeffer enjoyed many influential relationships, including friendships with the French pacifist Jean Lasserre and with fellow student Frank Fisher. Lasserre taught him a new way to think about Christ's commandments in the Sermon on the Mount. One could not be content merely to hear these commandments in faith; on the contrary, one needed to act upon them in obedience. Thus, the Sermon on the Mount was a call to a particular way of Christian life, which included as a central component the prohibition of violence. As Eberhard Bethge comments in regard to Lasserre's influence on Bonhoeffer: "after meeting Lasserre the question of the concrete reply to the biblical injunction of peace and of the concrete steps to be taken against warlike impulses never left him again."[11] Through his friendship with Frank Fisher, Bonhoeffer began attending Abyssinian Baptist Church, an African-American congregation in Harlem. Here he experienced authentic and lively Christian worship, rooted in the gospel. He also gained intimate knowledge of the racial struggle in the United States, an issue of immense practical importance that would take on a different form in his own country. These, and other experiences, eventually led to a decisive movement from being "not yet a Christian" to embracing the fullness of "the life of a servant of Jesus Christ."[12] Bethge referred to it as Bonhoeffer's transition from theologian to Christian, suggesting a shift

---

10. Pangritz's work provides a good starting point for exploring Barth's influence on Bonhoeffer; see, Pangritz, "'Within, not Outside,'" 245–82; Pangritz, *Karl Barth*.
11. Bethge, *Bonhoeffer*, 153; cf. DBWE 8:485–86.
12. DBWE 14:134.

from his largely academic interests in theology to a deep concern for and engagement with the life of the church.[13]

Bonhoeffer rarely spoke of this turning point and never gave it a precise date, although Bethge's observations regarding Bonhoeffer's increased church attendance and new attitude toward Scripture suggest a transformation having occurred by 1932.[14] What insight we do get from Bonhoeffer himself about the transformation comes from a letter he wrote years later. He recounts the following:

> But then something different came, something that has changed and transformed my life to this very day. For the first time, I came to the Bible. That, too, is an awful thing to say. I had often preached, I had seen a great deal of the church, had spoken and written about it—and yet I was not yet a Christian but rather in an utterly wild and uncontrolled fashion my own master. I do know that at the time I turned the cause of Jesus Christ into an advantage for myself, for my crazy vanity. I pray to God that will never happen again. Nor had I ever prayed, or had done so only very rarely. Despite this isolation, I was quite happy with myself. The Bible, especially the Sermon on the Mount, freed me from all this. Since then everything has changed. I have felt this plainly and so have other people around me. That was a great liberation. It became clear to me that the life of a servant of Jesus Christ must belong to the church, and step-by-step it became clearer to me how far it must go.[15]

The end of this passage makes clear that this transformation had the character of a gradual process, rather than a dramatic, revelatory moment that happened all at once. Moreover, Bonhoeffer's words throughout the passage reveal not just a change in theological attitude or a new conviction about a particular moral issue. On the contrary, he hints at a deep spiritual transformation, with both inward and outward manifestations.

---

13. One can find a slightly different interpretation of this event as a personal liberation from the problem of a powerful ego in Green, *Theology of Sociality*, 105–84 (esp. 105–7, 140–43).

14. For Bethge's comments on Bonhoeffer's transformation, including his attempt to date the experience, see Bethge, *Bonhoeffer*, 181–82, 203–4, 206. For Bethge's comparison between Bonhoeffer's transformation and Luther's "evangelical experience," the detail and dating of which is also difficult to determine, see ibid., 203.

15. DBWE 14:134. Bonhoeffer also notes in this letter that Christian pacifism, which he had previously questioned, "suddenly came into focus as something utterly self-evident."

Introduction

In particular, it is a transformation involving a new appreciation for the Bible and the Sermon on the Mount and a new sense of belonging to the church. He reflects on this new appreciation a few years later in a letter to his brother Karl-Friedrich. He writes that while theology had formerly been "more academic" for him, it now centered on his willingness "to take the Sermon on the Mount seriously."[16] Bethge elaborates on this in his own summary of the changes Bonhoeffer exhibited:

> Bonhoeffer now regularly attended church . . . He also practiced a meditative approach to the Bible that was obviously very different from the exegetical or homiletical use of it . . . He no longer spoke of oral confession merely theologically, but as an act to be practiced. This was unheard of in the church and academic circles in which he moved. He alluded increasingly to a communal life of obedience and prayer, which could perhaps renew the credibility of the individually isolated and privileged ministry . . . More and more frequently he quoted the Sermon on the Mount as a statement to be acted upon, not merely used as a mirror. He began taking a stand for Christian pacifism among his students and fellow clergy, although hardly anyone noticed at the time.[17]

Here, Bethge mentions Bonhoeffer's increased interest in the life of the church, his attention to spiritual exercises such as Bible meditation, oral confession, and prayer, and his new understanding of the Sermon on the Mount as an authoritative word demanding obedience. Bonhoeffer now had a sense that God could speak personally and directly to the individual. As one of his students remarked, commenting on a 1932 prayer meeting: "'[H]e [Bonhoeffer] said to us . . . that we should not forget that every word of Holy Scripture was a love letter from God directed very personally to us.'"[18] He also had a sense that one might best walk the way of discipleship, which centered on discerning God's voice and acting upon God's commandments, within the context of a disciplined, communal life. Some of these thoughts on discipleship and obedience begin to emerge in his writings as early as 1932.[19] In short, such emphases on the immediacy of God's word, the importance of community, and the practical nature of discipleship mark a significant change in Bonhoeffer, and remain part of his

16. DBWE 13:284–85; cf. Bethge, *Bonhoeffer*, 205.

17. Bethge, *Bonhoeffer*, 204.

18. Ibid. Bethge attributes this quotation to J. Kanitz via private communication in 1955; see ibid., 963n90.

19. See especially his lecture "Christ and Peace," DBWE 12:258–62.

thinking for the rest of his life.[20] Moreover, these changes contribute to the development of his thinking about discernment, as will become clear in the following chapters.

The second point of transition for Bonhoeffer comes much later in 1939 and once again corresponds to time spent in the United States. Of course, much had transpired between his return to Germany from Union Theological Seminary in 1931 and his second trip to the United States in 1939. During the early 1930s he was involved in several interrelated activities: teaching theology at the University of Berlin (out of which came his well known book *Creation and Fall*); advocating for peace through his association with the ecumenical movement; and ministering as a student chaplain, a preacher, and a confirmation class and youth club leader. In addition, he was deeply involved in the Confessing Church movement in Germany, which sought to oppose the German Christians who had acquiesced to the Nazi government. At stake were issues of authority (i.e., did the church owe her obedience to Christ alone or to other governing bodies as well?) and solidarity with the Jewish people (i.e., to what extent should the church oppose the unjust and inhumane policies of the Nazi government?). Bonhoeffer's deep convictions regarding the church situation and the treatment of the Jews in German society sometimes caused him to criticize even the Confessing Church for its failure to act boldly and decisively, and would eventually lead to the revocation of both his right to teach and to publish in Germany.

In late 1933, still near the beginning of the church struggle, he decided to leave Berlin and become a full-time parish minister for two German-speaking congregations in London. During this time he maintained his involvement in the German church struggle, and eventually returned to Germany in 1935 to take over as the director of the Confessing Church seminary, located first at Zingst and later at Finkenwalde. Living a disciplined, communal life with the seminarians and facilitating their training as ministers was one of the most significant experiences of his life; he reflects on these experiences in his book *Life Together*. Also notable during this time was his teaching on the Christian moral life, captured most fully in his book *Discipleship*. The Gestapo finally closed the seminary in 1937, which forced Bonhoeffer to find other means of working with the seminarians over the next few years. Meanwhile, his situation in Germany soon

---

20. For a persuasive account of how Bonhoeffer's year at Union influenced his thinking, see Pfeifer, "Learning Faith," 251–79; see also Marsh, *Strange Glory*, 101–35.

became more precarious. As war approached, the threat of his summons for military duty became imminent. He knew that if he were called up, he would have to refuse military service because of his theological conviction that Christ forbade war and called Christians to an ethic of peace. This would mean jail and probable execution, but more seriously in his mind, it would put his friends in the Confessing Church in jeopardy. The Nazi government would consider his personal refusal to serve as indicative of the Confessing Church's hostility toward the government and the nation and use it as an excuse for action. To avoid all of this, he eventually accepted an invitation to the United States to give a series of lectures and to do some teaching at Union. He left for New York in June 1939.

It is here that he experienced another decisive turning point in his life. While he had planned to stay in the United States for at least a year, he found himself returning to Germany just over a month later. Why the sudden reversal? From the diary he kept during his trip, we gain excellent insight into the inner struggle he experienced upon arriving in the United States.[21] Already on June 13, the morning after he arrived, he wrote about returning to Germany "after one year at the latest," noting that it was "entirely clear" to him that such a return trip was necessary.[22] Later that night, longing for the fellowship he enjoyed with his seminarians in Germany, he wrote: "I don't comprehend why I am here, whether it was sensible, whether the outcome will be worth it."[23] A few days later on June 15 he despairs again of having made a wrong decision. He writes: "The full force of self-reproaches about a wrong decision comes back up and is almost suffocating. I was filled with despair."[24] On June 16 he pens the following: "Disturbing political news from Japan. If turmoil now breaks out, I will definitely travel to Germany. I cannot be alone abroad. That is utterly clear to me. I do live over there, after all."[25]

At one point, Bonhoeffer even wonders if the intense homesickness he feels is a "sign from above" intended to guide him to a decision to return soon to Germany.[26] Indeed, prior to a decisive meeting on June 20, where he eventually turned down an offer to remain in the United States

21. DBWE 15:217–38.
22. Ibid., 220.
23. Ibid., 221–22.
24. Ibid., 222.
25. Ibid., 223.
26. Ibid., 228.

for at least three years as a pastor to German refugees, he longed for a sign indicating what he should do. In his own words, written on June 19: "I want to know how the work over there is going, whether all is going well or whether they need me. I want to have a hint from over there for tomorrow's decisive consultation."[27] Even after sharing his decision to return to Germany at the meeting on June 20, his mind remained unsettled and he wrote about feeling uncertainty about his resolution. His entry from June 20 reads: "It is strange that in all my decisions I am never completely clear about my motives. Is that a sign of lack of clarity, inner dishonesty, or is it a sign that we are *led* beyond that which we can discern, or is it both?"[28] He then writes out the daily texts from Isaiah 45:19 and 1 Peter 1:17, and continues with the following:

> The Daily Text today speaks with terrible severity of God's incorruptible judgment. God certainly sees how much personal concern, how much fear is contained in today's decision, as courageous as it may appear. The reasons that one puts forward to others and oneself for an action are certainly not sufficient. One can simply give reasons for anything. In the end one acts out of a level that remains hidden from us. Because of that one can only pray that God will wish to judge us and forgive us.[29]

While he had made the decision to return, the precise timing was still uncertain. But then, in a diary entry dated June 26, 1939, he mentions that he "happened to read" 2 Timothy 4:21, in which Paul closes the letter by writing to Timothy: "come before the winter."[30] Bonhoeffer immediately applied this verse to his own situation and believed that it might be telling him something about the timing of his return to Germany. In the final lines of his diary entry he writes: "'Come before the winter'—it is not a misuse of the Scripture if I allow this to be said *to me*. If God gives me the grace for that."[31] On June 28, two days after this experience reading the 2 Timothy text, he appears more certain about his course of action: "I cannot think that it is God's will that if war comes I should remain here without a particular assignment. I must leave at the first possible date."[32] And once again,

27. Ibid., 226.
28. Ibid., 227; Bonhoeffer's italics.
29. Ibid.
30. Ibid., 232.
31. Ibid.; Bonhoeffer's italics.
32. Ibid., 233.

when he is on the ship back home, he reflects that since the return journey began, "the internal tension about the future has stopped. I can think about the abbreviated time in America without reproach."[33]

Bonhoeffer would attempt to explain his decision in a letter to Reinhold Niebuhr:

> I have come to the conclusion that I have made a mistake in coming to America. I must live through this difficult period of our national history with the Christian people of Germany. I will have no right to participate in the reconstruction of Christian life in Germany after the war if I do not share the trials of this time with my people. My brothers in the Confessional Synod wanted me to go. They may have been right in urging me to do so; but I was wrong in going. Such a decision each man must make for himself. Christians in Germany will face the terrible alternative of either willing the defeat of their nation in order that Christian civilization may survive, or willing the victory of their nation and thereby destroying our civilization. I know which of these alternatives I must choose; but I cannot make that choice in security.[34]

These words give some credence to Bethge's comment that Bonhoeffer "struggled with his conscience" over the decision to return to Germany.[35] Andreas Pangritz, however, questions whether a struggle of conscience is an accurate description. He argues that it was not so much the internal voice of the conscience, but the external voices of friends, colleagues, and fellow Christians back in Germany that influenced his decision.[36] Or perhaps it was a sense of vocation that guided him home, as Robert Merrihew Adams suggests. He contends that Bonhoeffer's deliberation "was rooted in a sense of *belonging* in Germany, in his *caring* about certain people and projects and wanting to *participate* in a certain social process."[37] While it is difficult to evaluate these different characterizations, especially given the lack of detail Bonhoeffer provides, one can clearly see that at the very least, he was engaged in some manner of moral discernment, which included both rational reflection and an act of simple obedience to the perceived meaning of a biblical text.

---

33. Ibid., 238.
34. Ibid., 210.
35. Bethge, *Bonhoeffer*, 652.
36. Pangritz, "Theological Motives," 34.
37. Adams, *Finite and Infinite Goods*, 293.

Bonhoeffer wrote on his last day in New York before leaving for Germany that "[p]robably this journey will have a great effect upon me."[38] The next several years would show this to be true. Upon his return he averted the immediate crisis of military service by gaining an exemption from active duty with the help of his brother-in-law Hans von Dohnanyi, who worked for the *Abwehr*, the German military intelligence agency. In 1940 Bonhoeffer became a civilian member of the *Abwehr* and from 1940 to 1943 he lived a double life. Purportedly, he travelled abroad to meet his ecumenical contacts and gain intelligence for the German war effort; in reality, he met his ecumenical contacts in order to pass along information about the resistance movement in Germany. While doing this, he also helped smuggle Jews out of Germany as part of the clandestine "Operation 7." In addition, he found time to write his *Ethics* manuscripts and to develop a relationship with Maria von Wedemeyer, who would become his fiancé in 1943. Through it all, he was aware of the various assassination attempts on Hitler, and supported them not because he had abandoned his commitment to peace, but because he thought that the extraordinary time called for decisive and responsible action from Christians willing to commit sin and take on guilt for the greater good.[39] This period of his life lasted until 1943 when he was finally arrested, initially on suspicion of his involvement with "Operation 7." His famous prison writings, published as *Letters and Papers from Prison*, offer a unique glimpse into this final phase of his life from 1943 until his death on April 9, 1945 at the Flossenbürg concentration camp.

Previous Scholarship on Bonhoeffer and Discernment

Despite over 60 years of scholarly engagement with Bonhoeffer's work, surprisingly little exists on the theme of moral discernment.[40] However, this is not to say there are no precursors to the present study. While few scholars discuss discernment in any depth, and none take it up in a full-

---

38. DBWE 15:237.

39. Here I agree with Green's claim that Bonhoeffer exhibited a consistent peace ethic throughout his life, despite his involvement in conspiratorial activities against Hitler; see, DBWE 6, 14–16. For a different interpretation of the relationship between Bonhoeffer, pacifism, and the conspiracy against Hitler, see Nation et al., *Bonhoeffer the Assassin?*

40. For a solid overview of Bonhoeffer scholarship, see de Gruchy, "Reception of Bonhoeffer's Theology"; and Haynes, *Bonhoeffer Phenomenon*.

INTRODUCTION

length manuscript, there are a handful of texts that point toward the significance of moral discernment and offer brief interpretive comments. For instance, Heinrich Ott indicates the potential importance of discernment for Bonhoeffer's theology in his book *Reality and Faith*, one of the earliest studies of Bonhoeffer's thinking.[41] Ott argues that Bonhoeffer's discussion of discernment (*Prüfung*) in *Ethics* is "decisive . . . both for Bonhoeffer's ethical and his ontological conception."[42] Nevertheless, he does not pursue this theme, content merely to lament the fact that Bonhoeffer did not say more about simple discernment or describe some "teaching on methods" for "ethical proving."[43]

Larry Rasmussen, in another early study of Bonhoeffer's ethics, also singles out the topic of discernment by questioning the adequacy of Bonhoeffer's account of "proving what is the will of God" in a short section critiquing Bonhoeffer's methodological approach to ethics.[44] Additionally, in his later article, "A Question of Method," Rasmussen suggests that Bonhoeffer's thoughts on "proving the will of God" are one of four "methodological entry points" used to formulate his conception of ethics.[45] However, while he acknowledges that any of the four would be "worthy of study," he chooses to focus on "conformation" and "the command of God," leaving aside the theme of discernment. One can observe this pattern of identifying the theme of discernment, but not investigating it in any depth, in many other scholarly works on Bonhoeffer's theology. For instance, Marvin Bergman's 1974 work on Bonhoeffer and moral decision-making dances around the issue of discernment at several points, but surprisingly, never fully explores it.[46] Thomas Day, in his book *Bonhoeffer on Christian Community*, recognizes the tension in Bonhoeffer's theology between simple obedience and moral reflection, but falls short of a satisfying, theological explanation for the existence of such a tension.[47] In his 1985 book *Shaping the Future*, James

41. Ott, *Reality and Faith*. Ott's German text was originally published in 1966.

42. Ibid., 285.

43. Ibid.

44. Rasmussen, *Reality and Resistance*, 152–61 (first published in 1972). I will discuss Rasmussen's critique in chapter 6.

45. Rasmussen, "A Question of Method," 103.

46. Bergman, "Moral Decision Making," 227–43; Bergman, "Teaching Ethics," 367–80.

47. Day argues that, while Bonhoeffer believed in the necessity of moral reflection, he needed to encourage fellow conspirators to quick action without getting caught up in too much deliberation; thus, the apparent tension in his theology between moral reflection

Burtness hints at the importance of discernment when he contends that "a fascinating and potentially fruitful avenue of investigation" would be a study of Bonhoeffer's "ethical decision making."[48] Such a study, however, does not appear within the pages of Burtness' text.[49] Likewise, Ernst Feil goes so far as to argue in 1986 that a *Leitmotiv* for Bonhoeffer was the continual task of discerning what to do in the face of uncertainty and trusting in God alone for the outcome.[50] Despite this assertion, however, Feil does not delve further into Bonhoeffer's thoughts on discernment.

More recently, several scholars have engaged in more sustained explorations of Bonhoeffer and discernment. Rachel Muers, in her book *Keeping God's Silence*, speaks of Bonhoeffer and discernment on several occasions in the context of her larger attempt to develop a theological ethics of communication.[51] Though Bonhoeffer's view of discernment is not the focus of her study, she offers several insightful comments regarding the link between discernment and formation and the role of love as a guide for discernment.[52] Two other scholars, Michelle Bartel and Lisa Dahill, have explored Bonhoeffer's notion of discernment in even more depth. Bartel deals with the concept in her 1998 Ph.D. dissertation at Princeton Theological Seminary entitled "The Rationality of Discernment in Christian Ethics."[53] In seeking to demonstrate that discernment is both rational and teachable within the Christian community, she devotes a substantial chapter to Bonhoeffer. She argues that Bonhoeffer's view of discernment unites six key characteristics of discernment in Christian ethics: creativity, apperception, testing the spirits, intelligibility, shared loyalty to Christ, and objective verification in action.[54] Unfortunately, her methodology, evaluated strictly in terms of its impact on her treatment of Bonhoeffer, is questionable. By first articulating six characteristics of Christian discernment (drawn from her engagement with several theologians) and then arguing that Bonhoeffer's account of

---

and simple obedience is merely a byproduct of a particular historical situation. See Day, *Christian Community*, 142.

48. Burtness, *Shaping the Future*, 6.
49. Ibid.
50. Feil, "Gewissen und Entscheidung," 220.
51. Muers, *Keeping God's Silence*.
52. Ibid., 170–72.
53. Bartel, "Rationality of Discernment."
54. For a summary of these six characteristics, see ibid., 77–82. For Bartel's application of these characteristics to Bonhoeffer, see ibid., 122–28.

Introduction

discernment offers the prime example of how all six characteristics can exist together, she risks reading her own understanding of discernment into Bonhoeffer rather than letting Bonhoeffer speak for himself.

Dahill, who has easily written the most on Bonhoeffer and discernment, makes several important observations in her work.[55] For example, she emphasizes the significance of reading Bonhoeffer's views on discernment in light of his own biographical and historical context, as we already noted above. In addition, she recognizes the interconnectedness of discernment with many of Bonhoeffer's other ethical themes: reality, conformation, and discipleship, to name a few. She also understands discernment through Bonhoeffer's image of Christian life as a polyphony, in which Christ acts as the "cantus firmus."[56] As Dahill puts it: "To listen for the *cantus firmus* among all the other complementary or distracting melodies of our experience in this complex world—this is discernment."[57] Finally, she places great importance on the place of spiritual exercises in Bonhoeffer's account and their relation to the task of discernment.[58] More than any other scholar, Dahill's perceptive reading of Bonhoeffer and her insights into his understanding of moral discernment provide the impetus for further investigation, which this current book aims to provide.

Methodology and Argument

This study is an interpretative piece of research that pays close attention to Bonhoeffer's primary texts and relevant secondary sources in order to explicate and articulate what *he himself* thinks about the activity of discerning God's will.[59] Thus, it is not a comparative study of Bonhoeffer and

55. See Dahill, "Probing the Will of God," 42–47; Dahill, *Reading from the Underside*; Dahill, "Particularity," 68–76.
56. Dahill, "Probing the Will of God," 47.
57. Ibid.
58. Ibid., 45.
59. For the sake of simplicity and accessibility for the English language reader, I have chosen to make textual references to the English edition of the *Dietrich Bonhoeffer Works* (DBWE) whenever possible. Occasionally I reference the German edition, the *Dietrich Bonhoeffer Werke* (DBW), in order to emphasize a particular feature of the German text. Those wishing to consult Bonhoeffer's original German more frequently will benefit from the careful cross-referencing in the DBWE volumes, which allows one reading through the English translation to immediately locate the exact page number of the corresponding passage in the German edition.

other theologians, but rather examines other theological contributions only to illuminate aspects of Bonhoeffer's thinking.[60] This study also does not explore or evaluate other biblical or theological views of moral discernment or propose a new theory of moral discernment; again, the focus is strictly on Bonhoeffer's thought in the belief that he has something important to contribute to the larger discussion of discernment and Christian ethics.[61]

Bonhoeffer's *Ethics* manuscripts written from 1940–43 receive special attention throughout the book. Such a focus is justified because the collection of texts represents his mature ethical thinking, both incorporating themes from his earlier theology and developing new trajectories that carry into his writings from prison. Clifford Green remarks that even though the *Ethics* is incomplete and was only published posthumously, it is nevertheless "Dietrich Bonhoeffer's magnum opus."[62] Bonhoeffer himself indicated the prominent place of his *Ethics* in his own mind when he wrote to Bethge from prison: "Personally I reproach myself for not having finished the *Ethics* (at the moment it is presumably confiscated), and it comforts me somewhat that I told you the most important things."[63] He later writes: "I have the feeling that I am becoming significantly older here and sometimes think my life is more or less behind me and all I have left to do is to complete my *Ethics*."[64]

Of all his *Ethics* manuscripts, one holds particular importance and serves as the starting point for this study: Bonhoeffer's 1942 manuscript "God's Love."[65] This manuscript is an obvious starting point for our investigation for several reasons. In particular, the manuscript contains his most focused reflections on the dual activities that comprise Christian discernment: discerning or examining God's will (*prüfen den Willen Gottes*) and self-examination (*Selbstprüfung*). It therefore offers a fixed point from which

---

60. For a good introduction to comparative studies of Bonhoeffer and others, see Frick, *Bonhoeffer's Intellectual Formation*. This collection includes chapters on Bonhoeffer's relation to obvious figures such as Luther, Barth, Kierkegaard, Nietzsche, Kant, and Hegel, and less obvious individuals such as Augustine, Aquinas, and Thomas à Kempis, to name just a few.

61. For an introduction to the topic of discernment, particularly from the Protestant perspective, see Gustafson, "Moral Discernment," 17–36; Bartel, "Rationality of Discernment"; Wannenwetsch, "Fourfold Pattern," 177–90.

62. Green, "Editor's Introduction," 1.

63. DBWE 8:181.

64. Ibid., 222.

65. DBWE 6:299–338.

INTRODUCTION

to determine where discussions of discernment appear elsewhere in his writings, whether through the same or different terminology. This approach guards against the danger of importing a presupposed definition of discernment into the text prior to understanding what Bonhoeffer himself argues.

In addition to this, "God's Love" is a natural beginning point for the study because of the textual clues that suggest its prominence in Bonhoeffer's mind. The editors of the critical edition of *Ethics* point out that the manuscript, written approximately two years after he began work on his *Ethics*, is the only *Ethics* manuscript with Roman numeral pagination.[66] This feature indicates his possible intention to place it first as a preface to his completed work.[67] Both the form and content of the manuscript further strengthen this conclusion. For instance, the manuscript opens with a programmatic claim, setting the stage for the rest of the work, that one should approach Christian ethics as that which supersedes and critiques all other forms of ethics.[68] In addition, as we will see in chapter 2, the manuscript contains exegetical material from both Genesis 3 and Matthew 5-7, forming a natural bridge with Bonhoeffer's earlier works from the 1930s, *Creation and Fall* and *Discipleship*. As the editors assert, this evidence validates Bethge's decision to place "God's Love" first when he reordered Bonhoeffer's manuscripts for the sixth edition of *Ethics* and supports the decision to begin this study with an extended consideration of the manuscript.[69]

Despite the focus on Bonhoeffer's *Ethics*, however, it is certainly not the only one of Bonhoeffer's writings to deal with the issues surrounding moral discernment. Thus, while the current study deals substantially with *Ethics* and returns to it again and again at key junctures, it also draws from beyond this period when doing so will illuminate the issues under discussion. For example, while the theme of Christian formation is prominent in *Ethics*, one can hardly do it justice without some mention of its place in

---

66. Tödt et al., "Editors' Afterword," 445.

67. During Bonhoeffer's time, as today, Roman numerals commonly indicated prefatory material; see DBWE 6:299n1.

68. Ibid., 299-300. The fact that a similar methodological statement is found in Bonhoeffer's earliest *Ethics* manuscript, "Christ, Reality, and Good," is unsurprising and does nothing to undermine the argument concerning the prominence of "God's Love." Cf. ibid., 47.

69. Tödt et al., "Editors' Afterword," 446. The DBW and DBWE editions of *Ethics* present Bonhoeffer's manuscripts in strict chronological order (making "Christ, Reality, and Good" first, and "God's Love" ninth). For a reconstruction of Bonhoeffer's possible intended ordering, in which "God's Love" appears first, see ibid., 447-48.

Bonhoeffer's earlier book *Discipleship*. Moreover, the motif of God's commandment, while occupying a prominent place in *Ethics*, is also strongly present in his work in the early 1930s. Because part of the fascination with his theology is the way that it develops in some ways and remains constant in other ways throughout the years, one would be remiss even in a focused study not to offer some account of the historical development of his thinking.

Finally, a word concerning terminology will prove helpful. Throughout the book I employ the term "tension" to speak of the apparent incongruity in Bonhoeffer's theology arising from two different emphases: an emphasis on a simple, unreflective approach to discerning God's will and an emphasis on a rational, reflective, and deliberative approach to discerning God's will. These two emphases often seem to act in opposition to each other, resulting in a strained condition (e.g., how can a Christian disciple, in his or her approach to God's will, be simultaneously "unreflective" and "reflective"?). However, the very term "tension" not only indicates a strained condition arising from two opposing forces or themes, but also points to the possibility that someone or something might alleviate or finally overcome that strained condition; that is to say, a "tension" need not be a permanent state. Therefore, as already mentioned, a primary purpose of this book is to investigate the tension in Bonhoeffer's theology and to explore how the opposing themes that create the tension might find reconciliation.

With these methodological issues in mind, we turn now to a brief account of the argument ahead. Chapter 2 begins with a close analysis of Bonhoeffer's understudied 1942 *Ethics* manuscript "God's Love." Here, through an investigation of his theological anthropology and his concomitant understanding of two different approaches to the moral life and to moral discernment, I highlight a tension between a simple, unreflective obedience to God's will and a rational, reflective approach to God's will. I continue in chapter 3 by arguing that Bonhoeffer's Christology relieves the tension between simplicity and moral reflection and allows both to be combined into a coherent account of moral discernment. Here, the focus is on his understanding of the relationship between the two natures of Christ, which he expresses through his notion of Christ-reality and his conceptual innovation of the ultimate and penultimate. In chapter 4 I contend that this conceptual unity between simplicity and moral reflection becomes efficacious in the lives of Christians through the process of conformation to the form of Christ. In such a process one does not actively form oneself, but places

Introduction

oneself in a position, in part through spiritual exercises, where Christ's form can do its work. I explore the simplicity of discernment more fully in chapter 5 using as a guide the motif of God's commandment. I demonstrate the importance of simplicity and simple obedience for Bonhoeffer's conception of the Christian moral life and also argue that his understanding of simple obedience does not reject all manner of moral reflection, but merely redefines its purpose and purview. Finally, in chapter 6, I use the theme of natural life to address the place of discernment within the natural, penultimate world. I assert that Bonhoeffer's theology of the natural allows him to speak of the structure of the natural order as a relative guide to moral discernment. Moreover, human attributes such as reason and conscience, despite receiving some negative appraisals, also play a role in the process of discernment. I conclude the book in chapter 7 by reaffirming the centrality of moral discernment for Bonhoeffer's vision of Christian ethics and by considering what new picture emerges of Bonhoeffer given the contents of this study.

2

The Problem of Moral Discernment

BONHOEFFER'S MOST FOCUSED DISCUSSION of moral discernment occurs in his underappreciated *Ethics* manuscript "God's Love."[1] Here, in a section a little over halfway through the text, he explicates the task of discernment by discussing the interrelated activities of discerning God's will (*prüfen den Willen Gottes*) and self-examination (*Selbstprüfung*), both of which, he argues, are "legitimate and necessary" for Christian life.[2] He locates his discussion within a larger narrative of Christian ethics told through the language of theological anthropology. Understanding his contrast between the person in unity with God and the person in a state of disunity illuminates his distinction between two approaches to the moral life. The first approach, embodied by the New Testament Pharisees, depends upon the knowledge of good and evil to assist one's rational, moral reflection; the second approach, exemplified by Jesus Christ, consists of simple, unreflective obedience to God. However, it is here that a point of tension arises in Bonhoeffer's account of discerning God's will. While he wants to maintain an emphasis on a simple, unreflective approach to God's will that is independent of moral reflection, he also wants to speak of a kind of discernment that uses the best of human ability, moral reflection included. Investigating the nature of this tension in his theology and determining whether he alleviates the tension is the primary task of this chapter.

---

1. DBWE 6:299–338. I am unaware of any in-depth analysis of this particular manuscript in the secondary literature on Bonhoeffer, which is surprising given the manuscript's apparent importance to him.

2. Ibid., 320.

The Problem of Moral Discernment

Toward this end, I will begin the chapter by examining the opening portion of "God's Love," which employs theological anthropology as a lens through which to view the distinction between Christian ethics and all other ethics. In developing his distinction between unity and disunity and between Jesus Christ and the New Testament Pharisees, the opposition between simplicity and moral reflection becomes clear. Following this, I will analyze Bonhoeffer's specific discussion of Christian discernment in both its outward orientation (discerning God's will) and inward dimension (examining the self). Here, I will pay particular attention to his attempt to overcome the tension between simplicity and moral reflection and to include both within his account of discernment. Finally, I will consider the end of "God's Love" where Bonhoeffer reformulates the tension between simplicity and moral reflection in his discussion of "hearing" and "doing" God's will and hints at the Christological underpinning of moral discernment through his musings on the love of God.

Ethics From Anthropology

Bonhoeffer's treatment of theological anthropology in the first half of "God's Love" is an extended preparation for what he wishes to articulate about Christian ethics, and in particular, Christian moral discernment later in the manuscript. This is not the first time such a link between theological anthropology and ethics appears in Bonhoeffer's theological corpus.[3] In his first dissertation, *Sanctorum Communio*, he defines the human person in ethical terms: it is only through encountering the claim of the other that a person comes into being by moving into a place of ethical responsibility on behalf of the neighbor.[4] Thus, "[f]rom the ethical perspective, human beings do not exist 'unmediated' qua spirit in and of themselves, but only in responsibility vis-à-vis an 'other.'"[5] In this manner, ethical language informs theological anthropology, but the reverse is also true. As Bonhoeffer demonstrates in both *Sanctorum Communio* and more fully in his second dissertation, *Act and Being*, one's "being" either "in Adam" or "in Christ" carries direct ethical implications.[6] One is either self-centered, viewing

---

3. On the link between Bonhoeffer's theological anthropology and his ethical thinking, see Rüter and Tödt, "Editors' Afterword," 172; Green, *Theology of Sociality*.

4. DBWE 1:48–57.

5. Ibid., 50.

6. DBWE 2:136–37, 158–59.

others as mere objects of knowledge, or one is open and receptive to God and creation, seeking to meet the needs of others.[7]

In *Creation and Fall*, his theological commentary on Genesis 1-3, he focuses more specifically on how the fall transforms the human person from existing as a creature made in the image of God to existing as a creature who has become like God (*sicut deus*).[8] A distinction arises between Adam's simple relationship of obedience to God before the fall and Adam's grasping after his own knowledge of good and evil after the fall. Thus, Bonhoeffer believes that one's moral character and moral action stem, either consciously or unconsciously, from one's status as a human person vis-à-vis the Creator. One is either in a state of reconciliation and unity with God or in a state of fallenness and disunity with God. This fundamental distinction between unity and disunity, which illustrates the difference between Christian ethics and all other ethics, provides the starting point for his discussion in "God's Love."

He opens the manuscript with a programmatic statement that drives a wedge between Christian ethics and all other ethics:

> The knowledge of good and evil appears to be the goal of all ethical reflection [*ethischen Besinnung*]. The first task of Christian ethics is to supersede [*aufzuheben*] that knowledge. This attack on the presuppositions of all other ethics is so unique that it is questionable whether it even makes sense to speak of Christian ethics at all. If it is nevertheless done, then this can only mean that Christian ethics claims to articulate the origin of the whole ethical enterprise, and thus to be considered an ethic only as the critique of all ethics.[9]

Bonhoeffer is hesitant even to speak of Christian ethics because in his mind all ethics are a result of the fall, making the notion of Christian ethics a contradiction in terms. However, he stops just short of an outright rejection of the possibility of Christian ethics, likely due to practical considerations. The language of "Christian ethics," despite its problems, was still the most recognizable way to speak of the Christian moral life: thus, he chose to maintain the phrase, but only in careful distinction to other understandings

---

7. Ibid.

8. DBWE 3:116.

9. DBWE 6:299–300; cf. DBW 6:301. Pangritz suggests that this is an allusion to Barth's comment that the church's moral exhortation "can be naught else but a criticism of all human behaviour." See Pangritz, "'Within, not Outside,'" 273.

The Problem of Moral Discernment

of ethics. His opening statement is meant to clarify from the very beginning that Christian ethics has an entirely different point of origin and ultimately calls into question the legitimacy of "the whole ethical enterprise." He means that while all ethical inquiry inevitably seeks to obtain knowledge of good and evil in order to make moral judgments, Christian ethics takes a different approach, and thereby exists "as the critique of all ethics." However, his use of the verb *aufheben* to describe the relationship between Christian ethics and the knowledge of good and evil is intriguing.[10] On the one hand, he wants to argue that Christian ethics abolishes the knowledge of good and evil as an appropriate guide to the moral life, replacing it with a notion of simple obedience carried out in faith. This emphasis comes through strongly later in the manuscript when he says in no uncertain terms that one's unity with God and knowledge of God overcomes (*überwunden*) the knowledge of good and evil.[11] On the other hand, his use of *aufheben*, which he employs on several occasions throughout the manuscript, suggests a more Hegelian meaning in which Christian ethics supersedes the knowledge of good and evil precisely by incorporating it, in some manner, into itself.[12] Here, moral reflection, aware of the categories of good and evil, is not the ultimate source of moral knowledge, but retains some relative value even for those living in unity and simplicity with God. How exactly this works itself out in the life of the Christian disciple is not clear. But from the very beginning of the manuscript, one can perceive a tension in Bonhoeffer's thought between simplicity and moral reflection. This tension carries throughout the text and, as we shall see, manifests itself especially in his discussion of Christian discernment.

Despite this underlying tension, Bonhoeffer follows his introductory statement by clearly articulating a distinction between Christian ethics and all other ethics. He does this through a discussion of anthropology, and in particular, the notion of *Entzweiung*, which indicates disunion and separation as well as divisiveness and estrangement.[13] As seen from the full title of the manuscript, "God's Love and the Disintegration [*Zerfall*] of the World," he believes that disunion and disintegration is a real historical problem

---

10. For comments on Bonhoeffer's use of *aufheben* or *Aufhebung* in his writings, see DBWE 2:31n20; and DBWE 3:28n12.

11. DBWE 6:317; cf. DBW 6:319.

12. For other uses of *aufheben* in "God's Love," see DBW 6:319, 320, 321, 327, 329; cf. DBWE 6:317, 318, 324, 326.

13. DBWE 6:300n6.

occurring in a Western society that has rejected its Christian heritage. In another *Ethics* manuscript, "Heritage and Decay [*Verfall*]," he warns of the "abyss of nothingness" into which the West is sliding because of its rejection of Christ and its "desire for absolute freedom."[14] Certainly, his own experience of the dehumanizing impulses threatening to destroy Germany and much of Europe influenced his analysis in this regard. To counteract these self-destructive inclinations in society, the church must "stand in the middle of the dissolution of all that exists" by bearing witness to Christ.[15] In so doing, the church reminds the world of its reconciliation in Christ and calls it back to its true origin. However, while the problem of disunity is a serious historical concern, it is also a problem affecting individual morality: this is the topic of primary interest for Bonhoeffer in "God's Love."

He begins by arguing that while humanity before the fall lived in unity (*Einheit*) with God, and redeemed humanity after the fall can once again live in "rediscovered unity" with God in Christ, the fallen state of humanity, who is estranged from God and who does not yet know Christ, is a state of disunion (*Entzweiung*).[16] The fundamental characteristics of such a state are twofold. First, humanity's state of disunion means that humanity has fallen away from God as its origin.[17] For one to exist with God as origin means that all knowledge, all decisions, and all actions come from God alone. As Bonhoeffer puts it: "They know other human beings, things, and themselves only in the unity of their knowledge of God; they know everything only in God, and God in all things."[18] Here, the "reality of being elected and loved by God" and not the many "possibilities" of potential action and decision characterize one's life.[19] Thus, for Adam before the fall, there is no ethics or morality as such, but simply a direct relationship with the Creator marked by freedom and obedience. To fall away from God as one's origin, however, means to substitute the self as origin in God's place. This movement away from God and toward the self is initially prompted by the serpent's question, "Did God really say . . . ?" (Gen 3:1), furthered by the serpent's temptation masquerading as a promise, ". . . and you will be like God . . ." (Gen 3:5), and finally reflected in God's declaration in Genesis

14. Ibid., 122, 127–31.
15. Ibid., 132.
16. Ibid., 300.
17. Ibid.
18. Ibid.
19. Ibid., 302.

3:22, "see, the man has become like one of us . . . ." Having the self as origin means to become one's own creator and judge: it is to "become like God" by usurping God's rightful place at the center of life and presuming to operate according to one's own knowledge and skill.[20] For Bonhoeffer, Luther's theological understanding of *cor curvum in se* most accurately sums up this fundamental shift in humanity's relationship with God. Because the human heart is now turned in upon itself, it is cut off from anything outside of it.[21] This results in estrangement from God and others, and paradoxically, from the self as well.[22] The individual must now rely solely on his or her own knowledge of good and evil to negotiate moral situations.

This reliance on the knowledge of good and evil is the second characteristic that describes the state of fallen humanity. Bonhoeffer borrows this phrase from Genesis 2:9 and makes use of it throughout "God's Love" to indicate a fundamental inversion of knowledge, which is closely connected to the inversion of one's point of origin in falling away from God. For Bonhoeffer, to live out of the self as origin is to live according to the knowledge of good and evil.[23] "To know good and evil" does not mean to acquire a completely new body of knowledge, but to discover one's capacity to render moral judgment without recourse to God.[24] This is the sense in which knowledge is inverted: knowledge as a source of moral guidance no longer flows from God, who alone knows good and evil, but comes from the self, which has its own supposed knowledge of good and evil.[25] Thus, to know good and evil is to have the power to define and judge the self, other people, and the various situations one might encounter. One no longer relies on the simplicity of God's commandment, but turns instead to one's own human ability to recognize possibilities, make calculations, and render judgments in situations of ethical import. Bonhoeffer contends that this knowledge of

---

20. Ibid., 301.

21. DBWE 2:39, 137.

22. One aspect of Bonhoeffer's critique of German Idealism concerns the illusory freedom of the all-powerful self. While the self supposedly frees itself from anything transcendent by constituting its own being, this apparent "freedom" is actually a form of imprisonment whereby the self is completely closed off from anything outside. This means that when the fallen individual turns inward, away from God, this act results in an estrangement and isolation not only from God, but from others as well. Moreover, the self is estranged even from its own being, which can only exist in God. See ibid., 39.

23. DBWE 6:300.

24. Ibid., 301–2.

25. Ibid., 301.

good and evil is deceptive because it arises from a seemingly innocent and pious question: "Did God really say . . . ?"[26] This question does not directly contradict the authority of God's word, but subtly intimates that it might be in need of further clarification.[27] The question suggests the possibility of using human understanding as a basis for evaluating God's word, which is to say, the serpent introduces the possibility of moral reflection. No longer is a direct and immediate relationship to God's word sufficient. One must now verify the true meaning of God's word from a human basis before acting in response. Bonhoeffer decries "the real evil" of the question when he says that through the question:

> [T]he basic attitude of the creature toward the Creator comes under attack. It requires humankind to sit in judgment on God's word instead of simply listening to it and doing it. And this is achieved by proposing that, on the basis of an idea, a principle, or some prior knowledge about God, humankind should now pass judgment on the concrete word of God. But where human beings use a principle, an idea of God, as a weapon to fight against the concrete word of God, there they are from the outset already in the right; at that point they have become God's master, they have left the path of obedience, they have withdrawn from being addressed by God.[28]

Instead of "simply listening to it and doing it," the creature now wants to "sit in judgment" on the Creator's word. For Bonhoeffer, this is to leave "the path of obedience" and to withdraw "from being addressed by God." As he makes clear in "God's Love," seeking to reflect on and judge the true meaning of God's word is fundamentally opposed to God because it displaces God as Creator and Judge and puts the human individual into God's place.[29] Here, he clearly calls into question the very idea of moral reflection, which he views as a product of the serpent's temptation and fallen humanity's new relationship of disunion with God. But how does this relate to his hint at the beginning of the manuscript that knowledge of good and evil, while superseded in Christian ethics, might still retain some relative value? Put differently, is he rejecting all forms of moral reflection or does he allow a certain kind of moral reflection a limited role in Christian ethics?

26. DBWE 3:106.
27. Ibid.
28. Ibid., 107–8.
29. DBWE 6:301–2.

The Problem of Moral Discernment

Bonhoeffer does not immediately answer such questions, but turns instead to a further description of fallen humanity. He argues first that shame serves as a reminder of one's disunion from God and others. Shame compels one to try to alleviate the problem of estrangement, but in seeking to cover up this estrangement one merely reaffirms the underlying disunity that exists. Thus, as Bonhoeffer remarks, shame is both "an acknowledgment of and protest against disunion."[30] To overcome shame, one must endure "an act of ultimate shaming," which means confession before God and others.[31] God's forgiveness, received through confession, restores one's lost unity.[32] However, while, ontologically speaking, shame is overcome by forgiveness through confession, the phenomenon of shame continues to take observable shape in human life. Thus, the realities of shame and disunion are never fully eradicated in one's life, but continually exist in dialectical tension with the new human being who is reconciled in Christ. This suggests that Christian formation, which involves practices such as confession, is necessary because it helps one continually turn away from disunion and reorients the person toward his or her proper origin in God.[33]

Furthermore, Bonhoeffer states that conscience, in addition to shame, is a mark of fallen humanity and appears in the disunited person as the moral voice that impersonates God's voice and seeks to maintain unity within the self.[34] Conscience cannot be trusted because it originates from the self instead of from God, and in seeking unity with the self it unknowingly presupposes a state of disunity with God.[35] While the conscience is an essential moral guide for fallen humanity, Bonhoeffer dismisses it as a means of moral guidance for Christian ethics. To rely on the conscience is yet another way of turning inward toward the self and the self's own knowledge and away from the knowledge of God. While others might identify the voice of the conscience as the place where God's will becomes known, Bonhoeffer considers an appeal to the conscience to be misguided and unnecessary because one can just as well appeal directly to the voice of Christ in matters of ethics. But despite this critical appraisal, Bonhoeffer speaks elsewhere of a positive function of conscience in those who have

30. Ibid., 305.
31. Ibid., 306.
32. Ibid.
33. This points to the theme of Christian formation, which I discuss in chapter 4.
34. DBWE 6:307.
35. Ibid.

been redeemed by Christ; in fact, one might even construe his description of self-examination, which we investigate below, as part of this alternative account of conscience.[36] Thus, we once again observe a tension in Bonhoeffer's account, which reflects the larger tension between simplicity and moral reflection. On the one hand, he dismisses the conscience as an inappropriate aid to Christian discernment; on the other hand, he suggests that the conscience, if properly defined, might still have a necessary function in one's attempt to perceive God's will.

At this point in the manuscript Bonhoeffer has distinguished effectively between humanity in unity with God and humanity in disunity with God. The ethical implications of this distinction are clear. For those in unity with God, there is no need to rely on a supposed understanding of good and evil to make moral decisions because one enjoys a direct relationship of obedience with God and acts according to God's commandments. Such is not the case, however, for human beings in a state of disunion. These individuals become self-reflective (*Reflexion auf sich selbst*) in order to gain knowledge, ethical and otherwise, and this attempt to gain self-knowledge becomes the "essence and goal of life."[37] While the search for self-knowledge might be an attempt to find unity with the self, it nevertheless results in further disunity; moreover, it causes one to view the entire moral realm in terms of disunity. The starting point for ethical experience is not one of reconciliation, but instead one of conflict and division where "everything splits apart . . . is and ought, life and law, knowing and doing, idea and reality . . ."[38] The moral life becomes a series of ethical dilemmas that one must adjudicate and the disunited individual assumes the role of judge, using the knowledge of good and evil to evaluate alternatives and make decisions. Just as there are two states of being in relation to God, unity and disunity, so there are two ways of understanding the moral life, either as an obedient response to God or as an exercise in moral reflection apart from God.

Competing Approaches to the Moral Life

The ethical implications of Bonhoeffer's theological anthropology become even clearer when he moves from his general description of human beings in a state of disunity to his more specific discussion of the New Testament

---

36. Cf. Ibid., 278–79; 324–26. I return to the theme of conscience in chapter 6.
37. Ibid., 308; DBW 6:310.
38. DBWE 6:308–9.

The Problem of Moral Discernment

Pharisees. As he asserts: "It is the encounter of Jesus with the Pharisees that most clearly highlights the contrast of the old and the new."[39] For him, the Pharisees represent not only the historical individuals mentioned in the New Testament, but also contemporary human beings who exist in a state of disunity with God and who depend on the knowledge of good and evil.[40] It is only after describing the Pharisees and their misguided approach to the moral life that Bonhoeffer can finally turn to the life of Jesus and reveal what a proper approach to Christian ethics should be.

The Pharisee is "the epitome of the human being in the state of disunion" because he operates solely from the knowledge of good and evil.[41] The moral universe, seen through the eyes of the Pharisees, is a place of myriad possibilities in which many different ethical choices might be made with the help of reason, conscience, laws, and ethical principles.[42] Because of this, the Pharisees take on the role of moral arbiters, evaluating their own deeds and examining (*prüfen*) others with a critical eye.[43] Moreover, by considering countless moral scenarios and coming to many possible decisions in advance, the Pharisees exhibit what is for Bonhoeffer a troubling casuistic method and a tendency to treat moral thinking as a scientific exercise that breaks the moral realm into individual pieces of data that one can move around and manipulate until a desirable result appears.[44] His aversion to such an approach to ethics is evident later when he argues that "an ethic cannot be a chemist's laboratory for producing the ethical and Christian person."[45]

The Pharisees' desire to occupy the role of judge in the moral life receives particular condemnation from Bonhoeffer. He interprets Jesus' critique of judging in Matthew 7:1 ("Do not judge, so that you may not be judged") as a fundamental attack on the being of those who stand in disunity with God and live via a knowledge of good and evil.[46] He claims

---

39. Ibid., 309.
40. Ibid., 310n40.
41. Ibid., 310.
42. For Bonhoeffer's distinction between "reality" and "possibility," see DBWE 6:302; Feil, *Theology of Dietrich Bonhoeffer*, 30–32.
43. DBWE 6:310; cf. DBW 6:312.
44. For Bonhoeffer's definition of casuistry as an attempt to make moral decisions and judgments about particular cases in advance, see DBWE 6:99.
45. Ibid., 370.
46. Ibid., 313.

that the judging of the Pharisees "is always nothing but verdict, judgment, reproach, and accusation against others" and while it finds particular expression in their daily pronouncements, he claims that it is best understood not as "a particular vice" but as a deep seated characteristic of their "very nature."[47] One byproduct of this characteristic is a presumption to know the relative goodness of a particular action or decision as soon as it occurs instead of leaving this designation up to God. Thus, the judging of the Pharisees indicates a certain level of self-sufficiency. From Bonhoeffer's point of view, one must heed Jesus' command in Matthew 6:3–4 about giving alms without the left hand knowing what the right hand is doing.[48] One must exercise a measure of restraint in the moral life by refusing to employ one's own knowledge of good and evil as an a priori moral guide or moral evaluation. Overcoming the tendency to look at one's own goodness is possible only through Christ's call to a life of simplicity (*Einfalt*), which results in a transition from reliance on the knowledge of one's own goodness to a "knowledge which consists entirely in doing the will of God."[49] For Bonhoeffer, the elusive nature of moral certainty is important to recognize because it frees one to focus on *doing* God's will and trusting in God's gracious judgment.

Bonhoeffer's description of the Pharisees is intended to illustrate the path of disunity in the moral life. He contrasts this view with an alternative vision for ethics illustrated by the life of Jesus. Jesus stands as the antithesis of the Pharisees because he refuses to view life as a series of moral conflicts that need constant adjudication and instead approaches life from a place of reconciliation with God. In fact, despite the Pharisees' best efforts to force Jesus into making moral judgments based on ethical principles and moral distinctions, Jesus refuses to be drawn into ethics via a knowledge of good and evil.[50] Jesus embodies this refusal above all in his resistance to the first temptation in the desert in which he maintains unity with God's word over and against the devil's suggestion to move into conflict with God's word.[51] Because of Jesus' unity with God, his approach to the ethical life is one of

---

47. Ibid., 314–15.

48. Ibid., 317–19.

49. Ibid., 318. The term *Einfalt* is translated sometimes as "simplicity" and other times as "single-mindedness" depending on the context. It is an important concept for Bonhoeffer both in his *Ethics* and earlier in *Discipleship*. I return to it throughout the book, but especially in chapter 5.

50. Ibid., 312.

51. Ibid., 311.

freedom and simplicity (*Einfalt*). This freedom does not mean arbitrarily choosing between various ethical options, but instead means freedom to choose the one will of God.[52] Thus, Christian ethics is simple because it does not require deliberation between "several possibilities, conflicts, or alternatives," but obedience to "the one option, what is real, the will of God."[53] For the Pharisees, such freedom and simplicity appear as moral subjectivism; they believe Jesus is nothing but a nihilist.[54] Jesus, however, knows nothing of nihilism: he simply seeks to know and to do the one will of God and so remain in unity with God, self, and others.[55] Here, Bonhoeffer points to a distinction he will revisit at the end of the manuscript between the genuine "doing" of Jesus and the inauthentic "doing" of the Pharisees.

Despite his sharp critique against the judging of the Pharisees, Bonhoeffer indicates that not every act of judgment is morally problematic. There is a different kind of judging proper to Christians, as mentioned in 1 Corinthians 2:15: "The spiritual person judges all things and is not judged by anyone."[56] Whereas the condemnatory judging of the Pharisees depends on the self's own knowledge of good and evil and presumes to occupy a transcendent vantage point, Christian judging proceeds from "the vantage point of Jesus"[57] and takes form not as one's own independent judgment, but as the judgment of Christ.[58] Thus, the former kind of judging seeks to divide and condemn and presumes to know the goodness of a particular judgment before it occurs; the latter form of judging seeks to reconcile others and assist them on the moral path, while leaving ultimate judgment to God. By articulating such a distinction, Bonhoeffer avoids falling prey to

52. Ibid., 312–13.
53. Ibid., 318.
54. Ibid., 313.
55. Ibid. 318.
56. Ibid., 316. An acknowledgment of this more positive construal of judgment in Bonhoeffer's thinking is one of the elements lacking from Bartel's study mentioned in the previous chapter. It is a significant omission because, by not recognizing Bonhoeffer's distinction between two kinds of judging, one is ill prepared to appreciate his contrast between two kinds of moral reflection. Incidentally, Bartel also offers a negative, one-sided appraisal of conscience, which is justified through a reading of "God's Love," but insufficient to account for other passages in Bonhoeffer, as I discuss in chapter 6. See Bartel, *Rationality of Discernment*, 118n77.
57. DBWE 6:315.
58. As Bonhoeffer argues in *Discipleship* when commenting on Matthew 7:1, morally problematic judging occurs "from the distance of observation and reflection [*Reflexion*]," and is a place of blindness. See DBWE 4:170, 172.

his own critique against judging precisely because he grounds his critique in the knowledge of God received through the Holy Spirit and renders judgment with "the mind of Christ" rather than according to a knowledge of good and evil.[59]

In the end, Bonhoeffer's discussion of the Pharisees and Jesus solidifies his distinction between two different approaches to the moral life. In the first approach, the person in a state of disunity with God, such as the New Testament Pharisee, navigates the moral life using a presumed knowledge of good and evil to evaluate and judge people and situations. Continual self-reflection (*Reflexion auf sich selbst*) is crucial because in looking inward to reason, conscience, and one's knowledge of moral laws and principles, one can evaluate moral dilemmas, make moral judgments, and assess the goodness of moral decisions even before making them. This approach to ethics displays a mode of moral reflection that is overly casuistic and scientific and therefore inappropriate for Christian ethics. Moreover, a condemnatory and divisive nature characterizes the judgments arising from this manner of ethics. In fact, Bonhoeffer describes this whole approach to ethics as an ethics of conflict, which stands opposed to the way of Christian ethics.

In direct contrast to this, the person in a state of unity with God, Jesus being the prime example, embodies the second approach to the moral life by rejecting the knowledge of good and evil, and looking to the knowledge of God for moral guidance. Instead of relying on ethical principles, positive law, or one's own moral compass in situations of moral dilemma, the person in unity with God takes a much more streamlined approach: simply put, he or she looks to the one will of God and acts accordingly. The presupposition of this approach is that God's will in a particular situation is direct and unambiguous, thus requiring no interpretation or discernment: one chooses simply to obey or disobey. Therefore, the person in unity with God should forgo any attempts at self-reflection because one should not look at the self for moral knowledge, but only to God. Moreover, because Christian ethics should proceed from a point of reconciliation, the person in unity with God should exercise caution in passing moral judgment. While judgment in service of reconciliation may sometimes be appropriate, many acts of judgment presuppose a moral realm marked by continual conflict and thus betray their divisive nature.

---

59. DBWE 6:316–17. Interestingly, it is at this point in the manuscript that Bonhoeffer included, but then deleted, a sentence about the need for discernment despite the Christian knowing all things in Christ. He instead chooses to wait and speak about discernment a few pages later (as we shall see); cf. ibid., 317n62.

The Problem of Moral Discernment

Despite what appears to be a clear distinction between two approaches to the moral life, however, the careful reader of Bonhoeffer's manuscript will notice a few ambiguities: the first concerns his critique of the Pharisees and the second involves the point of tension already discussed between simplicity and moral reflection. To begin with the Pharisees, we have already seen the sharp nature of Bonhoeffer's critique, which reaches its height when he accuses the Pharisees of "apostasy" because of their audacity in usurping the place of God in judgment.[60] And yet, despite this charge of apostasy, Bonhoeffer also admits that the judging of the Pharisees can be lenient on some occasions and even have "noble motivations."[61] In fact, what is interesting about his polemic is its underlying respect, even empathy, for those he critiques. After all, the Pharisees are caught in a tragic situation because of their disunity from God; they "can do nothing else [*nicht anders können*]" but behave in the way they do.[62] One must not turn the Pharisees into a caricature, he says, for doing so "takes away the seriousness and importance of Jesus' controversy with them."[63] Thus, he is quick to point out the positive attributes of the Pharisees: they are "those human beings admirable to the highest degree, who subject their entire lives to the knowledge of good and evil and who judge themselves as sternly as their neighbors—and all to the glory of God, whom they humbly thank for this knowledge."[64] This mention of humility is especially striking given that some of his earlier critiques of the Pharisees focused particularly on their arrogant attitude of moral righteousness. For example, he speaks in one of his early sermons of the "Pharisaic self-satisfaction" and "incredible arrogance" of people like the Pharisees who stand "too comfortably" before God, thinking that their

---

60. Ibid., 315.

61. Ibid., 315; cf. Ibid., 310.

62. DBWE 6:311 (my translation); DBW 6:313.

63. DBWE 6:310. Whether Bonhoeffer himself avoids caricature and misrepresentation of the Pharisees in his interpretation of Matthew's gospel is another matter. Take, for example, his statement that Matthew 22 (specifically vv. 15–40) offers "the most forceful impression" of the Pharisees' approach to ethics. While he implies that the questions posed in the text about paying taxes to Caesar, the resurrection of the dead, and the greatest commandment all come from the Pharisees, the second question (concerning the resurrection of the dead) actually arises from the Sadducees. While perhaps a minor point, this nevertheless suggests that Bonhoeffer is more concerned with constructing a general, composite view of what the Pharisees represent than he is with detailed exegesis into Matthew's own account of the Pharisees.

64. Ibid.

moral superiority will justify them.⁶⁵ This assessment is quite different than saying the Pharisees have "no trace of thoughtless arrogance, presumption, or unexamined self-esteem," as he does in "God's Love."⁶⁶

The reason for such empathy becomes evident near the end of a passage where he speaks of the Pharisees' attempts to confront and tempt Jesus into adjudicating on situations of conflict.⁶⁷ Midway through the passage, he shifts his focus from the Pharisees and begins using the language of "we [*wir*]." He says:

> [A]ll these temptations repeat themselves in the questions with which *we too* always confront Jesus; questions with which *we* call on him for a decision in cases of conflict; questions, in other words, with which *we* draw Jesus into *our* questions, conflicts, and disunity, and demand that he provide a resolution.⁶⁸

This language points to the truth of Luther's *simul justus et peccator* and the fact that Christians also can fall prey to the knowledge of good and evil, as Bonhoeffer himself witnessed in the church struggle in Germany during the National Socialist period. His critique, therefore, blurs the lines between Pharisees and Christians, suggesting that both can struggle with the problem of disunity and both may be worthy of a mixture of criticism and understanding. But this illustrates another unresolved tension in the manuscript, for elsewhere he uncompromisingly distinguishes between those in unity and disunity. For example, he argues that human beings "cannot live simultaneously in reconciliation and disunity, in freedom and under the law, in simplicity and in inner conflict. Here there are no gradations and degrees, but only one or the other."⁶⁹ Helping to exacerbate this tension is his own increasing awareness, as a member of the conspiracy in the early 1940s, that it was often secular humanists, and not Christians, who were acting according to God's will.⁷⁰ Thus, one is left to wonder how sharp the distinction really is between Pharisee and Christian and whether the kind of discernment he describes in "God's Love" is inclusive or exclusive

---

65. DBWE 9:452.
66. DBWE 6:310.
67. Ibid., 311–12.
68. Ibid., 312; italics mine.
69. Ibid., 318.
70. See Bonhoeffer's *Ethics* manuscript, "Church and World," written just after "God's Love," in ibid., 339–51; cf. Bethge, *Bonhoeffer*, 857.

of those who are not Christians. While we cannot divert our focus to this question here, we will revisit the issue more fully in chapter 6.

The second ambiguity mentioned above points to the fundamental tension in Bonhoeffer's theology between simplicity and moral reflection. As we saw above, each of Bonhoeffer's two approaches to the moral life include a concomitant approach to discernment. In the approach of the Pharisees, moral reflection is of primary importance. One must carefully consider laws and situations and draw upon one's knowledge of good and evil in order to determine how to act in a particular instance. Put differently, one must consult a depository of moral knowledge in order to discern a correct decision and action from among a variety of possibilities. When describing the approach of Jesus, however, Bonhoeffer calls into question the very idea of moral reflection for Christian ethics. Deciding how to act in an individual instance is a matter of simple faith in God's immediate will, which is made known on each particular occasion to those who stand in unity with God. Moral discernment, if it even makes sense to use the term, consists of simple obedience to God's will and eschews a process of moral deliberation that takes into account human knowledge and experience.

But it is here that the tension in Bonhoeffer's account between simplicity and moral reflection is most pronounced. Immediately after concluding the section on abandoning the knowledge of good and evil and instead approaching God with simplicity, he makes a somewhat abrupt assertion that everything he has said about simplicity and single-mindedness is "completely misunderstood" if one thinks that it implies a naïve and unreflective approach to the moral life.[71] While he treats this crucial move in his manuscript as though it were self-evident, the reader is caught unaware. In a single sentence he announces that the unreflective, simple obedience to God's will that he had just championed for several pages may not be completely unreflective after all. He suggests instead the possibility of a third way: a kind of Christian discernment that makes use of the best of human ability and moral reflection while also remaining simple and faithful to Christ. What he had previously separated with careful distinctions, he now wants to combine in a single account of discernment. Here, the tension only hinted at by his use of *aufheben* at the beginning of the manuscript confronts the reader with full force.

Despite the suddenness of this transition, however, the reader familiar with Bonhoeffer's theology will realize that this is not the first time he has

---

71. DBWE 6:319.

dealt with such a tension; in fact, the roots of the tension in "God's Love" go all the way back to his early dissertation *Act and Being*, which deals with the epistemological problem of how one can know the being of God in revelation. There, he illustrates the tension between *actus directus* (direct consciousness) and *actus reflexus* (the consciousness of reflection), or in different terms, between *fides directa* (direct faith) and *fides reflexa* (reflexive faith).[72] On the one hand, he argues, there is a state of direct consciousness or a direct act of faith, in which the individual is unaware of the self and focused entirely on God; on the other hand, there is a kind of reflective act or reflexive faith in which consciousness itself becomes an object of reflection.[73] But how can each of these function properly in the Christian life, and how might they both come together? According to Bonhoeffer, Christ is the key. Christ resolves the tension between *fides directa* and *fides reflexa* by becoming, in the human person, both the subject and object of faith.[74] Thus, the epistemological discussion takes an anthropological turn, because the possibility of knowing God depends upon one's either being "in Christ," where Christ is the subject of one's believing, or "in Adam," where the self-enclosed I remains the subject.[75] In addition, Bonhoeffer continues the ecclesiological focus of his first dissertation, *Sanctorum Communio*, by arguing that the way one exists "in Christ" is through the church, which is the present Christ.[76] Only within the church, the body of Christ, do the dual aspects of *fides directa* and *fides reflexa* come together in the life of the Christian.

What is important for our purposes is something that both Ernst Feil and Hans-Richard Reuter have pointed out: the tension between *actus directus* (or *fides directa*) and *actus reflexus* (or *fides reflexa*) crops up many times in Bonhoeffer's later theology, though under different terminology.[77] In both *Discipleship* and *Ethics*, in particular, it appears in relation to practical moral reasoning as the tension between simplicity and moral reflection, as we have just seen in our exploration of "God's Love" up to this point. Though *Act and Being* is not without implications for ethics, it does not

---

72. For example, see DBWE 2:28, 158–60.

73. Ibid., 28.

74. Ibid., 92, 112.

75. Here, I agree with Green who argues that theological anthropology is the primary subject matter of *Act and Being*. See Green, *Theology of Sociality*, 70. See also Bonhoeffer's comment that "the meaning of epistemology [Erkenntnistheorie] is anthropology," DBWE 2:30.

76. Ibid., 111.

77. Feil, *Theology of Dietrich Bonhoeffer*, 29; Reuter, "Editor's Afterword," 181.

delve fully into what it might mean to live out a simple faith in the world while also reserving a space for rational, moral deliberation in one's life of Christian discipleship. Thus, we come back to our present discussion of "God's Love" to gain such insight. Having stated what this tension is, the question then arises: on what grounds can Bonhoeffer speak of simple obedience and moral reflection at the same time?

His initial justification for such a procedure centers on a distinction between psychological and theological realities. The problem, he suggests, is that many people view simplicity and single-mindedness as observable, psychological realities rather than theological truths.[78] Certainly, on a psychologically observable level, the left hand *does* know what the right hand is doing when making moral decisions and one *does* have some notion of the moral categories of good and evil when in the midst of moral deliberation.[79] However, on a much deeper, theological level, single-mindedness and simplicity are realities inherent to the life of the Christian. These qualities express the reality of the Christian's new life in Christ, which consists of the simplicity of a direct relationship of obedience to God characterized by the freedom to act according to God's will. It is not a contradiction for an individual to be both single-minded, in the theological sense, and a careful and critical thinker, in the psychological sense.[80] In other words, one must not confuse the simplicity of simple obedience with a "psychic simplicity" that is altogether different.[81]

At first glance this explanation is not wholly satisfying, as it seems to establish only that simple obedience is not a psychological category and therefore Christian reflection might, without contradiction, be simple on a theological level, but not on a psychological level. However, this is precisely Bonhoeffer's purpose: he means only to demonstrate that simplicity does not necessarily imply simplistic and uncritical Christian discernment; in fact, he twice asserts that the single-minded person *can* engage "in very complex reflection [*komplizierter Reflexion*]" and that "a single-minded discerning [*einfältige Erkenntnis*] of the will of God" does not preclude deliberation (*Überlegung*).[82] Thus, there is no inherent contradiction to a Christian being both simple *and* wise, as Bonhoeffer puts it in another of his

---

78. DBWE 6:319–20.
79. Ibid.
80. Ibid., 320.
81. Ibid.
82. Ibid., 320–21; DBW 6:322–23.

Ethics manuscripts.[83] The problem, then, is not whether simple obedience and moral reflection might theoretically co-exist, but *how* such an arrangement is possible in the life of a Christian, both theoretically and practically. So far in "God's Love" a clear explanation has not been forthcoming; we move now to Bonhoeffer's central discussion of discerning God's will in search of further clarity.

Discerning the Will of God

Throughout his discussion of discernment Bonhoeffer uses the noun *Prüfung* and the verb *prüfen* to speak of both the outward (discerning God's will) and inward (self-examination) dimensions of discernment. He adopts this language from the Luther Bible where Luther uses the verb *prüfen* to translate the biblical term *dokimázein* (to test), which appears at several points throughout Scripture with various shades of meaning.[84] For our purposes, it is important to note that in the New Testament *dokimázein* describes both the Christian's attempt to probe or discern God's will in order to act rightly and receive God's approval (Rom 12:2, Phil 1:10, Eph 5:9f, 1 Thess 5:21) and the need for Christians to examine or test themselves (2 Cor 13:5, Gal 6:4) and the situations in which they live (Luke 12:56).[85] Thus, while broadly speaking the verb *prüfen* has numerous meanings (test, examine, check, investigate), the English verbs "discern" and "examine" best capture the sense of *prüfen* as it appears in the biblical contexts just mentioned (i.e., one discerns God's will, and examines the self).[86]

---

83. DBWE 6:81–82; cf. chapter 4 below.

84. For an overview of biblical uses, see Kittel, *Theological Dictionary*, 255–60; Wannenwetsch, "Fourfold Pattern," 185.

85. Kittel, *Theological Dictionary*, 260.

86. In this regard I follow the practice of the translators of DBWE 6; cf. DBWE 6:320n74. The perceptive reader of both the German original and English translation of Bonhoeffer's writings will notice many occasions where the words "discern" or "discernment" appear in the English version in places where *prüfen* or *Prüfung* do not appear in the equivalent German text. This demonstrates that there are several other words in German that communicate aspects of what we mean when we speak of discernment in English: for example, *erkennen* (make out, recognize, perceive), a term that is especially prominent in Bonhoeffer's vocabulary; *wahrnehmen* (perceive, detect); and *unterscheiden* (distinguish, differentiate). See the following examples where translators render *erkennen* or *Erkenntnis* as discern or discernment: DBWE 4:68; cf. DBW 4:58; DBWE 8:40, 45, 196; cf. DBW 8:22, 29–30, 206; DBWE 16:264, 605–6, 629, 641; cf. DBW 16:252, 624–25, 654, 668. See also the following example where a form of *wahrnehmen*

The Problem of Moral Discernment

An examination of the references to *Prüfung* and its cognates listed in DBW 17, the index to the *Dietrich Bonhoeffer Werke*, reveals approximately one hundred appearances of the term, in its various grammatical forms, in Bonhoeffer's writings, of which seventy occur in a theological context.[87] Of these references, fifty-four occur in *Ethics* and, remarkably, fifty occur in "God's Love." A survey of all of these references reveals two matters of special interest. First, while almost all of the theological uses occur between the years 1938 and 1942, there are two notable exceptions, which occur in Bonhoeffer's 1932 essay "What is Church?" and in his 1933 essay "What Should a Student of Theology Do Today?"[88] Toward the end of "What is Church?" he affirms that the church is able to speak a concrete commandment to the world, but that a serious practice of self-examination must accompany the proclamation.[89] As he explains: "self-examination [*Selbstprüfung*] down to the smallest detail is always necessary as to whether this commandment was correctly heard or not."[90] Put differently, the church must discern whether it has correctly perceived God's concrete commandment for a particular time and place in order to proclaim it effectively to the world. In "What Should a Student of Theology Do Today?" he mentions that the study of theology should help prepare a person "to discern [*zu prüfen*] the spirits in Christ's church."[91] This means that students of theology must learn to distinguish between true and false doctrine: that is, between Christ's gospel and human teaching.[92] In both cases, these early uses of *Selbstprüfung* and *prüfen* indicate that while he does not fully employ the language of *prüfen* until "God's Love," he begins exploring it much earlier as a way to speak of the practice of discernment.

The second matter of interest when reviewing the references to *Prüfung* outside of "God's Love" is that the largest concentration of such

---

(*wahrnimmt*) becomes "discern," DBWE 6:184; cf. DBW 6:178. One can find an example of *unterscheiden* in Bonhoeffer's *Fiction from Tegel Prison*, although translators render it not as "discern" but as "discriminate," DBWE 7:66; cf. DBW 7:67.

87. DBW 17:775. For four additional references to *Prüfung* in Bonhoeffer's working notes for *Ethics*, see Bonhoeffer, *Zettelnotizen*, 218.

88. DBWE 12:262–66, 432–35.

89. Ibid., 265. For a discussion of Bonhoeffer's view of church and world, and in particular, the church's ability to speak a concrete commandment to the world, see Plant, "Sacrament," 71–87.

90. DBWE 12:265; cf. DBW 12:239.

91. DBWE 12:434; DBW 12:418.

92. DBWE 12:434.

references appears in a set of 1938–39 working notes on the New Testament notion of *Bewährung*.[93] This is unsurprising, given the intimate connection between the term *Bewährung* (tested or esteemed, from the Greek *dókimos*) and the verb *prüfen* (test, examine, or discern, from the Greek *dokimázein*). These notes, prepared only a few years before Bonhoeffer began his work on *Ethics*, clearly foreshadow his interest in exploring the concept of discernment more deeply. Towards the end of the notes, he organizes a brief outline in which the concept of "*selbst prüfen*" appears as the main heading with several subheadings underneath.[94] The outline appears as follows:

> III. To examine oneself [*Selbst prüfen*].
>
> a. to examine [prüfen] the will of God Eph. 5:9; Rom. 12:2
>
> b. situation Phil. 1:10; 1 Thess. 5:21; 1 John 4:1; Rom. 2:18; Luke 12:56
>
> c. oneself 2 Cor. 13:5; (Gal 6:4?): 1 Cor. 11:28[95]

Here he recognizes three aspects of discernment: discerning God's will, discerning correct actions and the nature of particular historical situations, and the reflective activity of discerning or examining one's inner self. The obvious comparison to this is his treatment of discernment in "God's Love," which employs a twofold division (discerning God's will and self-examination) representing the first and third of his 1938–39 subheadings. In "God's Love" he incorporates the second subheading from 1938–39, "situation," into the first subheading, "to examine the will of God," which one can see in part by his treatment of Philippians 1:10. This verse from Philippians, the first biblical reference used to support the subheading "situation," is now linked to the task of discerning God's will in "God's Love."[96] This rearrangement implies that Bonhoeffer began to view the task of "discerning God's will" as equivalent to the task of perceiving the nature of a particular situation in order to determine an action that is best. As we will explore more fully in the following chapter, the reason for this correspondence rests on his Christological understanding of reality.

With these early references to *Prüfung* and *prüfen* in mind, we turn now to the greatest concentration of references, which occurs in "God's

---

93. DBWE 15:357–60; DBW 15:343–45.
94. DBW 15:345.
95. DBWE 15:360; DBW 15:345.
96. Compare DBWE 15:360 and DBWE 6:320.

The Problem of Moral Discernment

Love." Bonhoeffer begins his extended treatment of discernment in this manuscript with a look at Scripture. Three texts that appeared in his 1938–39 musings on *prüfen* once again take center stage.[97] First, he quotes Romans 12:2: "Let yourselves be transformed [*umgestalten*] by the renewing of your minds, so that you may discern [*prüfen*] what is the will of God."[98] He follows this with a somewhat unconventional translation of Philippians 1:9-10a, where he renders the Apostle Paul's statement as: "I pray that your love may increase more and more with knowledge and full insight to help you examine [*prüfen*] the various situations."[99] The final passage is from Ephesians 5 where he combines the beginnings of verses 9 and 10: "Walk as children of light—discerning [*prüfend*] what is pleasing to the Lord." All of these texts illustrate for Bonhoeffer the seriousness of discernment in the Christian life. Determining God's will cannot be left up to intuition and does not require one to abandon moral deliberation (*Überlegung*); in fact, doing so betrays a certain naivety about the moral life and, as he already argued a few pages earlier, a "psychologizing misunderstanding" of what simplicity means for the Christian.[100]

Moreover, discernment cannot mean a casuistic application of moral rules and principles to particular situations. God's will is not "a system of rules that are fixed from the outset, but always new and different in each different life circumstance."[101] This idea of God's will being "new every morning," and therefore requiring continual discernment, is a constant refrain throughout Bonhoeffer's discussion, and indicates that his notion of God's will is particular and immediate, not general and universal. It is not a

---

97. A few pages earlier in "God's Love," Bonhoeffer also included, but then deleted, reference to two other texts mentioned in 1938–39: 1 Thess 5:21 and 2 Cor 13:5.

98. DBWE 6:320; DBW 6:323. Bonhoeffer deviates from the 1912 Luther Bible by using the verb *umgestalten* rather than *verändern* to render the Greek verb *metamórphein* ("Laßt euch umgestalten durch Erneuerung eueres Sinnes, um zu prüfen, was der Wille Gottes sei"). In *Discipleship*, he translates the verse differently, but still employs *Gestalt* language in the crucial phrase: "laßt euch zu einer andern Gestalt verwandeln . . .," DBW 4:263. We will explore the significance of this *Gestalt* language in chapter 4.

99. Bonhoeffer substitutes the word "*Wahrnehmungsvermögen*" (literally: "perception"), which is closer to the Greek *aesthesis*, for Luther's word "Erfahrung" (experience) in his translation. Bonhoeffer also uses "die verschiedenen Situationen" instead of Luther's "was das Beste sei" to render the Greek "*ta diaphéronta*." Bonhoeffer's translation, while perhaps too literal, nevertheless emphasizes that one cannot systematize the process of discernment, but must engage in it anew in every different situation.

100. DBWE 6:320–21.

101. Ibid., 321.

question of one's needing to perceive a general command (e.g., to love one's neighbor) in order to apply it to a unique situation; rather, it is God who forms the divine will into a concrete command in the immediate moment and calls the human person simply to obey. And yet, the immediate and concrete will of God is not always obvious: sometimes it lies "very deeply hidden among many possibilities that offer themselves to us."[102] This makes the task of discernment difficult not only because one must perceive God's will amidst other competing possibilities, but because these possibilities are enticing and solicit themselves as viable alternatives to God's will. These are not *true* possibilities, as if they held equal claim to God's will, but they *appear* as possibilities to the human individual persuaded by the serpent's temptation, "Did God really say?" Thus, as Bonhoeffer argues a few pages later, "genuine discernment . . . must consist precisely in eliminating all other sources of knowledge about the will of God."[103]

In order to engage in such discernment, one must draw upon "[h]eart, intellect, observation, and experience" as well as "cognitive ability, and attentive perception of the context."[104] In another manuscript, "History and Good," he argues that the goal for the Christian is "to discern what is necessary or 'commanded' in a given situation. One must observe, weigh, and judge the matter, all in the dangerous freedom of one's own self."[105] While he does not explicate each of these human attributes in any detail, it is clear enough that he wants to position discernment not only as a simple, spiritual activity, but as a noetic engagement with the reality of God's will within a particular situation. However, despite his emphasis on human ability, discernment is not a matter of human achievement. He believes the active principle of discernment is not one's own reason, but God's grace active through the Holy Spirit. Thus, while he speaks of the rational nature of discernment he likewise maintains that knowing God's will "is not at our human disposal" but depends upon our simple faith in

---

102. My translation differs from the DBWE by rendering "*anbietenden Möglichkeiten*" as "possibilities that offer themselves to us" rather than "competing possibilities," which is not an obvious translation of Bonhoeffer's German. The original text reads: "*Der Wille Gottes kann sehr tief verborgen liegen unter vielen sich anbietenden Möglichkeiten,*" DBWE 6:321; DBW 6:323.

103. DBWE 6:323.

104. Ibid., 321, 323–24.

105. Ibid., 221–22. Bonhoeffer's *Ethics* includes both a first and second draft of "History and Good," making it distinct among his *Ethics* manuscripts.

The Problem of Moral Discernment

God's Holy Spirit revealing the divine will.[106] Here we see the interplay of simplicity and moral reflection within his account.

He also argues that Romans 12:2 is of central importance because it speaks of a divine activity of human transformation, which serves as an essential prerequisite for discerning God's will. Bonhoeffer explains:

> Here the decisive and clear prerequisite is that such discernment can take place only on the basis of a "metamorphosis," a complete inner change of the existing form ... This "metamorphosis" of human beings can only mean overcoming the form [*Gestalt*] of the fallen human being, Adam, and con-formation [*Gleichgestaltung*] with the form [*Gestalt*] of the new human being, Christ.[107]

Bonhoeffer hearkens back to his earlier distinction between those who are in a state of disunion with God ("the fallen human being, Adam") and those who have been transformed into "the new human being, Christ." He claims that only the latter group can practice genuine Christian discernment because only they have experienced the transformative process of conformation to Christ. But this is only one of the points he wishes to convey. More importantly, he wants to link the practice of Christian discernment to the process of Christian formation; for him, the latter is the answer to the question of how the former takes place. In fact, all three Scripture passages cited by Bonhoeffer at the beginning of his discussion illustrate this link between discernment and Christian formation. Romans 12:2 connects the concept of transformation and renewal of the mind with one's ability to discern God's will. Similarly, in Philippians 1:9–10, one's growing in love and knowledge contributes to one's ability to "examine the various situations."[108] In Ephesians 5:8–10, Christians are told to "walk as children of light," which hints at Christian formation, and to "discern what is pleasing to the Lord." In short, Christian formation is not only a prerequisite to discernment, but an ongoing aid to discernment as well.

It is also important to stress that discernment is not enabled by just any manner of spiritual formation. Only as one moves deeper into life with Christ and becomes more closely conformed to the form of Christ—the *Gestalt Christi*—is one better able to discern God's will. Thus, as is true for many other aspects of his thinking, Christology is at the heart of discernment. We saw this already as we explored his contrast earlier in the

---

106. Ibid., 321.
107. Ibid., 322; italics mine.
108. Ibid., 320.

manuscript between those in disunity with God, represented by the Pharisees, and those in unity with God, embodied by Jesus. It is Jesus who brings together both freedom and simplicity in his attitude toward God's will, the same two characteristics that Christians must also learn to combine as they attempt to discern God's will. It is Jesus "who overcomes the knowledge of good and evil for us," and transforms us into his image so that we too can overcome our dependence on the moral categories of good and evil.[109] It is Jesus who is the foundation for discernment, defines the context of discernment, and is the person in whom one must participate in order to discern. As Bonhoeffer puts it, discernment can only happen "on the basis of Jesus Christ . . . within the realm defined by Jesus Christ, only 'in' Jesus Christ."[110]

In the first draft of "History and Good," we find an example of this Christological grounding. Bonhoeffer argues that because Christ became human, "responsible action has to weigh, judge, and evaluate the matter within the human domain . . . Responsible action must not want to be blind."[111] At the same time, because Christ is also divine, responsible action "must completely surrender to God both the judgment on this action and its consequences."[112] In the corresponding passage in the second draft of "History and Good" he repeats himself using slightly different terms: we need to "observe, weigh, evaluate and decide . . . with limited human understanding" in each particular situation; moreover, we must "attempt seriously to examine [*Prüfung*] our own motives and our own hearts."[113] Here, we see the twin emphases of moral reflection and simplicity at work. On the one hand, the moral agent must use the best of human understanding and experience to discern the reality of a particular situation and act accordingly: this is the way of moral reflection. On the other hand, one must ultimately surrender all evaluation and judgment of an action to God and depend on God's grace in discernment. This corresponds to the way of unreflective simplicity.[114]

---

109. Ibid., 313n53.
110. Ibid., 322–23.
111. Ibid., 225.
112. Ibid.
113. Ibid., 268.

114. Bonhoeffer speaks also of responsible action as that which "soberly and simply does what is in accord with reality" and also of "the plain and simple [einfältig] life that flows from reconciliation"; see, ibid., 238, 265.

The Problem of Moral Discernment

Bonhoeffer continues his treatment of Romans 12:2 by arguing that the transformation of which it speaks is not "a static entity," but a "living reality."[115] What he means is that conformation to the form of Christ is not a one time occurrence that, once complete, equips one to discern God's will correctly on all subsequent occasions. On the contrary, conformation to the form of Christ is an ongoing process. As he puts it: "With every new day, therefore, the question arises, how, today, here, in this situation, can I remain and be preserved within this new life with God, with Jesus Christ?"[116] He argues that this question "is the meaning of the concept of discerning the will of God."[117] This is a crucial statement, for it links discernment with ongoing Christian formation. And this ongoing Christian formation, to "remain and be preserved within this new life with God, with Jesus Christ," is another way to speak of the life of discipleship (*Nachfolge*), which includes both the justification and sanctification of the Christian.[118] The central purpose in discerning God's will, therefore, is not to obtain answers to particular problems or dilemmas, but to gain insight into how particular decisions and actions will strengthen and maintain one's relationship with Christ and move one forward on the path of discipleship.

Finally, Bonhoeffer ends this section by addressing the process of discerning God's will, though not through a list of detailed instructions.[119] For him, discernment is not a matter of method, but a matter of faith, and this means there is no blueprint for discernment, but rather some general guidelines. For instance, he affirms again that things such as reason, perception, and knowledge of past experience, all have a crucial part to play in discernment. Moreover, one must carefully considers both "possibilities and consequences" and attempt to maintain a "sober attitude" when trying to decide how God is calling one to act.[120] At the same time, one

---

115. Ibid., 323.

116. Ibid.

117. My translation. Bonhoeffer's original German reads, "Eben diese Frage aber ist der Sinn des Prüfens, was der Wille Gottes sei," which the DBWE 6 renders as: "This very question is what *gives meaning* to the concept of discerning the will of God" (italics mine). My more literal translation of "ist der Sinn" ("*is* the meaning") places a stronger emphasis on the connection between discernment and ongoing Christian formation, which Bonhoeffer wants to emphasize here. See DBW 6:325; DBWE 6:323.

118. See DBWE 4:258–60.

119. See, however, his 1942 letter to his Finkenwalde seminarians, which includes some basic guidelines for decision-making in the church, DBWE 16:264–65.

120. DBWE 6:324.

must exercise faith in God's willingness to make known the divine will.[121] This is not a faith in one's own ability to uncover God's will, but a simple faith that "to those who humbly ask, God will surely make the divine will known."[122] Lastly, one must always be prepared to act as a result of discerning God's will. God grants one freedom "to make a real decision" and respond with confidence that "it is not the human but the divine will that is accomplished."[123]

Bonhoeffer also issues a final warning about what discernment does not entail. He writes: "But in all of this there will be no place for the torment of being confronted with insoluble conflicts, nor the arrogance of being able to master any conflict, nor also the enthusiastic [schwärmerisch] expectation and claim of direct inspirations."[124] While he does not make it explicit, all three of these negative definitions correspond to a particular danger he sees for Christian ethics in general and Christian discernment in particular. In the first case, his reference to "insoluble conflicts" has two likely referents. On the one hand, it refers back to the New Testament Pharisees and their way of moral reflection that proceeds from a place of disunity and operates according to the knowledge of good and evil. He wants to make clear that the starting point for Christian ethics is not a situation of conflict or an either-or dilemma because this can never lead one to God's will. Discerning God's will can only be successful from a place of reconciliation and unity. On the other hand, another possible referent is the Lutheran tradition and its emphasis on guilt. He wants to maintain that one can receive real answers for Christian behavior through discernment; one it not caught in a situation of being "damned" no matter what choice is made.

In the second instance, Bonhoeffer says that discernment is not an arrogant activity that seeks to "master any conflict." Here, he is warning against the presumption that one can solve seemingly "insoluble conflicts" through accumulated knowledge or casuistic method. Thus, this is a subtle critique against both Kantian ethics and Catholic moral theology. Finally, he speaks against the danger of religious enthusiasm (*Schwärmerei*).[125] One cannot rely on direct inspiration from God every time one faces a decision while simultaneously ignoring the reality of the historical situation

121. Ibid.
122. Ibid.
123. Ibid.
124. Ibid.
125. Ibid.

and what it might be saying. While discernment is a spiritual activity, it is not a mystical and disembodied activity; rather, discernment is an activity deeply rooted in the reality of the world: an activity that remains faithful to God precisely by making good use of the best of human ability in order to discern God's will.

Self-Examination

Having spoken of what it means to discern the will of God, Bonhoeffer now turns to the activity of self-examination (*Selbstprüfung*), which, as Dahill rightly observes, is "one of the few instances in Bonhoeffer were *selbst-* (self-) is used in an unambiguously positive sense."[126] Here again, Bonhoeffer begins his discussion with reference to Scripture. As he did previously in the manuscript, he alludes to Jesus' warning against self-reflection in Matthew 6:3, on the one hand, but, on the other hand, quotes 2 Corinthians 13:5, "Test yourselves to see whether you are in the faith. Examine [*prüfet*] yourselves! Do you not realize that Jesus Christ is in you?"[127] These verses taken together point immediately to the same tension already noted above, between simple, unreflective faith (Matt 6:3) and moral reflection (2 Cor 13:5).

Bonhoeffer seeks to clarify his position by drawing a distinction between what he calls a "pharisaical kind of self-examination" and a "Christian self-examination," which mirrors his earlier contrast between two different kinds of judging. While the *act* of self-examination is the same for both the Pharisee and the Christian (i.e., the mind turning inward and reflecting on the self and its knowledge), both the *subject* and the *object* of reflection are different: for pharisaical self-examination, it is the disunited human being who turns inward to consider the isolated and disunited self and the knowledge of good and evil; for Christian self-examination, it is the self reconstituted in Christ who turns inward to reflect on the knowledge of Christ. Drawing on his understanding of Christian conformation to the form of Christ, Bonhoeffer puts all of this in very spatial terms: "Jesus Christ now occupies the very same space in them that had previously

---

126. Dahill, *Reading from the Underside*, 88. This is the aspect of discernment that Bartel passes over far too quickly, and which Rasmussen overemphasizes when he claims it is "the basic step in proving the will of God." See Bartel, "Rationality of Discernment," 102–7; Rasmussen, *Reality and Resistance*, 157.

127. DBWE 6:325. Bonhoeffer also mentions, but does not quote, Galatians 6:4: "But let each one test his own work, and then his reason to boast will be in himself alone and not in his neighbor" (NRSV).

been occupied by their own knowledge of good and evil."[128] Thus, when Christians look inward, it is actually Christ whom they see. As he puts it: "In examining themselves, the Christians' focus is thus not diverted away from Jesus Christ and onto their own selves. Instead, it remains completely focused on Jesus Christ."[129] One cannot help but notice somewhere in the background Luther's vivid image of the "happy exchange," whereby the life of the resurrected Christ takes the place of the sinful and egotistical self in the life of the Christian.[130]

The purpose of Christian self-examination, according to Bonhoeffer, is twofold. First, it has the obvious purpose of helping one examine one's own "faith and work."[131] While this is almost lost in his exposition because of his strong emphasis on looking inward at Christ, it is nevertheless crucial. It is helpful to consider his words in the second draft of his *Ethics* manuscript "History and Good," written just before "God's Love," where he says that in order to act responsibly in a given situation, "we must attempt seriously to examine [*Prüfung*] our own motives and our own hearts."[132] Later in the same manuscript, he discuses the concept of vocation and stresses the need for self-examination in order to determine the potential boundaries of one's responsible action. He even suggests that "there are criteria for self-examination [*Selbst-prüfung*], even though they cannot provide complete certainty about one's own self."[133] This is particularly striking because it demonstrates that he is not completely averse to incorporating careful reflection and common sense principles into the task of self-examination. In this case, he argues that by knowing one's usual temperament or disposition (e.g., one might be overly enthusiastic or overly cautious) one can more accurately discern God's will by not confusing one's own inclinations with what God might be calling one to do.[134]

This initial purpose of self-examination is linked to a second fundamental purpose: to reaffirm and renew the knowledge of Christ's presence within. When Christians turn inward they acknowledge their identity as people in whom Christ has taken form. Self-examination reminds a person

---

128. Ibid., 325.
129. Ibid.
130. See for example, Luther, *Galatians*, 283–84.
131. DBWE 6:325.
132. Ibid., 268.
133. Ibid., 294.
134. Ibid.

of his or her essential unity with God, which serves as the foundation from which one discerns God's will. This helps to orient one's moral vision because as a person gazes inward at the person of Christ rather than at his or her own presumed knowledge of good and evil, Christ becomes the prism through which one perceives morality and decides how to act responsibly in a given situation.[135] In addition, by focusing on Christ one learns to release one's grip on autonomous moral knowledge and to relinquish one's right to judge the validity or ultimate worth of a decision or action.[136] As Bonhoeffer puts it, self-examination will "always consist precisely in surrendering ourselves completely to the judgment of Jesus Christ."[137] He articulates this especially well in his discussion of responsible action when he speaks of the "*venture* [*Wagnis*] of concrete decision" in which one must act in faith and trust in God's judgment and grace, even though one might accrue guilt and not fully know the validity of one's action.[138]

Bringing Together Simplicity and Moral Reflection

In our exploration of "God's Love" up to this point we have seen Bonhoeffer develop a distinction between unity and disunity and between simplicity and moral reflection. At the same time, we have observed a tension in his account of Christian discernment, which seeks to include *both* simplicity and moral reflection within its sphere of activity. In our foregoing investigation of the activity of *Prüfung* we saw the interplay between simplicity and moral reflection and noted especially how both coexist in the person of Jesus Christ, suggesting the possibility that both might also come together in the human person. Thus, in answer to a question posed earlier in the chapter, it seems that Bonhoeffer's critique of moral reflection is not intended as a blanket rejection of *all* moral reflection, but as a targeted attack against one particular kind of moral reflection. Such an assertion finds support in the final portion of "God's Love" when Bonhoeffer reformulates the tension between simplicity and moral reflection in terms of the relationship between "hearing" and "doing" God's will and concludes his manuscript with a theological discussion of love.

135. Ibid., 325.
136. Ibid., 325–26.
137. Ibid.
138. Ibid., 257, 284.

According to Jesus in the Sermon on the Mount, the purpose of hearing God's will is to do God's will (Matt 7:25–27). Authentic Christian action immediately responds to God's command in obedience (doing) and does not seek to evaluate what God commands prior to acting (judging). For example, Bonhoeffer argues that the doer of the law recognizes its authority and "knows of only one single possibility for bringing the law to bear, namely, doing it oneself."[139] The judge, on the other hand, assumes that the law does not have "the power of the living word of God to assert itself" and therefore takes an active role in controlling and implementing the law in order to judge the self, others, and situations at hand.[140] These approaches to the law are mutually exclusive: the first accepts God's law as revealed and acts upon it in faith; the second questions God's law and seeks to improve or manipulate it.

The crucial difference between both approaches to the law concerns the relationship between hearing and doing. The doer of the law hears God's word not for the sake of gaining knowledge, but solely for the sake of putting the word into action; this is the only behavior that makes sense.[141] For the doer of the law, hearing becomes action directly ("*im selben Augenblick*"), without any mediating human influence.[142] Thus, one cannot construe hearing and doing as two separate and divided activities, but one must view them through one's relationship of unity with Christ. In contrast to this, the judge hears God's word in order to know God's word and thereby gain possession of God's word, cataloguing it in the mind for future use. There is not a direct line between hearing and doing, but instead one's knowledge of God's law mediates any subsequent action that might result.[143] The Pharisees are the prime example of those who hear God's law in order to know the law and cast judgments based on that knowledge. However, this knowing prevents the doing of the Pharisees from being genuine doing; instead, it is merely "pseudo-doing" or "hypocrisy" because the action is not "bound to Jesus Christ," but stems from a place of disunity with God.[144]

---

139. Ibid., 328.
140. Ibid.
141. Ibid., 330.
142. Ibid., 328–29; cf. DBW 6:331.
143. DBWE 6:329.
144. Ibid., 327.

The Problem of Moral Discernment

That much of this discussion sounds familiar is no surprise. When Bonhoeffer refers to James 1:22 midway through his criticism of those who hear the word rather than do the word, he mentions that James' polemic against the hearers of the word "exactly parallels Jesus' polemic against the Pharisees."[145] Likewise, Bonhoeffer's critique at the end of the manuscript of the one who seeks knowledge of God's word in order to pass judgment is the same critique he develops earlier again moral reflection. This connection is crucial because it finally helps us see more clearly that it is not moral reflection, per se, that stands opposed to his understanding of simplicity; instead, it is a particular kind of moral reflection, characterized by the activities of knowing and judging, that cannot coexist with simple obedience and cannot be a part of Christian discernment. Such reflection proceeds from and creates disunion between and within people. It is reflection that depends on one's own knowledge of good and evil, which serves as the criterion for all moral judgment. Moreover, it is reflection that draws upon an accumulated body of moral knowledge that one possesses in the intellect and uses the power of deductive reasoning and an overly scientific and casuistic method to apply rules to particular historical situations and arrive at judgments that constitute "God's will." Here, discernment becomes solely a human activity rather than an act of faith and obedience.[146] The great tragedy of this kind of moral reflection is its perceived transcendent vantage point from which it seeks to reflect on the self, on others, and on various situations; in reality, such a vantage point apart from Christ is illusory.

As we have seen, Bonhoeffer's way of Christian discernment is quite different from this and allows space for a more positive account of moral reflection. This kind of reflection proceeds from a presupposition of unity and reconciliation; thus, it results in evaluations and judgments that are never condemnatory, but always gracious even when serving a disciplinary purpose. It is not one's own knowledge of good and evil that gives rise to judgment and provides the criterion for moral reflection; on the contrary, it is the knowledge of God and the judgment of Christ that provide the basis for discernment. Looking inward to the self is to turn one's gaze upon Christ insofar as Christ has replaced the knowledge of good and evil in the individual. All moral evaluation is only preliminary with ultimate judgment being left to God's mercy. Furthermore, this kind of moral reflection can coexist with simplicity because it shares a common goal: to do the one will of God. In

---

145. Ibid., 329.
146. Ibid., 370.

short, the task of Christian discernment, which includes this more positive account of moral reflection, is not to discern how God's law should become immediate and concrete in a particular instance; God already performs this work in each historical situation. Christian discernment, therefore, means to perceive the one will of God amidst other enticing possibilities that offer themselves as options. To discern God's will is to recognize God's concrete commandment for the moment and to act on that command rather than try to catalogue it for future consultation. Such a process of discernment requires both simple obedience *and* moral reflection.

Bonhoeffer's theological discussion of love at the end of the manuscript brings his discussion full circle, and points once again to the importance of Christology for understanding how simple obedience and moral reflection might coincide in the life of the Christian. He asserts that love is "the decisive word that distinguishes the human being in disunion from the human being in the state of origin."[147] Without love "everything disintegrates and is unacceptable; in this love everything is integrated, united, and pleasing to God."[148] Thus, his discussion of love is the necessary counterpoint to his opening discussion of disunion. He explains that love is God's act of reconciliation chosen for humanity and embodied in the person of Jesus Christ. Insofar as one participates in this love and shares it with others, one approaches the moral life from a point of reconciliation rather than disunity.[149] The key is to understand that in loving one's neighbor, it is not one's human love that is active, but *God's* love within the person. To stress this point, Bonhoeffer speaks of a theological passivity that rules out an understanding of love as an "autonomous human doing, independent and free from the divine love."[150] Such passivity does not render a person inert in the moral life, but reminds a person that he or she loves others with the love that God has already graciously bestowed.

Moreover, because love distinguishes between those in unity with God and those in a state of disunity, it must also differentiate between Christian discernment and all other forms of moral deliberation. Philippians 1:9–10 suggests as much by identifying one's growth in love as an aid to successful discernment. Likewise, Bonhoeffer suggests in a 1929 address on Christian

---

147. Ibid., 332.
148. Ibid.
149. Ibid., 336–37.
150. Ibid., 337.

ethics that love might guide Christian moral action.[151] In a later *Ethics* manuscript he says that "God's love liberates human perception . . . for the clear recognition of reality, the neighbor, and the world."[152] In a 1944 meditation on 1 John 3:24 he speaks of love as that which helps people recognize whether they are keeping God's commandments and walking the path of discipleship.[153] All of this suggests that Muers is correct when she asserts that it is only "in and through love" that one can successfully discern God's will.[154] This is because "the divine love as gift shapes the exercise of hearing and discernment," which Christians rely upon to navigate the moral life.[155] Thus, to act according to God's will is to act according to divine love. Furthermore, because God's love is not "a general idea of love," but that which is "really lived in Jesus Christ," successful Christian discernment must rely on one's continual growth—or formation—in Christ, who reconciles the seemingly disparate elements of Christian discernment into one.[156] As we see yet again, one cannot fully understand Bonhoeffer's account of discernment without grasping its Christological underpinning: it is this connection between Christology and Christian discernment that we will begin to examine in the following chapter.

Conclusion

With his writing in "God's Love" Bonhoeffer sets the stage for his exploration of the Christian moral life in *Ethics*. He makes primary the question—what is the will of God?—and in so doing, positions discernment as the central task for Christian life. The possibility that he intended this manuscript as the preface to *Ethics* only makes the section on discernment all the more significant. Above all, the discussion is crucial not because it offers one of many ways that he speaks about moral discernment, but because it provides the key for how he handles the issue of discerning God's will

---

151. DBWE 10:365, 369.

152. DBWE 6:242. Bonhoeffer never completed his planned exposition of "Love and Responsibility" in his manuscript "History and Good"; see ibid., 298n191.

153. DBWE 16:629.

154. Muers, *Keeping God's Silence*, 171.

155. Ibid.

156. DBWE 6:83. Whether Bonhoeffer would have expanded on the connection between discernment, Christology, and love in "God's Love" is difficult to know, given the way his manuscript ends abruptly in the midst of his exposition.

throughout *Ethics*. Three important observations from "God's Love" will serve to summarize the foregoing investigation and point the way ahead to subsequent chapters in this book.

First, we see developing throughout the manuscript an obvious tension between a simple, unreflective approach to God's will and a rational, reflective approach. Bonhoeffer is aware of this tension, but seems to underplay its significance, arguing as though it were self-evident how Christian moral discernment can retain its simple character while still incorporating the best of human ability. There are certain theological presuppositions lying in the background, but by not fully explaining them, he leaves the reader at times uncertain about the coherency of his vision. However, he does offer some hints about the nature of these presuppositions. For instance, he clearly identifies Jesus as the prime example of one who brings together a single-minded approach to God and a freedom to make judgments before God. In addition, it becomes clear that conformation to the form of Christ is central to one's ability to discern God's will. If discerning God's will depends upon both simplicity and moral reflection, it follows that Christian conformation must have a role in facilitating their coming together in the life of a Christian. Thus, as we will see more fully in the following two chapters, Christology holds important resources for clarifying Bonhoeffer's view of discernment.

Second, the foregoing exploration of "God's Love" reveals that Bonhoeffer's understanding of moral reflection is more nuanced than it may initially appear. While he does not clearly articulate as much through precise terminology or definitions, his discussion nevertheless implies that there are two types of moral reflection, each with different presuppositions and goals. On the one hand, there is a moral reflection that assumes a knowledge of good and evil and seeks to possess God's word in the intellect in order to make judgments. This kind of moral reflection operates through a method of moral casuistry that attempts to apply universal moral principles to particular situations. In short, such moral reflection is self-centered because it looks only to the self and its own resources to navigate the moral life. It is this kind of moral reflection that leads him to maintain that discernment should be simple and *unreflective*. There is, on the other hand, a moral reflection that is proper to Christian ethics: one that relies on knowledge of God to make judgments and that seeks to hear God's voice only in order to act immediately upon it. This kind of reflection turns inward, but in doing so, discovers that Christ—not the self—is the object of reflection. Although Bonhoeffer does not go into detail in his description of this kind of reflection one might deduce a fuller account through studying material elsewhere in his corpus, as we will see in chapter 5.

Finally, there is a sense throughout the manuscript that moral discernment is a human activity, requiring the best of human abilities. One must not be carried away too far along the road of religious enthusiasm. Discerning God's will is not a disembodied act, but one grounded in the reality of the world. Indeed, one of the problems of disunity is not only that it draws one away from God and others, but away from true worldliness as well. The importance of the world is that it provides the context in which one's ongoing discernment of God's will occurs. As will become evident in chapter 6, it is Bonhoeffer's awareness of this context, and how it helps to guide moral discernment, that ultimately keeps his account of discernment from falling prey to a critique on the grounds of an alleged subjectivism.

With all three of these observations in mind, we turn now to the following chapter and embark upon a further exploration of the Christological presuppositions that undergird Bonhoeffer's view of moral discernment.

3

The Christological Foundation of Discernment

CHRISTOLOGY LIES AT THE heart of Bonhoeffer's understanding of moral discernment. Such a claim is not surprising given the centrality of Christology for his entire theological and ethical thinking.[1] In the previous chapter, we already saw indications of this Christological emphasis; for example, it is the life of Jesus Christ, in contradistinction to the Pharisees, that demonstrates what it means to overcome the knowledge of good and evil in order to correctly discern God's will; likewise, it is the form of Christ that determines the nature of one's transformation from living in Adam to living in Christ, thereby allowing one properly to discern God's will and engage in self-examination. In the current chapter, I will argue that it is also Bonhoeffer's Christology that provides the ground to alleviate the fundamental tension in his account of discernment between simplicity and moral reflection.

As noted in the last chapter, there is already a hint of this role of Christology in "God's Love" when Bonhoeffer contends that Jesus Christ embodies both freedom *and* simplicity in his approach to God's will.[2] For Bonhoeffer, Jesus Christ is free in that he is not bound by any predetermined course of moral action and is at liberty to reflect on a situation and

---

1. Among the most interesting and important discussions of Bonhoeffer's Christology are Dumas, *Theologian of Reality*, esp. 215–32; Feil, *Theology of Dietrich Bonhoeffer*, 59–96; Abromeit, *Das Geheimnis Christi*; Green, *Theology of Sociality*, esp. 185–246. For an insightful account of the link between Bonhoeffer's Christology and ethics, see Wannenwetsch, "The Whole Christ," 75–98.

2. DBWE 6:312–13.

The Christological Foundation of Discernment

respond accordingly, as he did when deciding to perform a Sabbath healing for the woman who had been sick for eighteen years (Luke 13:10–13). At the same time, he is simple insofar as he seeks only to carry out obediently the one will of God on every occasion without attempting to weigh several alternatives beforehand. Elsewhere in *Ethics*, he makes a very similar distinction, arguing that Christ is free because "he affirms God's will out of his very own insight with open eyes and a joyful heart," but also obedient "by blindly following the law he has been commanded."[3] What is crucial in both cases is that this freedom and simple obedience are not at conflict within Christ; instead, his freedom manifests itself in his simple obedience. Christ reminds Christians that they are not granted freedom *from*, but have freedom *for* God and others.[4] Thus, Christians exercise freedom through obedience, which keeps obedience from becoming slavery. Put differently, "freedom ennobles obedience" by giving it both practical and conceptual dignity.[5] The question is: how does Christ make it possible for Christians to combine freedom and obedience in their lives? To restate this in terms of our discussion of moral discernment: how does Christ allow a person to embody a simple, unreflective approach to God's will that also includes a space for a certain kind of moral reflection and deliberation?

To answer this question we first need to consider another question, which Andreas Pangritz says "forms the *cantus firmus* of Bonhoeffer's theological development from the beginning to the end."[6] This question, especially prominent in his 1933 *Lectures on Christology*, is the fundamental inquiry: who is Jesus Christ?[7] For Bonhoeffer, responding to this question points one in two directions: to the mystery of Christ as fully divine and fully human, which I investigate in the current chapter, and to the form (*Gestalt*) in which Christ takes shape in the world, which I take up in the following chapter. By reflecting on the former, Christ as fully divine and fully human, we come to understand the conceptual basis for combining simplicity and moral reflection. This becomes most obvious when considering Bonhoeffer's Christological description of reality and his conceptual scheme of ultimate and penultimate, both of which are extended reflections

---

3. Ibid., 287.
4. DBWE 3: 64.
5. DBWE 6:287.
6. Pangritz, "Who is Jesus Christ," 134–53.
7. On the centrality of the theme of Christ's presence in *Lectures on Christology*, see Pelikan, "Bonhoeffer's Christologie of 1933," 147.

on the two natures of Christ. Through considering the latter, the *Gestalt Christi*, we come to grasp in more practical terms how one's conformation to the form of Christ creates the necessary conditions for one to practice a discernment that is both simple and wise.

Reflecting on the Mystery of Faith: The Divine and Human Christ

Bonhoeffer's understanding of the relationship between the two natures of Christ provides a foundation for how to think about combining simplicity and moral reflection. For him, the Chalcedonian formula best expresses this mystery of faith when it asserts that Christ is both fully divine and fully human without confusion, change, distinction, or separation.[8] He argues that "nothing is further from being a product of Greek thinking than the Chalcedonian formula," by which he means that such a formula is not a philosophical construction aimed at explaining Christ, but an expression of the biblical truth about the person of Christ.[9] Moreover, such a formula is an example of negative Christology: it does not offer positive content for describing Christ, but it delineates boundaries beyond which one cannot go in one's attempts to characterize Christ. As Bonhoeffer puts it, the formula is a "living assertion about Christ that goes beyond all conceptual forms."[10] This is an important point for Bonhoeffer because he is convinced that Christological inquiry should not be an attempt at conceptual certainty or intellectual control of Christ. In fact, Christology represents the unique place where the divine Logos confronts the human logos and dethrones it.[11] This is because Christ, the Word made flesh, is beyond all classification or systemization. Christology is primarily about responding to the present Christ, not trying to reason out how Christ can be present in the first place.[12]

Bonhoeffer drives this point home throughout his *Lectures on Christology* by distinguishing between the "who" questions and the "how" questions of Christology. One cannot ask questions about *how* Christ's divine and human nature correspond to each other or *how* Christ can really be present in

8. DBWE 12:342.
9. Ibid., 352.
10. Ibid., 343.
11. Ibid., 302.
12. Ibid., 301–3.

the contemporary world because such questions are an attempt to gain mastery over Christ by interpreting him and classifying him into pre-existing human categories.[13] Thus, one can only ask questions about *who* Christ is because such questions recognize the limits of human reason, the supremacy of Christ, and the proper context of faith from which questions might proceed. Unfortunately, this procedure of distinguishing between questions of "who" and "how" is often confusing. It is not clear how questions about *who* Christ is, once answered, do not naturally become question related to *how* Christ exists. For example, Bonhoeffer's important description of Christ as Word, sacrament, and church-community might initially offer an answer to the question of *who* Christ is, but it is certainly also a response to the question of *how* Christ takes form in the contemporary world.[14]

Despite the potential confusion of Bonhoeffer's terminology of *who* and *how*, his distinction between these two kinds of questions intends to illuminate his underlying argument. He wants to convince us that Christological reflection is a matter of faith; thus, "God as human being, and human being as God, must be held together in our thinking at the risk of sacrificing the rationality of such an assertion."[15] At stake is how one approaches the two natures of Christ. The beauty of the Chalcedonian formula is that it does not begin with the human nature and divine nature, as such, considering each as isolated and objective "things," but it begins with the person of Jesus Christ, who is both divine and human. Thus, within the formula there is a presupposition of reconciliation at work. In a statement that has direct bearing on how we might think about moral discernment, Bonhoeffer says:

> We must carry on in this Chalcedonian sense. This can only happen when we overcome our way of thinking about the divinity and humanity of Christ as objects that are before us, when our thinking does not begin with the two natures in isolation, but rather with the fact that Jesus Christ is God. The *is* may not be interpreted any further. It has been established by God and is therefore the premise for all our thinking and not subject to any further constructions.[16]

13. Ibid., 302–3.

14. Jaraslov Pelikan exacerbates the confusion when he argues that the question of "who" can nevertheless include questions of "what" and "where," all the while avoiding the question of "how." See Pelikan, "Bonhoeffer's Christologie," 149.

15. DBWE 12:340.

16. Ibid., 350.

The premise of Christological reflection is the reality of the God-man, Jesus Christ, made known to us through faith. Such a premise means that Christology begins from a point of reconciliation, not disunity. It also means that Christological reflection happens within an ecclesial and doxological context, for only here can one truly understand the reality of Christ. Bonhoeffer suggests at the beginning of his *Lectures on Christology* that Christological reflection begins in "silence before the Word" and proceeds only within the church community where one learns to "reflect upon and analyze" the reality of Christ.[17] Later, in a 1939 Christmas letter, he says that theology arises from "prayerful kneeling before the mystery of the divine child in the stable."[18] Here, the task it not to "decode God's mystery," but "to keep the miracle of God a miracle, to comprehend, defend, and exalt the mystery of God, precisely as mystery."[19] Thus, Christology does not preclude all manner of reasonable reflection, but places it within the context of worship and of relationship with Christ; in addition, Christology subjects moral reflection to the particular presuppositions of reconciliation and divine authority, both of which guard against an unauthorized attempt to classify and systematize what cannot, by its nature, be classified and systematized.

In addition, Bonhoeffer's reflection on the relationship between the two natures of Christ manifests itself also in his view of reality: just as the divine and human natures come together in Christ, so also do the realities of God and world come together in Christ. This understanding of reality, described through his idea of Christ-reality (*Christuswirklichkeit*) and through his language of ultimate and penultimate, provides the conceptual tools by which we can grasp how simplicity and moral reflection come together. To better understand this, we turn now to an exploration of the ultimate reality of Christ and of the ultimate and penultimate.

---

17. Ibid., 300–301, 304. For a larger treatment of the theme of silence in Bonhoeffer's theology, and in theological ethics in general, see Muers, *Keeping God's Silence*. On silence and discernment, Muers remarks: "[T]he 'humble silence of the worshipping community' participates in God's act of hearing and is enabled thereby to discern, not only the person of Christ 'over against' the world, but the world in relation to Christ as its center," ibid., 121. Pangritz also notes the doxological setting in Bonhoeffer's Christology lectures; see, Pangritz, "Who is Jesus Christ," 142.

18. DBWE 15:528.

19. Ibid., 529.

The Christological Foundation of Discernment

The Ultimate Reality of Christ

It is quite telling that when Bonhoeffer began work in 1940 on his proposed book of ethics, the very first topics he addressed were Christology, reality, and how the two relate to Christian ethics. The result of this thinking is his earliest *Ethics* manuscript "Christ, Reality, and Good."[20] Though we have already argued that his later manuscript, "God's Love," was likely intended as the opening preface to his completed book on ethics, this earliest manuscript, "Christ, Reality, and Good," is a fitting first chapter because it lays out the core of his Christological understanding of God and world, which undergirds all of his ethical and theological thinking.[21]

During the final stages of his work on *Ethics*, Bonhoeffer penned the following Christological statement, effectively summarizing his Christocentric view of reality:

> *Jesus Christ, the eternal Son with the Father in eternity*—this means that nothing created can be conceived and essentially understood in its nature apart from Christ, the mediator of creation. Everything has been created through Christ and toward Christ, and everything has its existence only in Christ (Col. 1:15ff.). Seeking to understand God's will with creation apart from Christ is futile.[22]

This succinct passage highlights one of the primary dimensions of his belief in *Christuswirklichkeit*. One sees this dimension through his reference to Colossians 1:15ff, a text that speaks of Christ as the ontological ground of all being.[23] For Bonhoeffer the entire New Testament witness speaks of Christ as the foundational reality in which "all things hold together" (Col 1:17). All other so-called realities, such as the reality of "self," "world" or "ethical principle," have no autonomous existence or authority as such; to speak of them apart from Christ is to speak in abstraction.[24] Thus, all of creation is grounded in Christ at its inception, depends on Christ as its source of being, and finds final fulfillment only in Christ. As Bonhoeffer

---

20. DBWE 6:47–75.

21. For an account of the development of Bonhoeffer's thinking about reality, see Pfeifer, "Aesthetic Voyage," 63–81. For additional material on Bonhoeffer's view of reality, see Feil, *Theology of Dietrich Bonhoeffer*, 29–45; Dumas, *Theologian of Reality*, 215–35.

22. DBWE 6:399–400.

23. Ibid.

24. Feil asserts that philosophy and even theology fall under Bonhoeffer's category of "abstraction"; Feil, *Theology of Dietrich Bonhoeffer*, 32–37.

often writes by way of shorthand, Christ is the "origin, essence and goal" of all things.[25]

This view of *Christuswirklichkeit* rejects both a "positivist-empiricist" and an idealist approach to reality and ethics.[26] Regarding the former, Bonhoeffer claims that it is "vulgar" and unsuitable because it willingly accepts "what is at hand, given, accidental, and driven by temporary goals in any given time" without any awareness of the ultimate reality of Christ "beyond and in all that exists."[27] His dissatisfaction with the latter has roots as far back as *Sanctorum Communio* and especially *Act and Being*.[28] According to Hans Pfeifer, Bonhoeffer "considered it a failure of idealism that the ego as center of the consciousness could never reach reality itself, but remained in the realm of the spirit, circling perennially around itself. With Luther, he called it 'Cor curvum in se.'"[29] In short, one cannot arrive at a true understanding of reality by relying solely on sociological investigation into the empirical world or on philosophical speculation guided by the human ego. On the contrary, one must recognize in faith that only the incarnate, crucified and risen Christ makes real all that exists.

Perhaps his most effective illustration of this ontological truth is his portrayal of Christ as the center (*Mitte*).[30] He first uses this image in *Creation and Fall* (1932–33) when he offers a vivid description of Christ's cross firmly planted "[i]n the center [*Mitte*] of the world" where it becomes a "fountain of life" for all creation.[31] Shortly after this, in his *Lectures on Christology*, he identifies Christ as both the center (*Mitte*) and boundary of human existence, human history, and the natural world.[32] Echoes of this Christology occur again in *Ethics*, where he variously describes Christ as

---

25. Bonhoeffer uses this phrase throughout *Ethics* (though in the first reference he uses *Bestand* instead of *Wesen*); see, DBWE 6:70, 226, 251, 253, 259, 263; DBW 6:57, 225, 250, 252, 259, 262; Bonhoeffer, *Zettelnotizen*, 85.

26. DBWE 6:53–54.

27. Ibid., 54.

28. For Bonhoeffer's critique of Idealism and the problem of the *cor curvum in se* in *Act and Being*, see DBWE 2:46, 51, 58, 80.

29. Pfeiffer, "Aesthetic Voyage," 64–65.

30. Abromeit argues that, while Bonhoeffer's references to Christ as *Mitte* are relatively small, they are of primary importance for his Christology; see, Abromeit, *Das Geheimnis Christi*, 256–67.

31. DBWE 3:146. Bonhoeffer's allusion to the tree of life planted in the Garden of Eden is evident.

32. DBWE 12:324–27.

The Christological Foundation of Discernment

the center (*Mitte*) of the Bible, the church, and theology, but also of history, reason, justice, and culture.[33] His purpose in speaking of Christ as the center of all things is to illustrate the shape of reality and to affirm an expansive Christology. If Christ is the ontological foundation of all things, reality cannot consist of disparate principles competing against one another but must be a reconciled whole. In ethical terms, this means that the premise of Christian ethics cannot be a conflict between what is good and what is real or between what is spiritual and what is worldly. Christ has rendered any such distinctions obsolete, leaving a presupposition of reconciliation as the only possible starting point for Christian moral life. Moreover, Bonhoeffer's view means that Christ is not restricted to a spiritual realm accessible to a select group, but becomes manifest in every aspect of the world and available to all people. Theologically speaking, every encounter with reality is Christological, and this is because Christ not only has ushered in a new humanity, but has reconstituted all of creation and broken down any distinction between "Christian" and "worldly."[34] Thus, we see a clear rejection of two-realm thinking, which no longer makes sense given his conception of *Christuswirklichkeit*. As he states in "Christ, Reality, and Good": "To speak of the world without speaking of Christ is pure abstraction. The world stands in relationship to Christ whether the world knows it or not."[35]

Because Christ is the origin and essence of everything, one cannot conceive or understand anything apart from Christ, "the mediator of creation."[36] This image of Christ as mediator (*Mittler*) is closely linked with the image of Christ as the center (*Mitte*) and highlights the epistemological and existential dimension of Bonhoeffer's view of *Christuswirklichkeit*.[37] For him, there is no direct access to other people or things in the world: one has no immediacy with any reality apart from Christological immediacy. He expresses this notion most strongly in *Discipleship*, which is also the text in which the Christological title of mediator occurs most frequently.[38]

33. DBWE 6:58, 228, 341.

34. DBWE 6:400.

35. Ibid., 68.

36. Although the image of mediator does not appear in the passage from Colossians mentioned by Bonhoeffer, one finds it in 1 Timothy 2:5–6a and Hebrews 8:6; 9:15; 12:24. Interestingly, Bonhoeffer does not mention the Hebrews texts in his writings and only refers a few times to the 1 Timothy text; see, DBWE 14:799; DBWE 15:329, 336.

37. For a list of references to Bonhoeffer's use of *Mittler*, see DBW 17:721.

38. See DBWE 4:59, 80, 93–98, 153, 170, 207–8, 214; DBW 4:47, 72, 88–93, 157, 177, 221, 228. See also Bonhoeffer's discussion of "immediacy" in *Life Together*, DBWE 5:40–44, 106–7.

Here he speaks of Jesus' call to discipleship causing a break between the individual and all other realities: "He [Christ] is in the middle [*Mitte*]. He has deprived those whom he has called of every immediate connection to those given realities."[39] A few sentences later, in a statement that foreshadows his Christological understanding of reality in *Ethics*, he remarks that Christ is the mediator not only between humanity and God and between one human person and another but also "between person and reality."[40] To recognize Christ as the Son of God is to unmask the false immediacy of the world and thereby recognize reality as it truly is.[41] His polemic against unmediated relationship to the world reaches a climax when he argues that any "unmediated natural relationship, knowingly or unknowingly, is an expression of hatred toward Christ."[42] He repeats this line of thinking in *Ethics*, albeit with less rhetorical flourish and more ethical focus, when he suggests that it is "futile" to understand God's will in the world apart from Christ.[43]

Despite this emphasis on Christological mediation, however, Bonhoeffer does not view the world in negative terms; instead, he says that one should be grateful for "the gifts of creation" and "for the merciful preservation of this life."[44] Neither does he imply that Christological immediacy leads to disunity with the world: "He [Christ] separates, but he also unites. He cuts off every direct path to someone else, but he guides everyone following him to the new and sole true way to the other person via the mediator."[45] Thus, instead of creating a barrier to knowing and experiencing the world, Christ facilitates such an encounter by allowing one to see and experience the true nature of people and things. While *Discipleship* is sometimes criticized as a sectarian text, which appears to reject Christian involvement in the world, one must realize that Bonhoeffer's sometimes heightened rhetoric is serving a particular purpose—combating misunderstood notions of the created order, which legitimized the National Socialist regime—and is not intended as a complete rejection of the world. In short, while his view of the world became more overtly positive in his later

---

39. DBWE 4:93.
40. Ibid., 94.
41. Ibid.
42. Ibid., 95.
43. DBWE 6:399–400.
44. DBWE 4:96.
45. Ibid., 98.

The Christological Foundation of Discernment

writings after *Discipleship*, it is difficult to describe the transition from *Discipleship* to *Ethics* as a complete break.[46]

In "Christ, Reality, and Good" Bonhoeffer continues to argue that one can only experience the world through the mediation of Christ, but he does so with an added twist. He claims that while there is "no real worldliness outside the reality of Jesus Christ," neither is there "real Christian existence outside the reality of the world."[47] He expresses this same sentiment on another occasion when he claims the following: "Just as the reality of God has entered the reality of the world in Christ, what is Christian cannot be had otherwise than in what is worldly, the 'supernatural' only in the natural, the holy only in the profane, the revelational only in the rational."[48] Two things are happening here. First, Bonhoeffer repeats the basic understanding of Christological mediation just spoken of, but he also suggests a kind of reverse mediation: i.e., just as knowledge of the world comes to a person through relationship with Christ, so too does knowledge of Christ come to a person through relationship with the world. This highlights the significance of the natural realm to an even greater extent than we saw in *Discipleship*.

Second, in an insight not present in *Discipleship*, Bonhoeffer suggests that the relationship between Christ and the world, embedded within the notion of *Christuswirklichkeit*, provides the foundation for making sense of other paradoxical relationships such as those between the worldly and the Christian, the natural and supernatural, the rational and revelational—or, between moral reflection and simplicity. This is because the very nature of Christ as fully human and fully divine bridges the gap between the worldly and the spiritual realm and reconciles the two. The contrasts between worldly and spiritual, natural and supernatural, and moral reflection and simplicity become false dichotomies when viewed through a Christological lens. One can still appreciate the polemical relationship between these contrasts—for as Jürgen Moltmann reminds us Bonhoeffer does not posit a *complete* identification of God and world—but one cannot consider one side of a contrast in absolute isolation from the other, because of their common origin in Christ.[49] Thus, while the temptation is to view the way of simple obedience and the way of moral reflection as separate paths in the

---

46. For a cogent account of how the *Discipleship* tradition relates to *Ethics*, see Nation et al., *Bonhoeffer the Assassin?*, 161–88.

47. DBWE 6:61.

48. Ibid., 55, 59.

49. For Moltmann's defense of Bonhoeffer against pantheism, see Moltmann, "Wirklichkeit der Welt," 46–47.

Christian moral life, *Christuswirklichkeit* allows one to consider how both might come together at a point of reconciliation in Christ.

As is typical of Bonhoeffer, he is not content to leave a theological idea unattached from practical Christian experience; thus, he argues that the notion of *Christuswirklichkeit* fundamentally changes how one should approach Christian ethics. In fact, after reading through "Christ, Reality, and Good," it becomes clear that the purpose of the manuscript is not primarily metaphysical or ontological, but ethical. Because his view of *Christuswirklichkeit* assumes a fundamental link between the indicative and imperative elements of morality, his understanding of Christian ethics necessarily begins from a premise of reconciliation. A few pages into "Christ, Reality, and Good" he remarks:

> The place that in all other ethics is marked by the antithesis between ought and is, idea and realization, motive and work, is occupied in Christian ethics by the relation between reality and becoming real, between past and present, between history and event (faith) or, to replace the many concepts with the simple name of the thing itself, the relation between Jesus Christ and the Holy Spirit. The question of the good becomes the question of participating in God's reality revealed in Christ.[50]

A reconciled approach to ethics means that the reality of what *is* the case directly influences how one ought to act.[51] As we already mentioned above, this view of ethics rules out both an idealist approach, which overlooks the ethical import of reality in favor of ethical ideals yet to be realized, and a positivist-empiricist approach, which misconstrues whatever happens to be the empirical reality of the moment as a valid guide for ethical behavior.[52] Moreover, thinking in terms of two or more competing realms or realities can never determine ethical thought because it overlooks the true nature of reality reconciled in Christ. For Bonhoeffer, the beginning point for Christian ethics is always the concrete situation; thus, one's moral discernment is not a matter of discovering and applying universal principles, but perceiving the reality of what *is* the case and acting accordingly. We will see later that this same contextual thrust to his ethics takes shape already in

---

50. DBWE 6:49–50.

51. For an account of Bonhoeffer's reconciliation of the classic is/ought problem of ethics, see Burtness, *Shaping the Future*, 47–51.

52. DBWE 6:53–54.

his 1929 Barcelona address on Christian ethics and continues through his ethical writings into the 1940s.

As Moltmann rightly observes, Bonhoeffer expresses the ethical dimension of his view of reality by speaking about participation.[53] Throughout the manuscript he uses three primary terms—*teilbekommen, teilnehmen* and *teilhaben*—to speak of participating or partaking in ultimate reality; as he asserts on three different occasions, such participation is the way one approaches the ethical question.[54] And what is this ethical question? As he makes clear at the very beginning of the manuscript, it is the same question we already encountered in "God's Love": what is the will of God? To participate in reality is to participate in God's will realized through Christ and actualized through the Holy Spirit. *Christuswirklichkeit* means that one cannot grasp God's will from any other place than in the reality of the world constituted by Christ. Therefore, participating in reality is not optional, but mandatory if one aspires to act according to God's will. And, for Bonhoeffer, the possibility of such participation means that God's will is concrete and historical, not an ungraspable ideal.

However, such participation is not automatic: it requires discernment. While God's will is already realized through Christ, it nevertheless is "a reality that wills to become real ever anew in what exists and against what exists."[55] This means that acting according to God's will is not always easy. There is a contextual component at work as one must be sensitive to the reality of God's particular commandment for a particular situation. As André Dumas puts it:

> Once this affirmation of an ethic based on God's presence in reality has been proposed, there remains the difficult task of finding ways to recognize God's presence in the midst of a world that Bonhoeffer himself knew very well—a world that was no longer the reality first given in creation, and not yet the reality re-given in reconciliation, but the ambiguous and contorted everyday world where good and evil exist side by side.[56]

Christian ethics must "recognize God's presence" in the world; thus, as Dahill argues, the task of Christian discernment is to "perceive the real as that is revealed by and in Jesus and as his call opens to us our particular vocation

53. Moltmann, "Wirklichkeit der Welt," 53.
54. DBWE 6:53, 55, 74.
55. Ibid., 74.
56. Dumas, *Theologian of Reality*, 156.

in every new day, every concrete situation."[57] The meaning of Bonhoeffer's statement in "God's Love" about discernment happening "within the realm defined by Jesus Christ" now becomes clearer.[58] Dahill says, in reference to that passage:

> This means that an important aspect of the practice of discernment for Bonhoeffer is simply learning to live "in" the space Jesus Christ creates for us: to pay attention to where and how he reveals himself to us . . . to learn to distinguish his voice from others' voices and remain within earshot, to turn "toward" him and not be distracted by competing demands, etc.[59]

Thus, we are brought back to the theme of participating in the reality of Christ. In a paradoxical way, it is through the practice of discernment that one perceives Christ's presence in reality, but it is through that very reality, constituted by Christ, that one also finds guidance for discernment. Thus, it is crucial that one participate fully in the reality of both the spiritual and worldly realm because Christ, having reconciled both, reveals himself through each. This means that the context of one's Christian life is not only ecclesial, but worldly as well.

One must strike a proper balance between the ecclesial and the worldly. To participate in the world while rejecting the spiritual realm is to risk a legalistic and arbitrary approach to the moral life. To participate in the spiritual realm (i.e., the church) at the expense of the world risks an antinomian attitude marked by "unnaturalness, irrationality, [and] triumphalism."[60] In both scenarios ethics carries a presupposition of disunity and the moral agent becomes a person of "eternal conflict" always trying to reconcile and relate disparate realities.[61] Moreover, Christian ethics becomes subject to the "authority" of other realities apart from Christ whether these be static orders of creation or a triumphalist understanding of the church. Thus, the first task in participating in the reality of Christ is to break down the false dichotomy between opposing realms and to understand that *Christuswirklichkeit* precludes a sectarian or exclusive understanding of Christian ethics and

---

57. Dahill, *Reading from the Underside*, 89.
58. DBWE 6:323.
59. Dahill, *Reading from the Underside*, 89.
60. DBWE 6:61.
61. Ibid., 58; cf. "God's Love" where Bonhoeffer speaks of the Pharisees viewing life in terms of continual conflict, ibid., 310.

helps one imagine what it might mean for diverse elements, such as God and world or simplicity and moral reflection, to be brought together as one.

The Ultimate and Penultimate

We can see the theological grounding for combining simplicity and moral reflection even more clearly by considering Bonhoeffer's conceptual innovation of the ultimate and penultimate (*Letzte und Vorletzte*), which is perhaps his most creative contribution to Christian ethical thinking. For him, the relation between ultimate and penultimate things articulates the same fundamental truth expressed in his earlier discussion of reality: namely, that Christ has reconciled both the spiritual and the worldly realm and one can only understand one in relation to the other. However, using the language of ultimate and penultimate allows Bonhoeffer to go further in emphasizing the inherent connection between the two and in describing the nature of life in the penultimate realm. Moreover, as we shall see below, the concepts of ultimate and penultimate provide a helpful way to hold together the two approaches to God's will evident in his theology.

While his use of ultimate and penultimate traces back as far as 1926 and is found as late as 1943 in some of his prison letters, it is his *Ethics* manuscript "Ultimate and Penultimate Things" that best expresses his conceptual distinction.[62] The manuscript begins with a discussion of the event of justification whereby God's word of grace and forgiveness draws a human individual away from imprisonment to the self and into a restored unity with the divine.[63] This ultimate event of justification by Christ is the foundation of "life-in-Christ."[64] Conceptually speaking, this event is ultimate in two different ways. First, the event of justification is qualitatively ultimate because it describes an event (justification) and a condition (being justified) beyond which nothing is greater.[65] Justification entails a "complete break" with everything else: it does not naturally proceed from any prior process and it does not lead to anything that lies beyond.[66] Most importantly, there is no "method" to achieving justification because this

---

62. On the ultimate and penultimate distinction, see Liguš, "Ultimate, Penultimate," 59–77 and Burtness, *Shaping the Future*, 70–77.
63. DBWE 6:147–48.
64. Ibid., 149.
65. Ibid.
66. Ibid.

would result in the kind of "cheap grace" Bonhoeffer critiques in earlier writings.[67] Justification is instead dependent entirely on faith and on God's action in Christ.[68]

Second, the event of justification is ultimate in a temporal sense because it follows upon something that precedes it. From the human perspective there is always a time before one's justification, a time when one is still a sinner, and a time before the coming of God's kingdom in all its fullness, the time we live in now. Thus, for the event of justification to be truly ultimate it must be something entirely beyond the penultimate and yet simultaneously something that includes the penultimate as that which necessarily comes before. John Panteleimon Manoussakis suggests that John the Baptist is a fitting illustration for the relationship between ultimate and penultimate because John prepares the way for Christ and says in John 1:30: "After me comes a man who ranks ahead of me because he was before me." Thus, the penultimate (John) prepares the way for the ultimate (Christ), but at the same time, the ultimate is already present giving meaning to the penultimate (John 1:1).[69]

The important question for Bonhoeffer is whether Christian life is always lived in the ultimate realm of faith or whether it must engage with the penultimate realm of everyday experience.[70] His motivation for such a question is in part a matter of pastoral care. He wonders why it is often a penultimate response (sitting with a hurting individual in silent solidarity) that seems more appropriate and "Christian" than an ostensibly ultimate response (reciting familiar biblical passages to the suffering individual).[71] The reason is not that the ultimate is subordinate to the penultimate, but that the ultimate finds expression through the penultimate. Thus, a "genuine" Christian life proceeds from a place of faith in the ultimate reality of justification, but prepares for the coming of Christ through concrete actions in the penultimate world.[72] As Bonhoeffer will say later in a letter from prison sent to Bethge: "One can and must not speak the ultimate word

---

67. Ibid., 150–51; cf. DBWE 12:260; DBWE 4:43–44, 50–55.
68. DBWE 6:150–51.
69. Manoussakis, "Bonhoeffer's Eschatology of the Penultimate," 240–41.
70. DBWE 6:152.
71. Ibid.
72. Ibid.

prior to the penultimate. We are living in the penultimate and believe the ultimate, isn't that so?"[73]

In familiar form Bonhoeffer turns to Christology to explain the precise relationship between the ultimate and the penultimate.[74] In the person of Christ the reality of God (the ultimate) encounters the reality of the world (the penultimate) and allows both to exist alongside each other without conflict. He illustrates this through his common three-fold description of Christ's incarnation, crucifixion, and resurrection, which each illustrate an important truth about the relation of ultimate and penultimate.[75] The incarnation of Christ binds the grace of God to the created world in an intimate way and in so doing affirms humanity and the world and allows both to exist and to be taken seriously as the penultimate. Christ's crucifixion puts the penultimate in its proper place through judgment, but nevertheless shows grace to the penultimate by not abolishing it. Similarly, the resurrection of Christ brings the ultimate even more dramatically into the penultimate while vindicating the penultimate at the same time. In conclusion he writes:

> Christian life neither destroys nor sanctions the penultimate. In Christ the reality of God encounters the reality of the word and allows us to take part in this real encounter. It is an encounter beyond all radicalism and all compromise. Christian life is participation in Christ's encounter with the world.[76]

His reference to "radicalism and all compromise" indicates the two primary errors he is rejecting through his Christological understanding of the relationship between ultimate and penultimate. A radical relationship between ultimate and penultimate places too much emphasis on the ultimate at the expense of the penultimate, and views the penultimate as entirely sinful and opposed to Christ. A compromise relationship between ultimate and penultimate overemphasizes the penultimate and attributes to it an inherent value that renders the ultimate unimportant for everyday life.[77] Both of these relationships make mutually exclusive the ultimate and penultimate in different ways and both fail to realize how both ultimate and penultimate find their origin in Christ.

73. DBWE 8:213.
74. DBWE 6:157–59.
75. Ibid.
76. Ibid., 159.
77. Ibid., 153–54.

As already mentioned, the penultimate, understood in temporal terms, is everything that comes before the ultimate and is moving toward the ultimate. Nothing is penultimate in and of itself, but only in relation to the ultimate. Thus, for example, the condition of being human is penultimate because it precedes the ultimate event of justification, but this is only the case because justification (the ultimate) informs what it means to be human (the penultimate). The ultimate determines the penultimate, but the penultimate "must be preserved for the sake of the ultimate."[78] The penultimate is therefore a crucial arena for Christians, not least of all because it is the place where they prepare the way for the ultimate word of grace.[79] Through being human and being good, the two primary penultimate activities, Christians prepare the way in their penultimate existence for the arrival of the ultimate.[80] Such preparation takes on physical form in acts of love and mercy toward others, although one must remember that such acts can never bring forth the ultimate by their own power. Preparation also requires constant repentance that results in transformed behavior and requires new deeds.[81] Christians are to act within a "world preserved and maintained by God for the coming of Christ, a world in which we *as human beings* can and should live a '*good*' life in given orders."[82] Even so, Christians must remember that preparing the way is not a method from the penultimate to the ultimate; on the contrary, it can only be a pathway from the ultimate to the penultimate. One does not usher in the kingdom of God, but rather the ultimate breaks in of its own accord. And yet, both the ultimate and penultimate retain their seriousness. Bonhoeffer asserts the following as a final summary of the relation between ultimate and penultimate and their connection to the Christian life:

> Christian life is the dawn of the ultimate in me, the life of Jesus Christ in me. But it is also always life in the penultimate, waiting for the ultimate. The seriousness of Christian life lies only in the ultimate; but the penultimate also has its seriousness, which consists, to be sure, precisely in never confusing the penultimate with the ultimate and never making light of the penultimate over

---

78. Ibid., 160.
79. Ibid., 161–65.
80. Ibid., 165–66
81. Ibid., 164–65.
82. Ibid., 165; Bonhoeffer's italics.

The Christological Foundation of Discernment

against the ultimate, so that the ultimate—and the penultimate—retain their seriousness.[83]

Just as the two natures of Christ maintain their full dignity and relevance insofar as neither is confused with the other, so too does the seriousness of both the ultimate and the penultimate depend on careful distinctions that describe the relationship between them without encroaching on the integrity of either.

While Bonhoeffer uses the ultimate/penultimate distinction as a conceptual tool to help think about the relation of faith and life, the spiritual and the temporal, and the reality of one who is justified and yet still a sinner, one might also employ the distinction as a way to grasp his understanding of moral discernment. In fact, there is a clear indication in the manuscript that Bonhoeffer himself saw the potential of the ultimate and penultimate to help him relate the twin emphases of simplicity and moral reflection.[84]

To understand how this is the case one must remember the delicate balance between ultimate and penultimate. The problem with their relationship is that too often one or the other becomes absolutized. As described above, one either focuses too heavily on the ultimate, which Bonhoeffer calls the radical approach, or too much on the penultimate, which Bonhoeffer labels the compromise solution. Either way, the result is an "insoluble conflict" where "the very unity of God is itself dissolved."[85] One notices here very similar language ("insoluble conflict," "unity") to that used in "God's Love."[86] Bonhoeffer's point is that an improper and distorted understanding of ultimate and penultimate results in many things that should otherwise exist in unity being split apart. To illustrate this, he offers a series of contrasts such as: "Radicalism hates time. Compromise hates eternity" and "Radicalism hates patience. Compromise hates decision."[87] The most striking of these contrasts, given our concern with moral discernment, is the following: "Radicalism hates wisdom [*Klugheit*]. Compromise hates simplicity [*Einfalt*]."[88] Here the terms wisdom and simplicity stand in for the very two things one must bring together in moral discernment: moral reflection and simplicity. As we will see, this pair of terms will appear

---

83. Ibid., 168.
84. Friesen, "Comparative Analysis," 53.
85. DBWE 6:154.
86. See chapter 2.
87. DBWE 6:156.
88. Ibid.

again at several points in his writings when he wishes to express the tension we have been discussing. On this particular occasion, wisdom corresponds to the penultimate life (therefore radicalism hates it) and simplicity connects with the ultimate (and compromise hates it). Friesen makes this same connection in his early study of Bonhoeffer's *Ethics*. He links simple obedience with "ultimate ethics" and discernment with "penultimate ethics"; however, he wrongly identifies "God's Love" as an example of "ultimate ethics" in distinction from "penultimate ethics," thereby missing the tension within "God's Love" itself identified in chapter 2.[89] Overall, he is more interested in distinguishing competing approaches to ethics in Bonhoeffer's writings than he is with how Bonhoeffer might be attempting to integrate seemingly different approaches into a coherent whole. In particular, he does not consider how one might alleviate the tension between "ultimate ethics" and "penultimate ethics" through a careful look at the relationship between ultimate and penultimate.

For instance, Bonoeffer argues that "the penultimate must be preserved for the sake of the ultimate."[90] This is because any destruction or chaos in the penultimate realm hinders the coming of the ultimate. If a person lives in terrible conditions where fundamental bodily needs are not met, that person will have difficulty hearing God's word and coming to faith. This is why Bonhoeffer stresses the importance of "preparing the way" after the example of John the Baptist, who prepares the way for Jesus. Bonhoeffer says:

> [I]t is necessary to care for the penultimate in order that the ultimate not be hindered by the penultimate's destruction. Those who proclaim the word yet do not do everything possible so that this word may be heard are not true to the word's claim for free passage, for a smooth road. The way for the word must be prepared. The word itself demands it.[91]

This means that a life of simplicity, the goal of which is an ever-deepening relationship of unity with God through Christ, could be difficult to realize without a space for rational, moral reflection. Simple obedience to God's commandment (the ultimate) might not be possible if the best of human ability does not first "prepare the way." This is not to suggest that moral reflection can uncover an otherwise inaccessible word from God just as

---

89. Friesen, "Comparative Analysis," 53.
90. DBWE 6:160.
91. Ibid.

penultimate activity cannot force the arrival of God's kingdom. Neither is this to suggest the necessity of moral reflection to clarify an ambiguous commandment as if God were unable to speak clearly. Rather, moral reflection can prepare the way for simple obedience by assisting a person in perceiving God's unambiguous word amidst the many temptations and competing possibilities in the world. Thus, a wise and reflective approach to God's will does not compete against a simple approach to God's will, but works toward the same goal: renewed unity with God in Christ.

In the end, the final purpose of moral reflection, even when it seems to run counter to simplicity, is the affirmation of the ultimate (i.e., simple obedience and simple faith) just as sometimes the final purpose of a free act, which breaks the law, is the reaffirmation of the law, as Bonhoeffer claims elsewhere.[92] One engages in rational, moral reflection because Christ has given it penultimate significance and because it facilitates obedience to God's commandment, which is the same goal as the life of simplicity. One engages in simple obedience because it focuses one's gaze on Christ and frees one *from* the destructive hegemony of human reason and *for* the right use of human ability in the service of Christ.

Conclusion

The notion of combining simplicity and moral reflection appears throughout Bonhoeffer's theology. In *Discipleship*, as we will see later, he contends that disciples must "act wisely and simply at the same time."[93] Similarly in his *Ethics* manuscript "Ethics as Formation," which I explore in the following chapter, he speaks of the need to combine simplicity and wisdom in order to "recognize ethical reality."[94] In "Ultimate and Penultimate Things," as we saw above, he mentions wisdom and simplicity as opposites reconciled in a proper Christological balance.[95] As I have demonstrated in this chapter, these references to combining simplicity and wisdom are both viable and coherent given Bonhoeffer's Christological convictions. Because Christ is both fully divine and fully human and because he brings together the penultimate reality of the world with the ultimate reality of God, the

92. Ibid., 274.
93. DBWE 4:193.
94. DBWE 6:78, 82.
95. Ibid., 156.

foundation exists for a similar reconciliation of the seemingly disparate characteristics of simplicity and moral reflection in Christian life.

But Bonhoeffer is not content to leave things on a conceptual level. He does not only wish to provide theological grounds for combining simplicity and moral reflection, but practical grounds as well. The practical grounds become clear when one considers another way to answer the question "who is Jesus Christ?" Bonhoeffer argues that Christ is available and assessable to the human individual; he is "pro-me" in his very ontological structure.[96] Put differently, Christ is present in the contemporary world, primarily in three forms: as Word, sacrament, and church-community. Moreover, the Christ who is present in each of these three forms has yet another form: he is the incarnate, crucified, and risen one. Thus, to ask "who is Jesus Christ?" is also to inquire into Christ's form—the *Gestalt Christi*. It is his discussions of the *Gestalt Christi*, which occur prominently in his *Lectures on Christology*, *Discipleship*, and *Ethics*, that provide a more practical basis for us to conceive of how simplicity and moral reflection might come together in the Christian life. This is because, as mentioned previously, Bonhoeffer believes one's Christian formation is a process of conformation (*Gleichgestaltung*) to the form of Christ (the *Gestalt Christi*). Because Christ's form embodies both simplicity and moral reflection without conflict, Christians too begin to embody both characteristics as they move deeper and deeper into conformity with Christ. In many ways, then, Christian conformation is the key to effective Christian discernment. To this discussion we now turn.

---

96. DBWE 12:314–15.

4

Christian Formation and the Practice of Discernment

IN THE PREVIOUS CHAPTER I explored the conceptual grounds in Bonhoeffer's thinking for bringing together simplicity and wisdom in the Christian life. The current chapter will investigate, in more practical terms, *how* this joining together occurs; that is, how, according to Bonhoeffer, Christians can go about the task of moral discernment by becoming both simple and wise. The answer lies in his notion of Christian formation. As we observed in the analysis of "God's Love" in chapter 2, Bonhoeffer argues that conformation (*Gleichgestaltung*) to the form (*Gestalt*) of Christ is both the necessary prerequisite to discernment and an ongoing aid to discernment. For him, it is only by living life in Christ that one can discern God's will in order to act responsibly in the world. One does this through listening to the voice of Christ and allowing Christ to shape one's life, just as the original disciples did. This is not a process of self-formation, realized through human initiative, but is entirely dependent on Christ, who is both the active subject in the process (Christ forms us) as well as the object to which we are formed. Thus, it follows that discerning God's will is never a human achievement apart from Christ, but always relies on God's grace. Still, we can aid in the process of conformation through the regular practice of spiritual exercises, the purpose of which is to put us into a position where Christ can encounter us.

In order to explore these themes more fully I begin the chapter by investigating Bonhoeffer's notion of "ethics as formation," which is dominant among his ethical motifs. I will demonstrate how this approach to ethics identifies Christian conformation as the process through which the combination of simplicity and wisdom becomes efficacious for one's life. In so doing, I will also show how "ethics as formation" presupposes moral discernment as its central activity. Following this, I will address the theme of Christian formation itself. Here I begin by considering the importance of *Gestalt* terminology in Bonhoeffer's work before moving to investigate his thinking about the form of Christ (the *Gestalt Christi*) and the process of formation (*Gestaltung*) as it appears in *Creation and Fall*. I follow this with a discussion of conformation (*Gleichgestaltung*) to the form of Christ, explaining what Bonhoeffer means by this process and how it relates to moral discernment. Finally, I turn to an exploration of Bonhoeffer's understanding of spiritual exercise. I argue that for him, spiritual exercise is at the heart of moral discernment because it helps facilitate one's conformation to Christ, and in so doing, helps attune one to hear God's voice. Moreover, I contend that spiritual exercise informs his understanding of how a certain kind of meditative moral reflection might co-exist with a simple approach to God's will.

Ethics as Formation

As even his earliest commentators observed, the theme of formation is one of the primary approaches that Bonhoeffer takes to the problem of Christian ethics.[1] While the theme is present throughout his *Ethics*, it finds its greatest expression in his 1940 manuscript "Ethics as Formation [*Gestaltung*]," the text we will primarily focus on in what follows.[2] What is curious about this manuscript, however, is that despite its title and despite the use of *Gestalt* language in the first several pages, the specific discussion of *Gestaltung* does not make an immediate appearance, but emerges about two-thirds of the way through the text.[3] The manuscript begins instead with a shocking indictment of ethical theory, picking up on themes we have already explored in the previous chapter. Bonhoeffer argues that because of

---

1. For example, Müller, in one of the first studies of Bonhoeffer's theology, mentions formation as one of two primary approaches that Bonhoeffer takes to ethics; see Müller, *Kirche zur Welt*, 266. Similarly, Rasmussen, another early commentator, identifies "Ethik als Gestaltung" as a primary motif for Bonhoeffer; see Rasmussen, "A Question of Method."

2. The theme also arises in "Heritage and Decay," "Guilt, Justification, Renewal," and "History and Good."

3. DBWE 6:92; DBW 6:80.

the current historical situation and its unparalleled ethical problems, traditional ethical systems can no longer adequately address the concrete ethical questions besieging German society.[4] Things were different in the past when "firm orders of life" provided stability in society and guidance in the moral life.[5] Here, "the ethical as a theoretical problem could be interesting" because it did not encroach so drastically into the heart of society.[6] Now, however, with the National Socialist government and its policies throwing everything into chaos, people are deeply concerned with ethical problems, but "uninterested in ethical theory" because they believe it cannot provide concrete guidance for how to act in the current situation.[7] Now in a time where "the villain and the saint" are once again present in society and where good and evil find concrete embodiment, ethical theory alone can no longer suffice.[8] Clearly, his claim that people are "uninterested in ethical theory" is rather subjective, especially given his ensuing discussion of six types of people who all apparently think ethical theory is sufficient. Moreover, one wonders if his view of the past is overly romantic: as if society had never before experienced a serious disruption or manifestation of evil. Nevertheless, his assessment of the inherent limitation of ethical theory (it cannot provide concrete guidance) is significant and consistent with his overall vision for Christian ethics.

As he will do later in a letter he wrote to friends in the resistance movement at Christmas 1942, Bonhoeffer illustrates the problems with ethical theory by recounting how well-meaning people guided by reason, ethical fanaticism, conscience, duty, freedom, and virtuousness have all failed to engage ethical problems effectively.[9] These six "types" do not represent six different ethical theories, but the failure of ethical theory as a project.[10] In each case, a person depends upon a guiding principle, such as reason or duty, to govern moral behavior without taking into account the shape of reality. The tragedy of this is that each of the six guiding principles is

4. DBWE 6:76.
5. Ibid.
6. Ibid.
7. Ibid.
8. Ibid.
9. Ibid., 78–80; DBWE 8:38–40.
10. The editors of DBWE also suggest that each of these types likely describe not a generic ethical response to Hitler's regime, but an actual person's response (perhaps someone known by Bonhoeffer). It is notable that Bonhoeffer uses "der Mann" rather than "der Mensch"; see DBWE 6:78n9, 79n10.

commendable in and of itself: "Reason, ethical fanaticism, conscience, duty, free responsibility, and quiet virtue are goods and convictions of a noble humanity."[11] Thus, he is not critiquing inherently bad people with immoral approaches to life, but the very best people: "It is the best, with all they are and can do, who thus go under."[12]

The problem, at its core, is that these people look to ethical theory to perform a task it cannot possibly accomplish: i.e., to give, via universal principles, practical direction to human beings trying to navigate particular and concrete situations in the here and now. The following statement from later in the manuscript is helpful in grasping Bonhoeffer's position. He writes: "we are placed objectively by our history into a particular context of experience, responsibility, and decision, from which we cannot withdraw without ending up in abstraction."[13] Thus, ethical theory is not transcendent over, but rather embedded within, a particular context occurring "today and here."[14] The universal element of ethical theory is only helpful when one first knows the particular; that is, only after perceiving the reality of a particular situation through a Christological lens might one then employ ethical theory within that context and receive its relative benefit. It is not that Bonhoeffer means to eradicate all theoretical thinking from the field of ethics; he merely intends to redefine its purview. This is similar to his thinking about the notion of Christian ethics itself, which, despite its problems, remains useful if properly defined.

One can restate all of this in terms of moral discernment. Before even mentioning his six examples of ethical failure, Bonhoeffer argues that in the present historical situation good and evil are often difficult to distinguish, not least because evil often masquerades, quite effectively, as good.[15] Ethical theory is unable to discern good from evil and right from wrong because, as mentioned already, it depends upon "preconceived concepts" that do not always apply in a given instance and sometimes blind people to the true reality of a situation.[16] If ethical theory cannot adequately assist one in discerning

11. Ibid., 80.

12. Ibid.

13. Ibid., 100–101.

14. Ibid., 100.

15. Bonhoeffer writes: "That evil appears in the form of light, of beneficence, of faithfulness, of renewal, that it appears in the form of historical necessity, of social justice, is for the commonsense observer a clear confirmation of its profound evilness," ibid., 77.

16. Ibid.

"what is real" then one cannot depend upon it to address concrete ethical problems.[17] This is the same problem he associates with the Pharisees and their way of ethics and discernment, as we saw in chapter 2. What is needed, according to him, are people who learn to "experience and recognize [*erkennen*] ethical reality not by craftiness, not by knowing all the tricks, but only by standing straightforwardly in the truth of God and by looking to that truth with eyes that it makes simple [*einfältig*] and wise [*klug*]."[18]

He concludes that one "must replace rusty weapons with bright steel"; i.e., one must rid oneself of ethical theory and embrace a practice of moral discernment, for "[o]nly the person who combines simplicity with wisdom can endure."[19] But what does it mean to be simple and wise? Early in "Ethics as Formation" he argues that the simple person is one who "clings to the commandments, the judgment, and the mercy of God that proceed anew each day from the mouth of God. Not fettered by principles but bound by love for God, this person is liberated from the problems and conflicts of ethical decision, and is no longer beset by them. This person belongs to God and to God's will alone."[20] This passage parallels much of what he says in "God's Love" regarding the one who exists in unity with God. This person does not depend on ethical principles for guidance, but on a relationship of love with God. In responding to God's commandment in simple obedience, the person is freed from "conflicts of ethical decision" and finds the subject matter of ethics to be nothing less than God's will.[21]

In short, he is using the concept of simplicity, as he does elsewhere, to speak of the single-minded person (contra the double minded person of James 1) who enjoys immediacy with God through Christ the mediator and looks to God's truth and God's will alone for moral guidance. In so doing, the individual's focus rests solely on God in Christ and is not distracted by the world. To view God in Christ is to view reality while to cast one's gaze at the world is to be led astray. However, it is precisely at this point that one must remember what he has already written in his earlier manuscript "Christ, Reality and Good"; namely, that to look single-mindedly at God in

---

17. Ibid.

18. Ibid., 78. In a parallel passage in *Letters and Papers From Prison* he expresses this same sentiment slightly differently when he states, "the Christian who lives by the Bible" is not so easily confused by evil masquerading as good; see DBWE 8:38. He also speaks briefly of the virtue of wisdom (*Klugheit*) later in this same document; see ibid., 45.

19. DBWE 6:81.

20. Ibid.

21. Ibid.

Christ is not to cut oneself off from the world because the reality of God has been brought together with the reality of the world through the work of Christ.[22] His Christocentric ontology means that a single-minded looking at God in Christ is actually the best possible approach to ethics; through seeing God correctly through the lens of Christ, one also gains an understanding of the reality of the world.

At the point where one correctly perceives reality through Christ, simplicity becomes wisdom. Bonhoeffer writes: "The person is wise who sees reality as it is, who sees into the depth of things. Only that person is wise who sees reality in God."[23] Wisdom, for him, means developing the ability to perceive a situation accurately through a Christological lens. This, in turn, means to recognize the world as reconstituted and redeemed in Christ. Such recognition allows one to see through factual information into the essence of things and thus to perceive "the significant within the factual."[24] In pursuing this task, wisdom makes use of reason and experience, all the while recognizing its embeddedness in the natural, penultimate world. However, because it has its roots in simplicity, it does not look first and foremost to ethical theory and universal principles for guidance, but to the living God and the revealed commandment. What is most important to notice is that neither simplicity nor wisdom is enough on its own. One cannot live the Christian life solely in the realm of faith, ignoring the worldly context; at the same time, one cannot rely solely on natural human ability without enjoying a simple unity with Christ. Only through combining both simplicity and wisdom in the act of discernment can one accurately hear God's voice and respond accordingly. In short, just as in the last chapter we saw how moral discernment was central for a view of Christian ethics determined by *Christuswirklichkeit*, we now see again in the first part of "Ethics as Formation" that discernment is the foundational activity for the Christian moral life. However, we have yet to understand precisely what Bonhoeffer means by "ethics as formation" and how such a conception both requires and facilitates discernment. What, then, are the primary features of his view, which he explores throughout the remainder of the manuscript?

To begin, Bonhoeffer speaks of an ethic of formation because he believes the goal for Christians is not first and foremost a program of *imitatio*

---

22. Ibid., 47–75.
23. Ibid., 81.
24. Ibid.; cf. DBWE 8:265.

Christian Formation and the Practice of Discernment

whereby Jesus' life becomes a blueprint that, if followed faithfully, results in the correct approach to the moral life. While the life of Jesus does supply concrete examples of how one might live, these examples become important only because of an ongoing process of formation, effected by Christ's presence through the Holy Spirit, whereby one slowly learns how to respond to God's commandment and to understand the true nature of reality.[25] One can see this order of emphasis—formation first, then imitation—especially at the end of *Discipleship* when Bonhoeffer writes: "*since* we have been formed in the image of Christ, we can live following his example."[26] Thus, we do not imitate Christ in order to develop our own moral character, but Christ forms us, and in so doing, allows us to become "imitators of God."[27]

It is also important to realize that Bonhoeffer's ethic of formation has both an inward and outward dimension, which corresponds in some ways to the inward and outward dimension of moral discernment (self-examination and discerning God's will), as described in chapter 2. It is true that he speaks a lot about the inward dimension; that is, the fact that Christ takes form *in* the human individual. In *Discipleship* he says: "The incarnate, crucified, and transfigured one has entered into me and lives my life."[28] In "History and Good" he repeats this sentiment by saying that Christ is "*my* life, our life."[29] As we have already seen, he speaks in "God's Love" of Christ occupying "the very same space" in Christians "that had previously been occupied by their own knowledge of good and evil."[30] This is a vivid image of *Gleichgestaltung*, illustrating the intimate connection between the Christian moral life and the life of Christ. However, in "Ethics as Formation," he also asserts that the central question for Christian ethics is not an inquiry into what is "right" or "good," but a question about "*how Christ may take form among us today and here.*"[31] With this statement we see the outward dimension of a formation ethic; i.e., Christ not only takes form *in*

---

25. Wannenwetsch argues that Luther emphasizes Christ's sacramental presence before he emphasizes Christ's role as an example in the moral life, and this method influences Bonhoeffer's own thinking on the place of formation in Christian ethics. See Wannenwetsch, "The Whole Christ," 63–64, 88–89.

26. DBWE 4:287; italics mine.

27. Ibid., 288.

28. Ibid., 287.

29. DBWE 6:250; Bonhoeffer's italics. He references Philippians 1:21 and Colossians 3:4 in this context.

30. Ibid., 325.

31. Ibid., 99; Bonhoeffer's italics.

us in conformation, but *among* us in the world. This means that ethics as formation allows us to consider not only how Christ guides us by shaping our individual moral lives, but also how Christ guides us by structuring the reality of the world.

We can now understand what Bonhoeffer means when he asserts: "The starting point for Christian ethics is the body of Christ, the form of Christ in the form of the church, the formation of the church according to the form of Christ."[32] As is a strong theme in *Discipleship*, here also we see the importance of the ecclesial context for Christian life, and by extension, Christian moral discernment. It is by participating in the place where Christ takes form, i.e., the church, the body of Christ, that Christians position themselves to receive further formation via the form of Christ. However, we saw already in chapter 3 that one cannot ultimately separate this ecclesial context from the natural, worldly context in which Christian moral life proceeds. Therefore, as I will explore more deeply in chapter 6, the fact that Christ not only takes form as the church but also takes form in the world has strong implications for how the created structures of reality might act as both a crucial guide and interpretative context for moral discernment.

Finally, by speaking of a formation ethic Bonhoeffer wants to advocate once again a concrete ethic over an abstract ethic.[33] By using the term "concrete" he means to indicate an ethic that is historical and contextual, as well as personal and relational insofar as it deals with the living form of Christ. Above all, he wants to avoid the danger of abstraction. He outlines two ways in which ethics can become abstract.[34] The first is a kind of ethical formalism that deals with general rules and principles that guide ethical reflection. For him, such a system can only render ethical statements that are entirely formal and universal, and therefore useless for the variety and particularity of human experience.[35] Here we see the limitation, in Bonhoeffer's mind, of a Kantian approach to the moral life. The second is moral casuistry, which for him describes the activity of "taking up and elaborating all conceivable contents in order to say beforehand for every conceivable case what is good."[36] As with formalism, casuistry illustrates the inadequacy

32. Ibid.
33. Ibid.
34. Ibid.
35. Ibid.
36. Ibid.

of another general approach to the moral life: that of Catholic moral theology. Bonhoeffer sees in both formalism and casuistry an attempt to engage ethics from a place of conflict "between the good and the real," or as others might say, between the *is* and the *ought*.[37] In contrast to this, Christian ethics should begin from a place of reconciliation between *is* and *ought*, between God and world: the starting point for such an ethic can only be the reality of Christ, who forms us into real human beings.[38] While this call for concretion is not new in Bonhoeffer's thinking, as we have already seen, he believes that describing ethics in terms of *Gestaltung* and the *Gestalt Christi* lends itself well to avoiding abstraction.

Of course, all of this talk about an ethic of formation risks abstraction itself if it is not somehow made concrete. Bonhoeffer admits as much just after his words about the need for simplicity and wisdom. In what is a crucial transitional point in the manuscript, he announces that without a concrete grounding, what he has said about combining simplicity and wisdom is merely "theoretical" and "an impossible, highly contradictory ideal" that is "doomed to failure" as are the other six ethical approaches to reality.[39] Thus, he grounds his concept in the only possible source of concretion: the incarnate, crucified, and risen Christ. This introduces the remaining portion of the manuscript, which discusses the form of Christ as well as the process of Christian conformation to that form, both of which we explore below. Along with the question regarding the place of moral discernment in an ethics of formation, which has already been addressed to some extent in the present section, two further questions will guide the investigation: How does Christian conformation make efficacious in one's life the conceptual unity between simplicity and wisdom? What is the human role in what appears to be a largely passive process of Christian formation?

The Importance of *Gestalt* Terminology

Bonhoeffer's notion of Christian conformation (*Gleichgestaltung*) to the form (*Gestalt*) of Christ does not appear until the final chapter of *Discipleship*, and then again in *Ethics*. Even so, he begins speaking theologically of form (*Gestalt*) and formation (*Gestaltung*) much earlier. Altogether the index to the DBW indicates eighty-one references to the term *Gestalt* and

37. Ibid., 99–100.
38. Ibid.
39. Ibid., 82.

its variants in his corpus.[40] The earliest occurrence listed in the index is from a 1932 catechism written with Franz Hildebrandt, which refers to God encountering humanity in "earthly form [*irdischer Gestalt*]."[41] Shortly after, he uses *Gestalt* terminology in his discussion of creation in *Creation and Fall*, and in his *Lectures on Christology*, where he speaks of the present Christ by exploring Christ's form under three headings: Word, sacrament, and church-community.[42] As already mentioned, the specific notion of conformation (*Gleichgestaltung*) appears both in *Discipleship* and *Ethics* along with many other references to *Gestalt* and *Gestaltung*. Even as late as 1944 in his prison correspondence, one finds him referring to Christ's form.[43]

Dumas, in his book *Dietrich Bonhoeffer: Theologian of Reality*, claims that Bonhoeffer's *Gestalt* language defines his entire theology.[44] This is because, for Bonhoeffer, Christ is the "central structure [*Gestalt*] of the world."[45] Moreover, Christ's nature and being as the vicarious representative (*Stellvertreter*) determines the hidden structure of human existence; thus, Christian formation is not an existential event, but an ontological reality.[46] The strength of Dumas' argument is that it rightly illustrates Bonhoeffer's attempt to reconcile the divide between God and world without destroying the world or losing sight of God.[47] In addition, it realizes that Christology lies at the heart of any description of reality or moral formation. However, Dumas overstates his case on several points. For instance, while Bonhoeffer often refers to Christ as the *Stellvertreter* and uses a lot of structural and spatial language in his descriptions, he does not avoid, as Dumas suggests, terms such as "savior" and "language based on events,

---

40. DBW 17:586. There are other occurrences of *Gestalt* language not found in the index that one could nevertheless classify as "theological." For example, in 1929 Bonhoeffer speaks of human freedom that allows people to grasp the "forms [*Gestalten*]" of their ethical action; this contrasts with his later belief that one must allow Christ's form to determine such action. See DBWE 10:366; DBW 10:331; chapter 5.

41. DBW 11:230.

42. DBWE 12:315–24; DBW 12:297–307.

43. DBWE 8:363, 437–38, 475, 486, 501; DBW 8:404, 489–90, 529, 542, 558–59

44. Dumas, *Theologian of Reality*, 30–37, 215–35. The English translation of Dumas's work uses structure/structuring for the German *Gestalt/Gestaltung*; I will follow this pattern when considering Dumas's work in order to avoid confusion. Elsewhere throughout this book I use form/formation for *Gestalt* and *Gestaltung*, following the DBWE.

45. Ibid., 32n53.

46. Ibid., 31.

47. Ibid., 37.

encounter, decision."[48] Here, Dumas is guilty of overemphasizing Hegel's influence on Bonhoeffer and minimizing the influence of Barth. He also sees in Bonhoeffer's theology the danger of an ontological coherence between God, Christ, church, and world, that threatens to result in God and world becoming an undifferentiated unity.[49] However, he does not account for Bonhoeffer's belief that, while everything has being only through Christ, there can never be a strict ontological coherence between Christ and church or Christ and world because the incarnate, crucified, and risen Christ remains Lord *over* all things.[50]

While Dumas' text is helpful for illuminating the importance of *Gestalt* language in Bonhoeffer's work, Vivienne Blackburn's analysis of *Gestalt* language helps us understand how it assists Bonhoeffer in conveying a particular insight about Christ and Christian formation. Blackburn observes that unlike the English term "form," which is commonly used to translate *Gestalt*, the German word *Gestalt* carries the twin sense of "picture" and "structure."[51] Robert McAfee Brown agrees with this when he notes the limitations of the word "form": it "preserves, in Aristotelian terminology, an external meaning that is inappropriate, I believe, in relation to Bonhoeffer."[52] Thus, one must recognize in *Gestalt* a sense of both the outward and external image of something as well as the internal structure.[53] Blackburn points to several passages from Scripture where Luther uses *Gestalt* in this manner, to express both the inward and hidden reality of something as well as the outward appearance. For instance, in Mark 16:12 the resurrected Christ is said to appear "in another form [*in anderer Gestalt*]" to two of his disciples as they walk into the country. According to Blackburn, this use of *Gestalt* is meant to convey the dual reality of Christ's

---

48. For examples of references to Christ as Savior and to human salvation, see DBWE 6:96; DBWE 16:237, 378, 542, 644. For examples of "claim" and "encounter" language, see DBWE 6:378–79, 388. Cf. Dumas, *Theologian of Reality*, 32, 218.

49. Dumas, *Theologian of Reality*, 232–35.

50. See DBWE 6:401–2.

51. Blackburn, *Dietrich Bonhoeffer and Simone Weil*, 93n135.

52. Dumas, *Theologian of Reality*, 218n7. Despite these objections, the words "form" and "formation" have gained a currency in English usage (e.g., "Christian formation") that makes them more useful and less awkward than alternative translations for *Gestalt/Gestaltung* such as "structure" and "structuring."

53. Plant also notes that *Gestaltung* can refer to both "a spatial form" (outward dimension) or to "a character in a play, and thereby 'character' in the context of morality" (inward dimension). See Plant, *Bonhoeffer*, 120.

outward and visible form, but also the inner dimension of his resurrected self. She contends that this provides the "linguistic context for Bonhoeffer's adoption of the term *Gestaltung* to describe the transformation of the disciple who has responded to the call of Christ."[54] Although Blackburn is less convincing when she goes on to argue that important parallels exist between Bonhoeffer's use of *Gestaltung* and *Gestalt* psychology, her argument about *Gestalt* carrying both inward and outward dimensions is significant. As already mentioned above, both inward and outward dimensions exist in Bonhoeffer's conception of ethics as formation. In addition, we saw in the analysis of "God's Love" that a contrast between inward and outward dimensions of discernment was evident. It is therefore no surprise that Bonhoeffer chose to use *Gestalt* language in order to speak of conformation to the form of Christ as a dynamic process of formation, that affects not only the inner reality of one's being and character, but one's outward behavior as well.

The Form of Christ (*Gestalt Christi*)

Because Christ's form determines one's own form in the process of Christian formation, it is crucial to understand how Bonhoeffer describes the *Gestalt Christi*. He speaks of the form of Christ in two slightly different ways. First, he speaks of Christ taking form as Word, sacrament, and church-community; we see this explicitly in *Lectures on Christology*.[55] These "forms" are not so much forms to which one is transformed, but forms through which one encounters the present Christ. Second, he uses and often repeats the tripartite formula of Christ the incarnate, crucified, and risen one to speak of Christ's form. Each aspect of this three-fold form has direct bearing on one's own formation, as we will see later in the chapter.

To begin, Christ takes form as Word, sacrament, and church-community. As Word, he reveals himself not as a static idea but as a "living Word to humankind."[56] This means that Christ, in the form of the Word, is not a timeless, universal, and self-enclosed entity (Word as "idea"), but a person who actively addresses the human person in particular, historical circumstances and demands a response.[57] Insofar as the very nature of the Word is

54. Blackburn, *Dietrich Bonhoeffer and Simone Weil*, 96.
55. DBWE 12:315–23.
56. Ibid., 316.
57. Ibid., 316–17. One can see Bonhoeffer's aversion to German Idealism in his

to actively address humanity, the Word can only be present in community. This is because it is only in community that the Word as address can elicit a response from another person (the addressee). The content of this Word as address does not consist of ethical principles and new moral teachings, but of "commandment and forgiveness."[58] The Word as address allows people to know God's will in their historical experience and calls people to responsible action according to God's will. The particular way in which this Word of address takes shape in the church is through preaching. This results in the co-mingling of human and divine words such that the sermon, as Bonhoeffer puts it, is both the "the poverty and the riches of our church."[59]

Just as Christ is present through the form of the Word of proclamation so too is Christ present through the form of the sacrament. The sacrament embodies the Word and functions to make Christ present in "the sphere of our body's tangible nature."[60] In the form of the sacrament Christ the Word is the "restored creation of our spirit-bodily existence."[61] While one might be tempted to focus on *how* Christ is present in the sacrament, Bonhoeffer asserts that such a question is inappropriate: therefore, in his opinion, the Eucharistic debates of the Reformation are mostly misguided. His account of Christ taking form in the sacrament is significant because it is here that Christ's presence becomes most concrete. As he explains, the purpose of the sacramental form of Christ is to remind Christians that he is not "only an idea" but that he exists "in both history and nature."[62] Later, he will argue that it is the sacrament where Christian life together under God's Word reaches its culmination.[63] Furthermore, Christ's sacramental form is important because it suggests that Christ's presence in the sacrament is a place where nature overcomes its fallen state and connects back to its original created state. This, in turn, suggests that created nature vindicated through Christ might have a role to play in the Christian moral life. Nature, as such,

---

description of the Word as a living address, embodied in concrete proclamation, rather than the Word as timeless truth, that relates only to itself.

58. Ibid., 317.
59. Ibid., 318.
60. Ibid., 322.
61. Ibid.
62. Ibid., 319.
63. DBWE 5:118.

does not hold independent value, but insofar as it finds its fulfillment in Christ, it offers an important context for discernment.[64]

Both the form of the Word as proclamation and the form of the sacrament as the embodied Word are included in the form of the church-community. Between the time of the ascension and the second coming Christ is present in no other place than in his visible body, the church.[65] Here, Bonhoeffer continues to assert a position already developed in his early theology: an understanding of Christ existing as church-community.[66] The church is not a "mere *image*" of the body of Christ, but the church "*is* the body of Christ."[67] As he says in the words of his memorable phrase from *Sanctorum Communio*: "*Christus als Gemeinde existierend*."[68] And later, in *Act and Being*, he asserts: "God *is* present, that is, not in eternal nonobjectivity but . . . 'haveable', graspable in the Word within the church."[69] In short, the church, for Bonhoeffer, describes the spatial and visible presence of Christ and incorporates both the spiritual and bodily aspects of God's Word.

What is important about each of these three forms is that they serve, to borrow Dahill's phrase, as "loci of formation."[70] They are spaces where one encounters the present Christ and finds opportunity to participate in him. Thus, one participates in Christ the Word through active listening; one participates in Christ in his sacramental form by receiving the Eucharist and by engaging in the reality of the world; one participates in Christ in the form of church through regular worship, which includes both of the aforementioned participatory acts.[71] The reason one does this is simple: the form of Christ demands it. As Bonhoeffer explains: "A prophet and teacher would not need followers, but only students and listeners. But the incarnate Son of God who took on human flesh does need a community of followers

---

64. I return to this issue in chapter 6.

65. DBWE 12:323.

66. For example, see DBWE 1:121.

67. DBWE 12:323; Bonhoeffer's italics.

68. "Christ existing as church-community," DBWE 1:121, 141. See also Bonhoeffer's sixth graduation thesis, which states: "The church is to be understood as Christ 'existing as church-community' and as a collective person"; DBWE 9:440.

69. DBWE 2:91; Bonhoeffer's italics.

70. Dahill, *Reading from the Underside*, 101–8.

71. Dahill organizes her "loci of formation" slightly differently, speaking of "the Word, the Christian community (specifically the experience of friendship), and public life in the world"; ibid., 101.

who not only participate in his teaching but also in his body."[72] Through participation in Christ one occupies a space where the process of conformation can occur. It is not that Christians conform themselves by listening to a sermon or partaking of the sacrament, but they put themselves in a position to encounter Christ and allow his form to take shape within their lives. This points ahead to the discussion below about the significance of spiritual exercises for the Christian moral life.

In addition to speaking of Christ as Word, sacrament, and church-community, Bonhoeffer also focuses on the *Gestalt Christi* by way of another tripartite formula—Christ the incarnate, crucified, and risen one—which appears many times in both *Discipleship* and *Ethics* and even in *Letters and Papers from Prison*.[73] Abromeit highlights the significance of the formula by arguing that not only is the final chapter of *Discipleship* ("The Image of God") an extended explication of the formula, but it similarly functions as a structuring principle for Bonhoeffer's entire *Ethics*.[74] More specifically for our purposes, it functions as the structuring principle for Christian life. One can see this through Bonhoeffer's careful method of moving from Christology (the form of Christ) to its implications for anthropology (human conformation to Christ); this is most explicit in "Ethics as Formation" as he first describes the form of Christ as incarnate, crucified, and risen in a series of paragraphs before describing how one is conformed to each form in another series of paragraphs shortly after.[75] Because one should not artificially separate the *Gestalt* from the *Gestaltung*, I will reserve the more specific discussion of Christ as incarnate, crucified, and risen—and what this means for Christian formation—to the discussion of conformation below.

Formation (*Gestaltung*) in *Creation and Fall*

To introduce the discussion of Bonhoeffer's notion of conformation to the form of Christ, it is best to begin at the beginning with his doctrine of creation. This might seem an unlikely entry point for the discussion, but in fact his commentary on Genesis 1-3 in *Creation and Fall* offers a fascinating introduction to the concept of formation. Indeed, the core of the

72. DBWE 4:215.
73. Ibid., 285-87; DBWE 6:82-96, 157-58, 399-402; DBWE 8:501.
74. Abromeit, *Das Geheimnis Christi*, 230.
75. DBWE 6:84-92, 94-95.

Genesis narrative concerns God giving form to the unformed by bringing forth creation, structuring the world, and giving it life. Not surprisingly, Dumas understands Bonhoeffer's interpretation of Genesis 1-3 in terms of *Gestaltung*.[76] While God brings forth creation through formation, Adam rebels against creation by attempting to re-form it in a different way. Dumas claims that Adam "destroys the structures of the world by refusing to accept freedom-in-relationship."[77] While Bonhoeffer does not actually use the language of *Gestaltung* in reference to Adam's sin, he does express the radical shift in form brought on by Adam's actions. He argues that Adam's sin does not simply make the human creature "less good," but makes the creature one who begins to act like God.[78] Thus, the very ontological structure of the human being is re-formed from one thing (humankind in the image of God) into another (humankind as its own creator). Once this fundamental restructuring has occurred, it is left to Christ alone to reform humanity into the form of Christ, thus restoring unity with God.

In short, sin is fundamentally an act of de-formation, a falling back toward the formlessness that characterizes life apart from the form-giving Creator. Thus, for Bonhoeffer, the motif of formation in Genesis 1-3 not only addresses the divine act of creating the world, but applies much more broadly to the moral realm as well. It follows that his discussion of formation in creation holds some relevance for Christian conformation to the form of Christ, as described in his later theology. The fact that he insists that one can only understand creation through the lens of Christology, and that the events of creation and resurrection are really one and the same, only strengthen this assertion. He argues that "the God of creation, of the utter beginning, is the God of the resurrection . . . it is because we know of the resurrection that we know of God's creation in the beginning."[79] He also claims that it is God in Christ who both creates in Genesis out of nothing and "creates the new creation" via the resurrection.[80] With this in mind, we turn now to a description of his primary discussions of formation in *Creation and Fall* followed by an analysis of how these passages connect to the concept of conformation to Christ.

---

76. Dumas, *Theologian of Reality*, 149–54.
77. Ibid., 149.
78. DBWE 3:115–16.
79. Ibid., 34–35.
80. Ibid.

The concept of *Gestalt* or *Gestaltung* appears a number of times in his exposition of Genesis 1-3. This seems understandable given that Genesis speaks of the earth as a "formless void" (Gen 1:2) and of God having "formed man from the dust of the ground" (Gen 2:7). What is interesting, however, is that a closer inspection of Luther's German translation, which Bonhoeffer used, reveals not a single instance of *Gestalt* language anywhere in Genesis 1-3 (instead, the earth was *"wüst und leer"* and God *"machte"* man). The fact that Bonhoeffer purposefully employs *Gestalt* language in a place where it does not originally appear suggests its significance.[81] As we argued above, he wants to capture the dynamism implied in the transformation from formlessness to form by pointing to both internal structure and external image, both of which find expression in his account of formation in Genesis.

He begins early in *Creation and Fall* by differentiating between two moments in creation. God's first act of creation is best described not as an act of formation, but as an act of bringing into being that which is formless (Gen 1:1–2a).[82] Bonhoeffer describes this formless and empty creation in different ways. For instance, it is subject to God and praises God through its very formlessness.[83] It holds within it a power that, if removed from its origin in the Creator, embodies rebellion.[84] In addition, it cannot form itself and is therefore entirely dependent on the Creator to give it form.[85] Finally, it has existence as such, but it does not exist in a differentiated or "particular" way.[86] It simply stands before God as an undifferentiated mass, a deep, dark abyss.[87]

In contrast to this formless creation stands the second moment of creation, indicated by the image of the Holy Spirit hovering over the formlessness; this moment of creation involves creation's release from a state of formlessness and its simultaneous binding into a state of formation. This transition from formlessness to form is dependent on God's word, which

81. Bonhoeffer also differs from the 1912 Luther Bible on other occasions by using the terms *Gestalt* and *gestalten* although they do not appear in the text: see, for example, his translations of Romans 8:29 (DBW 4:297) and Romans 12:2 (DBW 4:263; DBW 6:323); cf. Blackburn, *Dietrich Bonhoeffer and Simone Weil*, 97.

82. DBWE 3:36.
83. Ibid.
84. Ibid., 37.
85. Ibid.
86. Ibid., 38.
87. Ibid., 37.

calls forth form out of the formless.[88] The word differentiates creation and gives structure to that which exists.[89] One cannot speak of form without also speaking of God's word. As Bonhoeffer asserts:

> God speaks and by speaking creates. Strangely enough the Bible first says this when it comes to the creation of form, the wrestling of form out of the formless. Form corresponds to the word. The word brings into relief; it outlines and limits the individual, the real, the whole. The word summons that which comes to be out of nonbeing, so that it may be.[90]

This new creation, given form by God's word, is distinct from formless creation in that it can praise God not through necessity, but in freedom. The very form, given by the Creator, allows this creation to exist "over and against" God.[91] Nevertheless, it continues to be a creation that is totally subject to God: it cannot form itself. While Bonhoeffer makes no overt reference to it in this particular passage, it is difficult to ignore the connection between the word, which addresses creation and gives it form, and the word which calls one to be a disciple, forming that person after the image of Christ.

In addition to drawing this basic distinction between formless and formed creation, Bonhoeffer also distinguishes between different kinds of formation within creation. For instance, in speaking of the creation of the first day, Bonhoeffer points out the "great rhythm" or "natural dialectic" inherent in that act of formation.[92] In giving form to creation by creating day and night God's word instills into the fabric of creation a natural tension between formation and formlessness.[93] The day stands in contrast to the night, but neither exists as a static entity. Instead, this act of formation—or perhaps better, the structure of this formation—entails movement between day and night, light and dark, and between "times . . . of wakening and of slumbering in nature, in history, and in the nations": it is within this rhythm that creation rests and finds its form.[94]

---

88. Ibid., 43.
89. Ibid., 43–44.
90. Ibid., 43.
91. Ibid., 39.
92. Ibid., 49.
93. Ibid.
94. Ibid.

He sees another kind of formation in the creation of the firmament, distinct water and dry land, and the heavenly bodies: all of this indicates that which is fixed.[95] He appeals especially to the structures and laws of the universe and the realm of numbers to express the fixed nature of this kind of formed creation. Creation that is fixed praises God precisely through its inflexible regularity and remains entirely unaffected by humankind: "[T]he stars go their way, whether or not human beings endure suffering, guilt, or bliss."[96] While one might assume that fixed creation enjoys autonomy, he is adamant that even the world of numbers is upheld by God's commandment and has no autonomy apart from the divine being.[97] The final type of formed creation finds expression through the creation of living things: plants, animals, and human beings.[98] Here, creation takes on living form and praises the Creator not only through its very existence, but particularly through its ability to create life.[99] Bonhoeffer writes: "God does not will to be Lord of a dead, eternally unchangeable, subservient world; instead God wills to be Lord of life with its infinite variety of forms."[100]

His final reference to *Gestalt* in *Creation and Fall* comes in the following statement, which serves as a partial summary for the discussion to this point:

> [T]he peculiar being of the creature, that is, its creaturely being, is wholly suspended and sustained [aufgehoben] in God's being and is fully obedient to God. After all, the being of that which is without form—of that which in greater and greater intensification of its own being is given form as rhythm, as what is fixed, and as what lives—always remains wholly created being, that is, obedient being. It never knows about its own being except by looking at the word of God, at the freedom with which God creates and upholds.[101]

Here, he reiterates his view that there are different kinds of creation and views God's act of formation as a process of "intensification": beginning with formless creation, moving to that which has rhythm and that which is

---

95. Ibid., 50–55.
96. Ibid., 52.
97. Ibid., 53.
98. Ibid., 56–59.
99. Ibid., 57.
100. Ibid.
101. Ibid., 59.

fixed, and culminating with that which lives. He also makes an important ontological statement about the status of creation, in any form, vis-à-vis God, which rules out any notion of created autonomy apart from God. While God structures creation in particular ways, some of which manifest themselves to us in our lived experience, this does not imply any kind of ontological priority for those structures. If anything has priority, it is surely God's word, which gives whatever relative worth is appropriate to the structures, but nothing more. Finally, he links the discussion of creation to ethics by asserting that creation always remains obedient to the Creator and thereby experiences freedom. This is not to say that disobedience is impossible, but merely that God's act of creative formation has as its aim obedient creation. The fact that the process of *Gestaltung* has inherent ethical implications is merely a repetition of his belief, expressed already in *Sanctorum Communio*, that one can only understand the structure of the human person in ethical terms: one becomes a person precisely through an ethical encounter with another.[102]

Given these early musings on the first moments of creation, what might one say about their connection to Bonhoeffer's later understanding of Christian formation? To begin, it is interesting to note the two primary characteristics that the transition from formlessness to form entails. First, formation entails a movement from undifferentiated existence to a state of distinct and particular being that remains subject to, but now stands over and against, God. Thus, formation involves freedom, but this depends precisely on obedience. Moreover, this relationship of freedom and obedience only finds its proper balance in formed creation or the formed individual: unformed creation remains subject to God, but does not experience freedom in the same sense as formed creation. One might say in an analogous way that in "God's Love," the Pharisees, while "formed" in the sense that all natural life is "formed life," represent those who are "unformed" insofar as they are not conformed to the form of Christ. Thus, while the Pharisees enjoy a relative freedom made possible through natural life, they do not experience the absolute freedom found only through obedience to Christ.[103] Only through an act of formation can freedom and obedience co-exist.

Second, neither formation in creation nor formation made possible through the resurrection occurs through self-agency: formless creation cannot form itself and depends instead upon the action of the Word. Put

---

102. See DBWE 1:48–49.
103. Cf. DBWE 6:171–218 (esp. 171–74 and 178–81); see also chapter 6.

Christian Formation and the Practice of Discernment

differently, one must not forget that the same Holy Spirit who hovers over the waters in Genesis 1:2 is also at work in the contemporary world, actualizing Christ's presence in the Christian life. The human being in a state of disunity from God, who is formless to the extent that he or she is not conformed to the true form of Christ, is entirely passive in the activity of formation. This does not mean that humanity does not desire formation. As Bonhoeffer says in *Creation and Fall*: creation waits "impatiently to be bound into form."[104] This brings to mind Augustine's statement, which Bonhoeffer refers to in more than one sermon during his time in Barcelona, that humanity waits impatiently and experiences restlessness until it finds rest in God.[105] The problem with this restlessness, however, is that humanity is impatient and tries to create its own form and structure in the world. As Bonhoeffer maintains in a lecture given earlier in 1932 (the same year his lectures on Genesis 1-3 began), such activity amounts to inauthentic forms (*unechten Gestalten*) that stand opposed to the authentic or genuine forms (*echten Gestalten*) that come only from God.[106] In anthropological terms, one obtains the true form of humanity only through Christ.

Bonhoeffer's comments about the rhythm inherent in formed creation also come to bear on his later thoughts on Christian formation. The inherent dialectic between form and formlessness, light and dark, day and night expresses the same kind of dialectic within the human person who is both justified and a sinner, or in the terminology of "God's Love," the one who is in unity with God and the one who is in disunity with God. This is not to deny the fundamental, ontological distinction between unity and disunity, but to recognize that for those united to Christ, the problems of disunity continue to manifest themselves. Those formed after the image of Christ must be mindful not to drift back toward formlessness, or to express it in Bonhoeffer's terminology from elsewhere in *Ethics*, they must be careful not to drift from the "natural" (that which is open to Christ) to the "unnatural" (that which is closed to Christ).[107] As already mentioned in chapter 2, it is not a mistake that in his polemic against the Pharisees, he uses "we" language. Christians are not immune to the problem of disunity; in fact,

---

104. DBWE 3:37.

105. DBWE 10:481, 505. Augustine's quote: "[Y]ou made us for yourself and our hearts find no peace until they rest in you," Augustine, *Confessions*, 21.

106. Bonhoeffer's discussion appears in his lecture "The Nature of the Church," which survives in the form of student notes; see, DBWE 11:291.

107. DBWE 6:173.

during the time of the Nazi government in Germany, they may have been especially susceptible.

Finally, it is interesting to consider how the process of Christian formation might correspond to Bonhoeffer's notion of the "intensification" of formation that happens in creation. In *Discipleship* he appears to argue for a similar kind of intensification in the life of Christian discipleship, which moves along through various stages of formation. In *Ethics* he minimizes talk of intensification, although the teleological thrust to the moral life remains. Moreover, he begins to argue that one moves deeper into the reality of the world as one moves deeper into the process of Christian formation.

In summary, one cannot assume a direct correspondence between Bonhoeffer's description of *Gestaltung* in the context of creation and his later uses of *Gestaltung* in the context of moral and spiritual formation. Nevertheless, one can see interesting parallels, such as the contrast between form and formlessness in *Creation and Fall* and a similar contrast between unity (those conformed to the form of Christ) and disunity (those who have not been conformed) in *Ethics*. Moreover, the importance of *Gestaltung* as a description of God's creative activity and its obvious ethical implications points ahead to Bonhoeffer's later use of *Gestaltung* or *Gleichgestaltung* as a description of one's metamorphosis from life in the old human being, Adam, to life in the new human being, Christ, and the moral component inherent in this transformation. Finally, it is clear that the *Gestaltung* spoken of in *Creation and Fall* depends entirely on God's word. Reading Bonhoeffer's commentary on Genesis 1:3—"Then God said, 'Let there be light'; and there was light"—one cannot help but think of Christ (which is what Bonhoeffer expects). Most striking is his statement: "Form corresponds to the word."[108] One could imagine this phrase appearing in the midst of his later discussion about Christian formation in which one's form is nothing else but the form of Christ, the Word of God. Thus, the act of *Gestaltung*, in all its expressions, always occurs within a Christological context.

Conformation (*Gleichgestaltung*) to the Form of Christ

We move now to the heart of our discussion of Christian formation by considering Bonhoeffer's two great texts on the moral life, which are also the two documents that deal most heavily with the theme of Christian conformation to the form of Christ: *Discipleship* and *Ethics*. In both documents,

---

108. DBWE 3:43.

many of the themes already touched upon in describing ethics as formation come to light once again. For instance, Bonhoeffer insists that Christians cannot form themselves, but must rely on the form of Christ taking shape within them (Gal 4:19). The goal, he says, "is to be shaped into the entire *form* of the *incarnate,* the *crucified,* and the *risen one*."[109] This means, in turn, that Christian conformation is not conformation to the world (Rom 12:2) or to some human or divine ideal: that is to say, it is not conformation to the form of Adam, but to the *Gestalt Christi*—the form of Christ.[110] In addition to this, conformation to Christ involves, as Romans 12:2 suggests, a radical metamorphosis: a transformation from one state of being to another, which carries both internal and external implications.[111]

Aside from these characteristics, it is important to note that for Bonhoeffer, the process of Christian formation is ongoing: "The community is called to be ever increasingly transformed into this form [of Christ]."[112] His penultimate chapter in *Discipleship*, "The Saints," while not using *Gestaltung* language directly, does speak extensively of the same reality when it refers to the life of sanctification and its sense of growth and progression. David Ford rightly notes this connection between the justified and sanctified life of discipleship and the concept of *Gleichgestaltung* when he argues that the closest definition of holiness (i.e., sanctification) that one finds in Bonhoeffer's theology is his discussion of *Gleichgestaltung* in "Ethics as Formation."[113] Thus, when Bonhoeffer speaks of the realization of both one's justification ("the new creation of the new human being") and sanctification ("preservation and safekeeping unto the day of Jesus Christ") through the work of Christ and the Holy Spirit, this does not negate the fact that one's new, sanctified life in Christ, i.e., the life of Christian discipleship, is still an ongoing process of participation in Christ's Body.[114] For instance, he mentions that one gains maturity in the life of sanctification, that "the fruit of sanctification grows" within a person, and that the life of sanctifica-

---

109. DBWE 4:285; Bonhoeffer's italics.

110. Ibid., 4, 103, 247; DBWE 6:93, 322.

111. It is not clear what Burtness means when he maintains that this "transformation" does not indicate a "radical personal change" for Bonhoeffer as it does for Paul. One can only say that it is difficult to imagine Bonhoeffer not understanding a movement from disunity to unity with Christ, or in fact his own experience of inner transformation in 1931–32, as both "radical" and "personal." See Burtness, *Shaping the Future*, 88.

112. DBWE 4:247.

113. Ford, "Bonhoeffer, Holiness and Ethics," 361–80.

114. DBWE 4:260.

tion is a journey.[115] There is a teleological element at work: a sense that one is always moving forward seeking to "[p]ursue . . . holiness[,] without which no one will see the Lord."[116]

This sense of progression in his account of Christian formation is especially strong in *Discipleship*, where he presents it as a process of intensification that is similar in some ways to the intensification of creative formation in *Creation and Fall*. One first learns to be truly human, then to live a cruciform life, and finally to radiate the glory of God. He writes:

> The transformation into the divine image will become ever more profound, and the image of Christ in us will continue to increase in clarity. This is a progression in us from one level of understanding to another and from one degree of clarity to another, toward an ever-increasing perfection in the form of likeness to the image of the Son of God.[117]

Here the process of conformation sounds almost like a pursuit of Christian perfection. One is drawn deeper and deeper into a sanctified life and begins to resemble the form of Christ more and more closely. However, he is careful to note that this is not a matter of pious individualism: it is only within the church community that one becomes "like Christ."[118] Still, this description of conformation, while not necessarily excluding an outward orientation, appears to be more focused on the inward aspect of Christian life as lived out within the context of community.

The sense of progression in the life of discipleship is also present in *Ethics*; for example, Bonhoeffer says in one of his latest *Ethics* manuscripts that God's commandment allows one "to be actually on the way," moving forward in a "unified direction" in the Christian life.[119] However, in *Ethics* his former emphasis on moving deeper into the life of Christ with increasing intensification takes on a new emphasis because of his understanding of *Christuswirklichkeit*. Now, as one moves deeper into the life of Christ one also moves deeper into the reality of the world. Thus, in *Discipleship* conformation to Christ does not necessarily run away from the world, but perhaps takes a parallel track, focusing more on the inner life. In *Ethics*, and later in his prison letters, conformation to Christ means direct engagement

---

115. Ibid., 267, 269, 279.
116. Ibid., 276. This is Bonhoeffer's rendering of Hebrews 12:14.
117. Ibid., 286.
118. Ibid., 287; cf. DBWE 6:96–102.
119. DBWE 6:385.

in the world and focuses more on the outward dimension of one's encounter with the world. However, while this shift in emphasis might suggest a new focus for his theology, one should understand it more in terms of a natural expansion of his thinking: it is not that he rejects the emphasis on the inner life in *Ethics*, he simply chooses to take it for granted as he moves on to explore its worldly implications.[120] In short, the life of discipleship in conformation to Christ becomes much more expansive and all encompassing.

Finally, Bonhoeffer argues that a constant companion on the road of discipleship—and, in fact, an impetus for the journey—is the reality of sin. As he succinctly puts it: "We journey under God's grace, we walk in God's commandments, and we sin."[121] While Christ's work of redemption means Christians are no longer slaves to this sin, "the struggle of the Spirit against the flesh" nevertheless continues to characterize the sanctified life.[122] One must daily die to the flesh under the cross of Christ and seek instead the good works that God has prepared in advance for one to do.[123] To accomplish this, Christians must rely on things such as church discipline, personal confession, and other spiritual exercises for their ongoing orientation.[124] Such acts of spiritual discipline do not make formation happen, but they draw people closer to the Christ who alone has the power to transform an individual. A more detailed discussion of the role of spiritual exercise will follow, but first, we must finally consider the specific manner in which conformation occurs according to the three-fold form of Christ.

The first thing to note about Bonhoeffer's tripartite formula is its use as a shorthand expression for the entire Christ narrative, which always functions as a unity. This means that while one aspect of the narrative (e.g., the incarnation) might hold particular implications for Christian formation and moral action, one can never divorce it from all other elements in the narrative. He explains:

---

120. In a similar way, Green suggested in a 2008 address that *Ethics* presupposes the place of the Sermon on the Mount at the core of Christian identity (spoken of in *Discipleship*) and, given this presupposition, attempts to work out its implications for Christian action in the world. Green, "Beyond Fundamentalism."

121. DBWE 4:279.

122. Ibid., 267.

123. Ibid., 269, 278–79.

124. Ibid., 270–71. Although not mentioned explicitly here, Bonhoeffer speaks earlier in *Discipleship* of the central role of prayer and other spiritual disciplines in helping to overcome the flesh. I will speak below of the role of spiritual exercise in Christian life.

> The unity and differentiation of incarnation, cross, and resurrection should be clear. Christian life is life with Jesus Christ who became human, was crucified, and is risen, and whose word as a whole encounters us in the message of the justification of the sinner by grace. Christian life means being human [Menschsein] in the power of Christ's becoming human, being judged and pardoned in the power of the cross, living a new life in the power of the resurrection. No one of these is without the others.[125]

The tripartite formula of incarnate, crucified, risen helps to isolate and emphasize individual aspects of Christ's person and how each impacts one's conformation to Christ without losing sight of the unity of Christ's person. Thus, the use of the formula by Bonhoeffer is both functional, expressing a larger narrative in a shorthand way, and also theological, stressing both the unity and diversity inherent in Christ and in the human person.

Bonhoeffer first speaks of conformation to the form of the incarnate Christ in "The Image of Christ," the final chapter of *Discipleship*. He begins by describing the incarnate Christ—the "miracle of all miracles"—as the one who takes on human form.[126] A sinful flesh and lowly stature, both of which Christ accepts in order to fully bear the human condition and restore the image of God within human individuals, characterize this human form.[127] In *Ethics*, he is even more specific, insisting that the incarnate Christ embodies not an ideal humanity, but real humanity. This means that Christ bears in a bodily way "the nature, essence, guilt, and suffering of human beings."[128] In doing so, Christ expresses God's unfathomable love toward humanity and offers us hope within our human situation.[129] After all, as Bonhoeffer says in another *Ethics* manuscript, Christ's becoming human reinforces the truth that God is always "for us."[130]

The foregoing description suggests that conformation to the incarnate Christ is a process of becoming a real human being. Because of Adam's attempt to transcend his humanity and become like God, he lost his true human nature. It is only the saving work of Christ that can restore this fallen human nature. Thus, by taking on human flesh Christ does not seek

---

125. DBWE 6:158–59.
126. DBWE 4:214.
127. Ibid., 285.
128. DBWE 6:84.
129. Ibid., 87.
130. Ibid., 400.

Christian Formation and the Practice of Discernment

to raise us above our human nature, but to help us realize our real human nature and to live more fully *as* humans. Bonhoeffer writes in "Ethics as Formation" that "human beings are not transformed into an alien form, the form of God, but into the form that belongs to them, that is essentially their own. Human beings become human because God became human."[131] This statement has generated much debate regarding its relationship to the classic patristic formula of *theosis* (divinization). While some argue Bonhoeffer's view stands in contrast to the patristic formula, others claim that his theology corresponds well with the doctrine.[132] What is most interesting about this discussion, however, is that both sides of the issue often miss Bonhoeffer's primary purpose in the passage: namely, to counter what he perceives as the widespread contempt for humanity or misguided idolization of humanity pervading German society. Early in the manuscript he made the veiled reference to Hitler, "the tyrannical despiser of humanity," who functions as the antithesis of Christ, the "form of God become human."[133] His strong emphasis on Christ as the true form of real humanity is not an attempt to enter into patristic debates, but to correct the radically distorted views of humanity threatening his contemporary society.

The result of one's conformation to the incarnate Christ, through which one realizes true human nature, is twofold. First, one turns away from the self and discovers a connection with all of humanity. As Bonhoeffer says in *Discipleship*: "Inasmuch as we participate in Christ, the incarnate one, we also have a part in all of humanity, which is borne by him."[134] One becomes better able to love human beings as God loves them and to avoid the dual temptations, especially prevalent during the National Socialist period, of either despising humanity or idolizing humanity.[135] Second, one begins to bear the troubles and sins of others through one's conforma-

---

131. Ibid., 96.

132. For example, both Green and Manoussakis point out the contrast between Bonhoeffer's view and the patristic formula. Manoussakis, in particular, contends that Bonhoeffer's position results in a minimalist eschatology that denies one's ultimate participation in the life of God. Both Harvey and Zimmermann argue to the contrary, claiming that Bonhoeffer does not reject a doctrine of *theosis*. Zimmermann claims that the church fathers embrace a strong humanism not unlike Bonhoeffer's and that Bonhoeffer speaks on many other occasions of participating in the reality of God. See DBWE 6:96n86; Manoussakis, "Bonhoeffer's Eschatology of the Penultimate," 226–44; Zimmermann, "Suffering with the World," 313ff; Harvey, "Augustine and Thomas Aquinas," 29.

133. DBWE 6:85–87.

134. DBWE 4:285.

135. DBWE 6:85–86.

tion to Christ.[136] This is because the very structure of Christ's life, which Bonhoeffer defines in terms of responsibility, has become the structure of human life. This structure includes four elements: 1) "vicarious representative action"; 2) action in "accordance with reality"; 3) accountability (i.e., a willingness to assume guilt); and 4) freedom for a "*venture [Wagnis]* of concrete decision."[137] While one's obligation to God and others determines the first two characteristics, one's freedom before God and others determines the final two.[138] He describes the unavoidable reality of this responsible life when he states that "all human life is in its essence vicarious representation . . . Even if a life resists this intrinsic character, it nevertheless remains vicariously representative, be it with regard to life or with regard to death, just as a father remains a father for good or for ill."[139] Thus, while one might act contrary to one's human nature, this cannot change the fact that human existence will always have a particular, intrinsic structure insofar as the incarnate Christ, who acts vicariously and takes on guilt on behalf of others, forms it according to his image. Moreover, all of this impacts the nature of one's moral discernment. As Muers suggests, discernment that proceeds from one conformed to the form of the incarnate Christ will take on the "complexities of reality," rather than try and escape reality by living solely in the spiritual realm.[140] Thus, one will understand discernment not as an isolated spiritual activity, divorced for the reality of the natural world, but as a human activity fully embedded in the world.

Aside from the incarnate one, Bonhoeffer also speaks of Christ as the crucified one who must become subject to judgment, suffer, and experience rejection, all for the sake of humanity.[141] Christ is so utterly rejected that there is no value or dignity that might attach itself to the suffering such that one might construe it in a heroic manner.[142] Christ's form as the crucified one "remains alien, and at best pitiable, to a world where success is the measure and justification of all things"; nevertheless, the crucified one is not concerned with success or failure, but only with accepting God's judgment

---

136. DBWE 4:285.
137. DBWE 6:257, 288; Bonhoeffer's italics.
138. Ibid., 257.
139. Ibid., 258–59.
140. Muers, *Keeping God's Silence*, 171.
141. DBWE 4:285–86; DBWE 6:88.
142. DBWE 6:85.

CHRISTIAN FORMATION AND THE PRACTICE OF DISCERNMENT

at the cross.[143] He also asserts that Christ the crucified one is both judgment and grace for humanity. He describes this in "Ultimate and Penultimate Things" using his conceptual contrast: "The ultimate has become real in the cross—as judgment on all that is penultimate, but at the same time as grace for the penultimate that bows to the judgment of the ultimate."[144]

In *Discipleship*, one's conformation to the crucified Christ means taking on the form of death and living a crucified life, which for some will end in martyrdom. As Bonhoeffer writes: "It is by Christians' being publicly disgraced, having to suffer and being put to death for the sake of Christ, that Christ himself attains visible form within his community."[145] Moreover, such conformation means a "daily dying in the struggle of the spirit against the flesh," which implies the necessity of continual formation in the life of discipleship.[146] In "Ethics as Formation" he highlights a slightly different aspect of this conformation: he argues that conformation to the form of the crucified Christ helps Christians recognize themselves as judged and reconciled by God. We are reminded that the Christian should not be concerned with success or failure precisely because the Christian has no vantage point from which to evaluate success or failure. The Christian cannot judge the self, but must proceed with a "wiling acceptance of the judgment of God."[147] Once again, Muers proposes that conformation to the crucified Christ corresponds to discernment as "the exercise of judgment."[148] In fact, we already saw in "God's Love" how Christian judgment, which seeks to facilitate reconciliation, is a valid and important function in the Christian moral life. This significance of judgment is particularly interesting to note given that in both *Discipleship* and *Ethics*, one's conformation to the crucified Christ and one's following the way of the cross receive more emphasis than conformation to the incarnate or the risen one. One gains further proof of the importance of this strand of Bonhoeffer's thinking in his prison musings where he suggests that only through conformation to the suffering Christ can one fully engage in the world.[149] And yet, this way of the cross is

---

143. Ibid., 88–91.
144. Ibid., 158.
145. DBWE 4:286.
146. Ibid., 285.
147. DBWE 6:90.
148. Muers, *Keeping God's Silence*, 171.
149. DBWE 8:480–81. For a commentary on how the "suffering Christ" helps one respond to a "world come of age," especially a world heavily influenced by the nation

never divorced from the reality of the resurrection. Indeed, without the resurrection, Bonhoeffer's theology falls apart and a proper balance between simplicity and wisdom in moral discernment becomes impossible.

Thus, Bonhoeffer argues that the form of Christ is also a glorified and risen form. We see the truth of this in Scripture at the transfiguration and the resurrection and ascension of Christ. Although Christ has taken on sinful flesh, he nevertheless remains the image of God and his form reflects God's glory and represents God's "Yes" to both Christ and humanity.[150] Christ's risen form is the creation of the new humanity and represents victory over the power of death.[151] The risen Christ now offers "the liberating call to come under the lordship of Jesus Christ" and reveals himself as the one who is the "origin, essence, and goal" of all things.[152] In *Discipleship*, he does not offer a very concrete description of what conformation to this form entails, mentioning only that one begins to "reflect the glory of Jesus Christ."[153] In *Ethics* we get a more interesting comment: he says that the resurrection of Christ overturns the "idolization of death," meaning that one no longer anxiously holds onto life at all costs and neither does one cast it away too easily.[154] In a sense, conformation to the risen one is about hope and trust and it affirms the reality of Christ's image inside a person even as he or she continues in the world of pain and death in the present. While Muers speaks about conformation to the risen Christ pointing toward discernment as "the practice of patience," I would also argue that discernment becomes more attuned to the structure of reality as a source of guidance.[155] Christ's victorious resurrection radically reconstitutes creation: it is no longer a fallen creation devoid of any hope; it is a redeemed creation, still bearing the marks of its falleness, but moving slowly toward its final consummation. As we will see in chapter 6, such a creation holds many resources for the disciple trying to navigate the moral life.

It should be clear from the foregoing discussion that conformation to the form of Christ is not merely a "theoretical process" or something that happens only internally in the realm of faith; instead, it is a process

---

state and market economy, see Pugh, *Religionless Christianity*.

150. DBWE 4:286; DBWE 6:91.
151. DBWE 6:91.
152. Ibid., 401–2.
153. DBWE 4:286.
154. DBWE 6:92.
155. Muers, *Keeping God's Silence*, 171.

with an outward dimension—something that happens concretely in one's life. Thus, it is through one's conformation to Christ that the conceptual unity between simplicity and wisdom becomes efficacious. As the *Gestalt Christi* shapes the inner structure of one's being, this results in outward implications regarding the shape of one's moral character and moral discernment in the world. Put differently, as one moves deeper into life with Christ through a process of Christian conformation, one becomes more adept at perceiving the reality of relationships and situations and knowing how to respond to them rightly. The more Christ-like one becomes, the more one's life exhibits both the simplicity of communion with God and the wisdom of discerning the significant from the factual. As one learns to embody and express this simplicity and wisdom, one learns how to engage in moral discernment. And, paradoxically, it is through engaging in such discernment that one perceives how to move deeper into life with Christ, in part, through the practice of spiritual exercise.

The Place of Spiritual Exercise

As already mentioned above, one of the reasons for Bonhoeffer's emphasis on *conformation* is to remind us that it is never human action as such, but the work of Christ through the Holy Spirit, that effects one's moral formation. At the same time, he does not want to suggest that human beings are entirely inert in the formative process. In fact, human activity is crucial precisely because it places one into a position where Christ's form can do its work. In the present section, I will argue that it is the regular practice of spiritual exercise that plays a central role in continually placing Christians into situations with formative potential.[156] Moreover, I will contend that spiritual exercise is significant for Bonhoeffer because it gives him the language to speak about a kind of moral reflection proper to the life of simplicity. Finally, I will argue that although he does not articulate the details of the relationship, it is clear that spiritual exercise helps to facilitate moral discernment in several ways.

In his final *Ethics* manuscript, left incomplete due to his arrest, Bonhoeffer critiques the German Protestant church in part for its failure to take

---

156. Not many have written on the theme of Bonhoeffer and spiritual exercise. However, the following works offer an introduction to certain aspects of the theme: Altenähr, *Lehrer des Gebets*; Dahill, "Particularity"; Dahill, "Probing the Will of God"; Pelikan, *Die Frömmigkeit Dietrich Bonhoeffers*; Northcott, "Human Identity," 11–29.

seriously "the significance of disciplined practices [*Zuchtübungen*], such as spiritual exercises [*geistlicher Exerzitien*], asceticism, meditation, and contemplation."[157] If the inner life of the church is lacking, he argues, its outward proclamation will lose its effectiveness.[158] To find such a statement in 1943 is surprising for those who assume Bonhoeffer held an interest in spiritual exercises only during his years at the Finkenwalde seminary in the mid 1930s. Contrary to this misperception, however, he spoke of spiritual exercise, using the common German term *Übung* and sometimes the Latin *exercitium*, on many occasions beginning in 1928 and continuing into the 1940s.[159] During the course of these years he came to understand spiritual exercise as an essential aspect of the Christian life, with direct bearing on the task of moral discernment.

His earliest discussion of spiritual exercise occurred at age 22 in a 1928 sermon on Psalm 62:1, preached during his time as an assistant pastor in Barcelona.[160] What is striking about the sermon, which speaks of the human soul waiting before God in silence, is its spiritual, almost mystical, tone.[161] He speaks of the soul expectantly yearning for God's beneficent hand, waiting in silence to breathe in God's will, and becoming "completely free . . . to travel to the house of the Father."[162] While this is certainly metaphorical language, he means to indicate a concrete discipline of prayerful meditation that must be "practiced through serious work."[163] Speaking near the end of the sermon as though he were a spiritual director, he discusses potential difficulties, offers practical suggestions, and exhorts his congregation to action, for only "those who seriously apply themselves to such exercises day after day will amply experience the golden abundance of the

---

157. DBWE 6:407.

158. Ibid., 407–8.

159. For specific references to the Latin *exercitium*, see DBW 10:591; DBWE 3:23n11; DBWE 12:231–32; DBWE 4:46–47.

160. DBWE 10:500–505. Psalm 62:1 is numbered 62:2 in Luther's translation.

161. Pelikan contends that Bonhoeffer's description in this sermon of a free meditative practice before God does not have a mystical feel (*mystische Stimmung*) due to his aversion to mysticism. I would argue, contra Pelikan, that it is more precise to say that Bonhoeffer's sermon *does* have a mystical feel ("breathing in God's will"; allowing one's soul to "travel to the house of the Father"), but nevertheless refrains from falling into the error that Bonhoeffer associates with mysticism: the presumption that humanity, through its own potential, can bridge the gap between human beings and God. See Pelikan, *Die Frömmigkeit Dietrich Bonhoeffers*, 76; DBWE 10:356.

162. DBWE 10:500–504.

163. Ibid., 503.

Christian Formation and the Practice of Discernment

fruit such hours yield."[164] He does not develop the potential link between spiritual exercise and discernment despite his language of "listening" to God's word. Nevertheless, his description of this free, meditative approach to God confirms his early awareness of spiritual exercise and his recognition of its potential for Christian growth. Herbert Rainer Pelikan is right to observe, however, that his view of meditation quickly changes: while he advocates a free meditative practice not grounded in Scripture in 1928, he begins to champion a meditation grounded solely in the Bible in the mid 1930s, as we will see below.[165]

While his interest in spiritual exercise did not originate from his experience of transformation in the early 1930s, this event did result in an even greater appreciation of spiritual exercises such as Bible meditation, prayer, and oral confession.[166] Not surprisingly, references to spiritual exercise appear in two of his lecture series at the University of Berlin during this period in the early 1930s: "Theological Anthropology" and *Creation and Fall*. Of particular interest are his comments on *exercitium* in his introduction to *Creation and Fall*. He remarks:

> The word of God [is] neither fiction nor fairy tale nor myth; on the contrary one must read it word for word . . . like a child and learn to rethink *completely* what the historical critical commentaries teach us. One can never hear it, if one does not at the same time live it—and this involves especially *exercitium* ["practice"]. For *us* the word of God always lies hidden like a treasure in a field . . . for we always have to come to the knowledge of God via the cross of Christ.[167]

He mentions in this brief introduction the necessity of a careful, thorough reading of God's word and the inaccessibility of God's word outside of Christ's mediation: he will continue to develop these themes in later works, as we have already seen. Of particular interest, however, is his assertion that in order to hear God's word one must "live it—and this involves especially *exercitium*." This implies not only that living by God's word (i.e., the life of discipleship) includes disciplined, spiritual practice, but that spiritual practice assists one in perceiving God's word in the first place. Here, for the first time, we see a subtle link between spiritual exercise and discernment.

164. Ibid., 503-4.
165. Pelikan, *Die Frömmigkeit Dietrich Bonhoeffers*, 76.
166. See the discussion in chapter 1 of Bonhoeffer's spiritual transformation.
167. DBWE 3:23n11; Bonhoeffer's italics.

By the time he reaches the mid-1930s, Bonhoeffer is clearly convinced that spiritual exercise is an essential aspect of the Christian moral life. In his book *Discipleship*, which represents much of his thinking during this period, he recognizes that despite its negative development, monasticism in the early church was a positive example of a disciplined Christian life of "daily exercise."[168] However, such exercise needs to be "hidden" lest it become self-serving.[169] To be demonstrative and overly pious in one's spiritual practice is to betray a self-righteous arrogance rather than a humble and repentant demeanor. It is typical of the kind of prayer practiced by "the hypocrites" who pray in public not in order to grow closer to God, but to be visible before the crowd (Matt 6:5–8). As Albert Altenähr puts it, prayer, for Bonhoeffer, is the gift of freedom from the imprisonment of the egotistical I.[170] Thus, a spiritual practice such as prayer loses its purpose of placing one into a space of encounter with Christ if it becomes merely "a deed, an exercise, a pious attitude" to be seen by others.[171] It also loses its purpose when it becomes a criterion to evaluate the self or others, rather than retaining its rightful status as God's gift.[172]

Despite the danger of overly pious practice, Bonhoeffer points out that Jesus himself takes it for granted that the disciples will engage in spiritual exercise.[173] It is not, *if* you fast or pray, do it this way, but, *whenever* you fast or pray, do it accordingly.[174] The purpose of such exercise is to overcome the will of the flesh, which obstructs Christian discipleship: it is "to make disciples more willing and more joyous in following the designated path and doing the works required of them."[175] Thus, spiritual exercises are a part of sanctification: they are penultimate activities that prepare the way to hear and act upon God's word by creating space for Christ to take form

---

168. For Bonhoeffer's positive and negative comments in *Discipleship* regarding monasticism, see DBWE 4:46–47; DBW 4:32–33. For his comments on a "new monasticism" that might restore the church through concrete obedience to the Sermon on the Mount, see DBWE 13:273.

169. See Bonhoeffer's frequent reference to Luke 18:9–14, which illustrates two mutually exclusive approaches to God in prayer, DBWE 9:455–56; DBWE 10:352, 567; DBWE 6:314, 317.

170. Altenähr, *Lehrer des Gebets*, 268–72.

171. DBWE 4:153.

172. Ibid., 161.

173. Ibid., 158.

174. Ibid., 152; cf. Matthew 6:5–8.

175. DBWE 4:158.

within a human life.¹⁷⁶ For example, it is only through the practice of mutual confession that one enters into a place of communion with Christ at the altar.¹⁷⁷ Thus, just as Peter had first to leave his nets in obedience in order to experience Christ in faith and to pursue a life of discipleship, so also must we obediently pray, meditate on Scripture, and confess our sins in order to fully experience Christ's transformative action in our lives. This is what Bonhoeffer means when he says in *Discipleship*: "*only the obedient believe.*"¹⁷⁸ Christians should not forsake penultimate acts of obedience thinking they can simply "take refuge" in the realm of faith; on the contrary, it is precisely those who are obedient who will experience the realm of faith.¹⁷⁹ Of course, his opposite statement—"*only the believers obey*"—is also crucial:¹⁸⁰ it reminds us that despite their significance, spiritual exercises, in and of themselves, cannot cause Christian formation to happen. One engages in spiritual exercises in the first place only through God's grace.

One can find many examples of spiritual exercises in Bonhoeffer's book *Life Together*, which describes his attempt to organize a disciplined, communal life with his Confessing Church seminarians. Here he speaks of prayer, intercession, Bible meditation, communal Bible reading, singing, keeping silence, mutual confession, Christian service, and breaking bread together. The book's focus has caused some to designate it a classic work of Christian spirituality akin to *The Imitation of Christ* by Thomas à Kempis or the *Rule of St. Benedict*.¹⁸¹ It is far more, however, than a work of spirituality: it is also an apology for the importance of spiritual exercise for Christian life. The following passage captures the main line of Bonhoeffer's argument in this regard. He writes:

> Moreover, we will see at this point whether Christians' time of meditation has led them into an unreal world from which they awaken with a fright when they step out into the workaday world, or whether it has led them into the real world of God from which they enter into the day's activities strengthened and purified. Has it transported them for a few short moments into a spiritual

---

176. Ibid., 160.
177. See Bonhoeffer's final chapter of *Life Together*, "Confession and the Lord's Supper," DBWE 5:108–18.
178. DBWE 4:63; Bonhoeffer's italics.
179. Ibid., 160.
180. Ibid., 63; Bonhoeffer's italics.
181. Müller and Schönherr, "Editors' Afterword," 128.

ecstasy that vanishes when everyday life returns, or has it planted the Word of God so soberly and so deeply in their heart that it holds and strengthens them all day long, leading them to active love, to obedience, to good works? Only the day can decide.[182]

He poses two possibilities in this paragraph. The first is that spiritual practice acts as an escape from reality by leading one into an "unreal world" of "spiritual ecstasy." Here, a disjunction exists between the spiritual benefits of meditation and the everyday decisions and actions Christians engage in. The second possibility, however, is that spiritual practice leads Christians more deeply into the "real world of God" out of which they "enter into the day's activities." This possibility suggests a connection between one's spiritual practice and one's moral life—or between one's private, inner life and one's public, outer life—and does so on the basis of a particular view of reality that rejects thinking in terms of autonomous realms.[183] Thus, far from pulling Christians away from the reality of God's will, spiritual exercise ushers them into this reality by creating space in their lives for Christ's form to take root. Spiritual exercise is not a human achievement, but a humble participation in Christ, who conforms Christians ever more into the divine image. As Christians pray, read and meditate on Scripture, and confess their sins to one another, they prepare themselves to better hear and act upon God's word in obedience.

Two interconnected practices in particular—Bible meditation and prayer—are helpful in further illuminating some of Bonhoeffer's thinking. Regarding Bible meditation, he offers both practical instruction and theological reflection on the topic at various points in the 1930s and 40s.[184] We saw above the change from his earlier recommendation of free meditation, present in his Barcelona sermon, to his belief during the 1930s and 40s that Scripture must always ground meditation.[185] This shift happened because of an increased awareness that Christ is not a static entity, but a "living address" who meets human beings through Scripture, and speaks to individuals in their "personal situation" and in their "particular tasks, deci-

---

182. DBWE 5:92.
183. See chapter 3.
184. See especially DBWE 14:494–95, 931–36; DBWE 15:517–18; DBWE 16:254–55.
185. For Bonhoeffer's distinction between Ignatian meditation, which he recommends because it stays closely bound to the biblical text, and Sulpician meditation, which derives from the Jesuit Jean Jacques Olier and takes the form of free prayer, see DBWE 14:484–95.

sions, sins, and temptations."[186] As he says in *Life Together*: "[W]e read the text given to us on the strength of the promise that it has something quite personal to say to us for this day and for our standing as Christians."[187] This is especially true when using the daily devotional texts of the Church of the Brethren (*Losungen der Brüdergemeine*), which Bonhoeffer loved and often found helpful for thinking through particular situations in his daily life.[188] When considering these texts from Scripture, he always found them quite lucid and demanding. This is because the perspicuity of Scripture does not depend upon one's own interpretive framework, but solely upon Christ present through the Holy Spirit, the subject who addresses individuals and communities through the text.[189] Christ's words are clear and authoritative and demand a response from contemporary individuals, just as they did when Jesus called Levi the tax collector, whose only option was to follow Jesus in simple obedience or remain in disobedience.[190]

While much of Bonhoeffer's thinking on meditation remains consistent from the mid 1930s into the 1940s, a new development does emerge in 1939. When speaking of meditating on God's word as part of his commentary on Psalm 119, he describes meditation as "reflection [*Besinnung*]."[191] He does the same later, in 1942, when he speaks of meditation as "daily silent reflection [*Besinnung*] on the word of God as it applies to me."[192] This introduction of the notion of *Besinnung* in relation to Christian meditation, on the eve of beginning his *Ethics*, is quite telling. It suggests that he saw in the concept of meditation a way to speak about a certain kind of moral reflection within the Christian life that does not fatally contradict the simplicity of one's relationship with God through Christ. Moreover, it suggests

186. DBWE 5:89; DBWE 12:317.

187. DBWE 5:87; cf. DBWE 14:931–33.

188. These readings were first prepared in 1731 by the Herrnhut community of Count Nicholas Ludwig von Zinzendorf and have provided Christians ever since with daily devotional readings from Scripture (a short text from both the Old and New Testaments). For the history of the daily texts, see DBWE 5:58–59n27. For examples of Bonhoeffer relating a daily text to a particular situation, see DBWE 14:309–10; DBWE 15:232; DBWE 16:253, 256–57. For examples of circular letters sent by Bonhoeffer to the Finkenwalde seminarians that included lists of daily readings, see DBWE 14:220, 320; DBWE 15:25, 41, 52, 61, 85, 167–68.

189. DBWE 14:417; cf. Webster, *Word and Church*, 98–107.

190. DBWE 4:57–76. Bonhoeffer also speaks of Christ the Word demanding a response from the hearer in *Lectures on Christology*, DBWE 12:313–18.

191. DBWE 15:517; DBW 15:524.

192. DBWE 16:254.

that at least by 1939, he began to see more direct links between a spiritual exercise such as Bible meditation and the task of moral discernment, which lies at the heart of Christian ethics. I will return to this important matter in the following chapter when I take up the theme of simple obedience and explore in more detail Bonhoeffer's work on Psalm 119 and his understanding of meditative reflection.

Along with Bible meditation Bonhoeffer speaks often about prayer. He believes that just as a child learns to speak by listening carefully to the language of his or her parents, Christians learn to pray by first hearing God's words spoken through Christ.[193] Because God's speech in Christ addresses Christians in Scripture, the Lord's Prayer and the Psalter become prime training grounds for prayer, because here one discovers the appropriate language to address God.[194] Not surprisingly, this emphasis on the Psalter and the Lord's Prayer corresponds to Luther's high regard for both; in addition, Bonhoeffer's understanding of prayer as a learned discipline also finds support in Luther, as evidenced by the Reformer's letter to his barber offering advice about how to pray.[195]

But what is happening when one learns to pray? Here, Bonhoeffer offers an answer that helps to clarify his understanding of spiritual exercise. When a person prays, he argues, that person does so through Christ the mediator, who alone grants access to God.[196] However, it is not *one's own* prayer that one speaks to God through Christ, but actually *Christ's* prayer in which one participates.[197] "If Christ takes us along in the prayer which Christ prays," writes Bonhoeffer, "then we are freed from the torment of being without prayer . . . [and] certain and glad that God hears us."[198] Of course, for Bonhoeffer, the best example of this participatory prayer is the Psalter, which expresses the full range of petitions or thanksgivings one might offer to God. Because the Psalter is both God's word addressed to humanity and also human words addressed to God, the only person who

---

193. DBWE 5:156. Cf. Bonhoeffer's thoughts on truth telling as a learned activity, DBWE 16:603.

194. DBWE 5:156.

195. See Luther, "A Simple Way to Pray," 193–211. One might also note that the very title of Luther's letter, "A Simple [*einfältige*] Way to Pray," and his statement that good prayer requires both "concentration and singleness of heart" (ibid., 199) point to Bonhoeffer's own emphasis on simplicity in prayer and other spiritual disciplines.

196. DBWE 4:153.

197. DBWE 5:156.

198. Ibid.

can truly pray the psalms is the divine and human Christ, who alone can speak a truly divine word and a truly human word simultaneously.[199] Thus, to pray the psalms is to participate in Christ's prayer and to recognize that Christ—not the self—is the ultimate origin and ground of one's spiritual life.[200] We see through this language of participation another way to speak about the purpose of spiritual exercise in moving people into a place of formative potential.

While this middle period of Bonhoeffer's life was undoubtedly the high point of his thinking about spiritual exercise, the theme does not disappear in his later writings. We have already seen at the beginning of this section his reference to the significance of spiritual exercise in *Ethics*, and a look at his preparatory notes for *Ethics* reveals many other references both to prayer and to spiritual practice.[201] Moreover, many of his letters during the late 1930s and early 1940s offer helpful insight into his thinking.[202] For instance, in a circular letter to his former seminarians, he mentions that spiritual exercise must not become oppressive: one must acknowledge that some life situations, such as active military duty, simply do not allow for the regular practice of spiritual discipline.[203] Freedom, therefore, and not law, determines the practice of spiritual exercise. With pastoral wisdom, he encourages his former students by saying: "God knows your present life and finds a way to you even in the most strained and overburdened days, when you can no longer find the way to God."[204] In another letter, Bonhoeffer admits his own struggle with reading Scripture regularly, and his

---

199. The fact that Scripture suggests a Davidic authorship for the Psalms is not a problem for Bonhoeffer because he sees an intimate link between David and Christ. He says: "In the Psalms of David it is precisely the promised Christ who already speaks (Heb. 2:12; 10:5) or, as is sometimes said, the Holy Spirit (Heb. 3:7). The same words that David spoke, therefore, the future Messiah spoke in him. Christ prayed along with the prayers of David or, more accurately, it is none other than Christ who prayed them in Christ's own forerunner, David," ibid., 159.

200. See also Bonhoeffer's thoughts on intercessory prayer, which allows one to participate in the vicarious representative action of Christ. DBWE 1:184, 186–87; DBW 1:121, 124.

201. For example, see Bonhoeffer, *Zettelnotizen*, 36, 63, 124, 132, 142.

202. See, for example, Bonhoeffer's discussion of daily prayer, Bible reading, and spiritual practice in general in the following letters: his 1940 and 1942 Finkenwalde circular letters (DBWE 16:46–47, 254–55); his 1940, 1941, and 1942 letters to Eberhard Bethge (DBWE 16:78, 133, 329).

203. DBWE 16:46–47.

204. Ibid., 47.

satisfaction when he finally comes to it again.[205] In prison, he writes to his parents about his appreciation of the contemplative tradition, his regular Bible reading, and especially his love of the Psalms.[206] Thus, far from leaving spiritual exercise behind during his final years, he continues to think about, and to practice, the same disciplines that had grasped his attention for the majority of his adult life.

We have seen from the foregoing discussion that spiritual exercise is crucial for Bonhoeffer because it describes the way Christians can put themselves into a place where conformation to Christ can occur. But this is not the only significance of spiritual exercise for the Christian life: spiritual exercise also assists Christians in the task of moral discernment. As Dahill argues, Bonhoeffer's notion of discernment depends upon his belief in the efficacy of spiritual disciplines, such as prayer, meditation, and mutual confession, to shape and teach Christians to be attentive listeners to the Word of God.[207] In effect, discernment becomes *the* primary spiritual activity that orientates all other spiritual discipline.[208] One can see the connection between spiritual exercise and discernment in at least three ways.

First, in his primary discussion of discernment in "God's Love" Bonhoeffer posits self-examination as a crucial element of discerning God's will in the Christian life.[209] As mentioned in chapter 2, turning inward in self-examination is not about looking to one's own moral knowledge or analyzing possible decisions and outcomes. Instead, turning inward means to focus one's gaze on the person of Christ within, who then becomes the prism through which one perceives morality and decides how to act responsibly in a given situation.[210] For Bonhoeffer, renewing the knowledge of Christ within is not simply an intellectual exercise, but something that takes place through worship, through receiving the sacraments, and through spiritual exercises that help one grow in love and in conformity to Christ. Thus, when one prays or meditates on Scripture, one is focusing on the presence of Christ within, and this assists one's discernment by forcing the individual to abandon the many self-generated possibilities of moral decision and action and focus instead on the single reality of Christ and

---

205. Ibid., 133, 329.
206. DBWE 8:81.
207. Dahill, "Probing the Will of God," 45.
208. Ibid.
209. DBWE 6:324–26.
210. Ibid., 325.

how such reality shapes an understanding of God's will in the concrete situation. While Bonhoeffer does not make the entire connection explicit in his writings, the link between spiritual exercise and self-examination and between self-examination and discerning God's will are enough to suggest that without the regular practice of spiritual discipline, discerning God's will becomes more difficult.

Second, when Bonhoeffer speaks of hearing God's word or perceiving God's will, it is never an isolated activity, but always inherently linked with decision and action. God's will is not a set of static instructions that one can contemplate at leisure, but a dynamic address that demands one's response. Thus, as he consistently points out, authentic Christian discernment is not about acquiring knowledge of God's will in order to possess it in the intellect, but perceiving God's will for the purpose of doing God's will. And herein lies the connection with spiritual exercise, one purpose of which is to bridge the gap between hearing and doing God's word.[211] In *Discipleship*, Bonhoeffer, following Galatians 5:17, describes the process of sanctification (i.e., the life of discipleship) as a struggle of "the Spirit against the flesh."[212] While "[t]he spirit knows the path of discipleship and is ready to follow it . . . the flesh is too fearful; the path is too difficult for it, too uncertain, too arduous."[213] And so, while a disciple might hear God's word in the spirit, the "selfish and lethargic will" of the flesh makes sure that this hearing does not result in doing; thus, a failure in discernment.[214] But there is a solution to this struggle in the life of discipleship: namely, spiritual exercise. He argues that through daily prayer, meditation, fasting, and other spiritual disciplines, one can overcome the will of the flesh and thereby prepare oneself not only to hear God's word, but to put that word into action. Thus, through enabling concrete discipleship, spiritual practice becomes a means of discernment by helping Christians avoid the hypocrisy of knowing God's will without doing God's will. And, paradoxically, this also demonstrates how the disciplined practice of spiritual exercise, which might seem an affront to Christian freedom, is actually a means to Christian freedom, insofar as true freedom exists only in doing God's will.[215]

---

211. DBWE 4:159–61.
212. Ibid., 267.
213. Ibid., 159.
214. Ibid., 158.
215. Ibid., 159.

Finally, as mentioned in chapter 1, a striking link between spiritual practice and discernment occurs in Bonhoeffer's own life in 1939. It is through an encounter with Paul's words from 2 Timothy 4:21—"'Come before the winter'"—that Bonhoeffer is able to discern that he, too, must leave the United States as soon as possible and return to Germany.[216] Such a verse would seem highly inconsequential for many, having no apparent theological or even practical significance; Bonhoeffer, however, believed that God was speaking to him directly through the text. Granted, it is difficult to say with certainty whether his chance encounter with the 2 Timothy text was the single decisive factor in helping him discern the timing of his return to Germany. However, it is equally difficult to deny that when he spoke earlier of prayer being "an unbroken, indeed continuous, process of learning, appropriating and impressing God's will in Jesus Christ on the mind" or when he encouraged Bethge to practice morning prayer because it "clarifies what one is to do and say throughout the day," he did not intend a clear link between spiritual exercise and discernment.[217] Whatever the case, it is clear that Bonhoeffer took seriously God's ability to speak in a direct and immediate way through spiritual exercise, the practice of which indicated a readiness to "appropriate the Word" by letting it speak personally.[218]

Conclusion

I have argued in this chapter that the conceptual unity between simplicity and wisdom becomes efficacious in the lives of Christians through the process of conformation to the form of Christ. Christian conformation is not a theoretical process, but a concrete transformation in the life of an individual that shapes not only the structure of one's being, but the form of one's moral behavior as well. Thus, as one moves deeper into life with Christ both simplicity and wisdom begin to manifest themselves through one's communion with Christ and through one's accurate perception of reality. Through investigating Christian conformation, and the notion of ethics as formation, we also saw once again the centrality of discernment for Bonhoeffer's vision of Christian ethics. Discernment is necessary because an ethic of formation deals with the concrete: how Christ is taking form here and now. Ethical theory is inadequate for determining good and

---

216. DBWE 15:232; cf. chapter 1.
217. DBWE 5:57–58; DBWE 16:153–54.
218. DBWE 5:89.

evil in such a concrete ethic; the task is left to a practice of discernment that is both simple and wise. In addition to this, I argued that spiritual exercise plays a prominent role in this process by placing individuals into a space where Christ's form can act upon them and by assisting them in the task of discernment. Such a life of spiritual discipline is not opposed to a life of active engagement in the world; in fact, it helps to facilitate such a life by helping one participate in what is real.

However, while the reality of Christian conformation to Christ's form might alleviate the tension between a simple, unreflective approach to God's will and a rational, reflective mode of moral deliberation, it can also threaten to obscure the importance of each particular point of emphasis. There is a reason Bonhoeffer spoke on many occasions of simplicity, simple faith, and simple obedience: these terms name something fundamental about the proper character and purpose of Christian life. In the same way, there is a reason he spoke of wisdom and the human ability to reason and reflect on moral situations: such an emphasis recognizes the natural, penultimate context of discernment, without which the Christian life would be unintelligible. Moral discernment is not only a matter of faith, taking place within an ecclesial context; it is also a matter of human nature, implanted in the real and historical world. Therefore, the following two chapters will address the significance of both simplicity (chapter 5) and the penultimate nature of discernment (chapter 6).

5

The Simplicity of Discernment

SOME OF BONHOEFFER'S STRONGEST expressions of the simple, unreflective approach to the moral life appear during discussions of God's commandment (*Gebot Gottes*). He argues in *Creation and Fall*, for example, that God's commandment demands from the human being one of two options: either a questioning and reflective approach, which asks along with the serpent, "Did God really say . . . ?," or an approach of simple obedience, which responds directly and immediately to God's word.[1] This belief that God's concrete commandment encounters the human person at each particular moment and calls him or her to respond in simple obedience runs throughout Bonhoeffer's work in the 1930s and, as we saw in chapter 2, continues into his *Ethics* as well. For him, there is something essential about the simplicity of a relationship with God that one cannot sacrifice without risking a fall back into disunity. One of the tasks of the present chapter, therefore, is to demonstrate why an emphasis on simplicity is so crucial for Bonhoeffer in his account of the Christian moral life.

A second task, however, is to determine whether Bonhoeffer's view of simplicity and simple obedience, at least as he expresses it in the 1930s, eliminates space for any practice of moral reflection for Christians. As we saw in chapter 2, Bonhoeffer realized in 1942 that one must employ the best of human ability along with a simple faith in order to successfully discern God's will and act upon it. Moreover, I claimed in the previous chapter that in 1939 he was beginning to speak of meditating on God's word as a legitimate form of moral reflection for Christians. But what about earlier

1. DBWE 3:107–8.

The Simplicity of Discernment

in the 1930s, particular during his work on *Discipleship*: did Bonhoeffer sense even then that his stark understanding of simple obedience required a more nuanced explanation?

Finally, a third task of this chapter, which will point ahead to chapter 6, is to show that despite Bonhoeffer's view that simple obedience should be direct and implicit, he recognizes that one cannot divorce simple obedience to God's commandment from the natural world, which provides a necessary interpretive context.

I will pursue all three of these tasks through a chronological survey of the God's commandment motif in Bonhoeffer's corpus, from his early days as a student to his *Ethics* manuscripts in the 1940s. As I describe his early views on God's commandment and his later focus on simple obedience in the 1930s, the importance of simplicity in the Christian life will begin to emerge. Not only do Bonhoeffer's discussions of simplicity and simple obedience clarify the proper relationship between the Christian disciple and God, but they also emphasize the immediate and concrete nature of Christian ethics and the seriousness of Christ's call to discipleship, and train Christians to focus on responding to God's will rather than on the demands of ethical precepts. In addition, as I discuss Bonhoeffer's view of God's commandment in 1932 and his later focus on simple obedience in *Discipleship*, I will argue that even in the midst of developing his thinking about simple obedience to God's commandment, he recognized the dangers of overemphasizing simple obedience in the Christian moral life to the exclusion of all manner of rational reflection. His notion of meditative reflection, discussed in 1939, was his attempt to alleviate the tension between simple obedience and rational reflection in his account of Christian discipleship. Finally, I will highlight several points in Bonhoeffer's earlier and later work where an understanding of the reality of the world serves as a guide for Christian discipleship. This will be especially clear in one of his final *Ethics* manuscripts: "The 'Ethical' and the 'Christian' as a Topic."[2] This text explores the theme of God's commandment as a methodological entry point for Christian ethics. As I will argue, it is in discussing a theory of ethics often criticized on the grounds of an alleged subjectivism that Bonhoeffer makes his boldest move toward an objective foundation for Christian ethics and moral discernment. Put differently, it is in "The 'Ethical' and the 'Christian' as a Topic" that he positions moral discernment as an activity deeply rooted in the reality of the penultimate world.

2. DBWE 6:363–87.

Early Thinking About God's Commandment

Although easily forgotten amidst the intoxicating rhetoric of *Discipleship*, Bonhoeffer did not always advocate the way of simple obedience to God's commandment. In fact, prior to 1932 God's commandment was not an important theological category for him, a fact evidenced by the scant reference to the *Gebot Gottes* in his early work.[3] Nevertheless, at least two early texts warrant special attention and help to illustrate both the unity *and* disunity of Bonhoeffer's early thinking in relation to his later formulations.

The first text is a student paper from 1926 comparing Johannine and Pauline theology. During the course of the paper Bonhoeffer briefly explores what it means to keep God's commandment for both John and Paul.[4] He observes that in John 15, one keeps the commandments in order to maintain one's "mystical unity" with Christ.[5] As Jesus says, "If you keep my commandments, you will abide in my love, just as I have kept my Father's commandments and abide in his love" (John 15:10). For Paul, by contrast, one keeps the commandments for the sake of "absolute obedience": "Have this mind among yourselves, which is yours in Christ Jesus, who . . . humbled himself and became obedient unto death, even death on a cross" (Phil 2:5, 8).[6] Leaving aside the accuracy of Bonhoeffer's analysis of Johannine and Pauline theology, what is interesting is how he focuses not on the manner or method of keeping God's commandment, but rather on the *purpose*. Should one be obedient to God's commandment for the purpose of obedience itself, either to the commandment or to the commander, or because such obedience draws one deeper into unity with Christ? He does not explore the question in his student paper, content to merely highlight what he sees in John and Paul, but in noticing the potential connection between obedience to God's commandments and deeper unity with Christ, he unknowingly anticipates a crucial aspect of his later understanding of simple obedience and moral discernment.

The second early text is his 1929 Barcelona lecture entitled, "Basic Questions of a Christian Ethic."[7] Rasmussen chooses this lecture as a suitable beginning point for his survey of the *Gebot Gottes* motif because,

---

3. For the few early references to God's commandment during Bonhoeffer's student days, see DBWE 9:260, 400, 474.

4. See Bonhoeffer's "Paper on John and Paul," in DBWE 9:395–404.

5. Ibid., 400.

6. Ibid.

7. DBWE 10:359–78; DBW 10:323–45. Hereafter referred to as "Basic Questions."

The Simplicity of Discernment

although it does not mention "God's commandment" as such, it contains "some affinities in terms such as 'being addressed,' 'God's call' and 'claim.'"[8] Although unmentioned by Rasmussen, the lecture also contains several instances where Bonhoeffer uses the term commandment (*Gebot*): he speaks of "Jesus's ethical commandments," "the commandments of the Sermon on the Mount," "Jesus's new commandments," and "the commandment of love."[9] Moreover, "Basic Questions" is Bonhoeffer's first attempt to address the problem of Christian ethics, making it especially intriguing not only for those exploring the theme of God's commandment, but also for those wishing to trace the development of his ethical thinking.

Just as he does over a decade later when writing his *Ethics*, Bonhoeffer expresses near the beginning of this 1929 text his hesitancy to even speak of "Christian ethics."[10] He argues that the two terms, "Christian" and "ethics," contradict each other because the former focuses on the way of God to humanity and eschews the knowledge of good and evil, and the latter, resulting from the fall in Genesis 3, describes the way from humanity to God and embraces the moral categories of good and evil.[11] This means, for Bonhoeffer, that Christian ethics is not concerned about whether something is "good" or "bad," "right" or "wrong" in and of itself, but only whether something corresponds to God's will.[12] He explains as follows:

> Christians act according to how God's will seems to direct them, without looking sideways at others, that is, without considering what is usually called morals . . . Only in the realization that we have been addressed by God, that God is making a claim on us, does our self [Ich] awaken. Only through God's call do I become this 'self,' isolated from all other people, called to account by God, confronted, alone, by eternity. And precisely because I am face to face with God in this solitude, I alone can know what is right or wrong for me personally.[13]

---

8. Rasmussen, "A Question of Method," 115. For an earlier example of such "affinities" in language, see Bonhoeffer's 1925 sermon on Luke 17:7–10 where he says that God "demands, speaks, and gives" while the human individual is to "perform, listen, and receive"; DBWE 9:454–55.

9. DBWE 10:365, 367, 368, 369–70; DBW 10:329, 332, 333, 334–35.

10. DBWE 10:362–63; cf. chapter 2.

11. DBWE 10:362–63.

12. Ibid., 367.

13. Ibid.

Here one finds the language of "claim" and "address" that Rasmussen highlights in his survey of God's commandment. God's claim or address encounters Christians and creates an immediate relationship with God's will in each historical moment. The Christian must respond to this address of God and can do so only by taking seriously "the decisive moment at hand."[14]

Thus, Christian ethics cannot rely on universal norms or general moral principles for guidance, nor on a literal application of Scripture to the present situation; on the contrary, Christian ethics is entirely contextual and situational and depends on what is happening here and now. Bonhoeffer speaks again of this contextual nature in a summary passage near the end of the text:

> Ethics is a matter of earth and blood, but also of God, who made them both . . . The ethical can be found only within the bonds of history, in concrete situations, in the moment of the divine call, of being addressed, of the demands made by concrete crisis and the concrete circumstances of decision, of a demand I must answer, to which I am accountable.[15]

Again, the Christian must take into account both divine and human realities at the moment of ethical decision. As Bonhoeffer puts it near the end of his address, Christians can make ethical decisions only when they have "entered into the situation of crisis itself and are conscious of being addressed by God."[16] However, on many occasions God's will does not clearly reveal itself; it does not come fully formed as a direct imperative requiring only one's simple obedience in response.[17] This means that moral discernment is necessary to take stock of a situation and decide on an appropriate decision that corresponds to God's will. God's love, exemplified in the cross, informs such discernment, as does one's knowledge of a situation.[18] In addition, despite Bonhoeffer's adamant rejection of ethical principles, it seems that they too have a role in one's discernment. For example, he reasons that the demand to protect one's family and friends always outweighs the broader call to love one's enemy—he says it would be "an utter perversion of one's

---

14. Ibid., 365.

15. Ibid., 376–77. Rasmussen hints at a connection between this statement and Bonhoeffer's later understanding of the divine mandates, though he does not make it explicit. Rasmussen, "A Question of Method," 115–16.

16. DBWE 10:377.

17. Ibid., 368.

18. Ibid., 365, 369.

ethical sensibility" to think otherwise—and this alleviates the apparent conflict between Jesus' commandment for peace and the need to fight to defend one's own people.[19] Here, his use of a principle (i.e., protecting one's people must come before loving one's enemy) not only highlights his not yet abandoned nationalistic thinking, but appears to contradict his statements in the same manuscript rejecting universal norms and principles.[20] We will return to this apparent contradiction in chapter 6 when we consider his discussion of natural rights in *Ethics*.

In short, the Barcelona lecture displays both similarities and contrasts to what will come later. Bonhoeffer's description of God's claim as direct and absolute bears similarity, as Rasmussen argues, to how he will later describe God's commandment as an all-encompassing address that confronts the human person in a particular situation. Additionally, his emphasis on concrete ethics that looks not to universal principles, but to the ethical moment itself for guidance, corresponds to his later mention of "reality" and the natural world as guides for ethics. We will see this stress on reality appear prominently in his *Ethics*, but also during the 1930s when he develops his theme of simple obedience. At the same time, his strong emphasis on freedom in the moral life leads him to suggest that Christians "draw the forms of their ethical activity out of eternity itself" and thereby "provide the justification for their acts."[21] As we have already seen in the previous chapters, such an ability to form and justify one's own ethical action stands at odds with Bonhoeffer's later characterizations of Christians who seek *con*-formation to Christ, which includes a relinquishing of any attempts to justify or evaluate ethical activity. In addition, his radical notion of freedom causes him to devalue the role of Scripture, particularly the Sermon on the Mount, for ethical deliberation. In the Barcelona text, Jesus' ethical commandments in Scripture remind Christians of their place before God, but do not demand their obedience in a direct and immediate manner.[22] This will soon change, as Scripture becomes much more important for him as a source of God's concrete commandment for the human situation here and now.

---

19. Ibid., 370–71.
20. Ibid., 371n32.
21. Ibid., 366; DBW 10:331.
22. DBWE 10:365–67.

A shift begins to occur in the early 1930s around the same time that Bonhoeffer experiences his decisive life transformation.[23] References to God's commandment sharply increase and Bonhoeffer begins to emphasize the immediate and direct character of God's commandment and its very specific demand for obedience. For example, the nature of God's commandment for peace cannot simply be a general prohibition against war, but must be a specific command to refrain from *this* or *that* particular war.[24] In addition, Scripture, and in particular the Sermon on the Mount, begins to take center stage, as seen especially in his book *Discipleship*, which consists largely of an exposition of Matthew 5–7. For Bonhoeffer, the way of discipleship, at its core, demands simple obedience unencumbered by moral reflection that seeks to drive a wedge between the disciple and the concrete commandment.[25] This shift in his thinking, however, is not a smooth one. His new understanding about these issues does not develop all at once, and while themes such as simple obedience to God's commandment are dominant within this 1930s period, he continues to question and explore his formulations, aware of difficulties and unresolved issues. As we shall see below, even his book *Discipleship*, which contains his most explicit discussion of simple obedience, also includes subtle indications that one can overemphasize the role of simplicity in the life of the disciple, resulting in a misguided account of the Christian moral life.

A helpful starting point to explore his emerging view of the *Gebot Gottes* in the 1930s is his 1932 address entitled "On the Theological Foundation of the Work of the World Alliance," which he delivered in Ciernohorské Kúpele (former Czechoslovakia) at an ecumenical youth conference on peace.[26] This was one of the many gatherings he attended in 1932 as his interest in ecumenical relations, particularly as a way of avoiding another war, steadily increased. Moreover, this address was a testing ground for many of his burgeoning ideas about the nature of God's commandment, first presented in a seminar entitled "Is There a Christian Ethic?," taught during the 1932 summer semester at the University of Berlin, just prior to

---

23. Bethge, *Bonhoeffer*, 205; DBWE 14:134–35; cf. the discussion of this transformation in chapter 1.

24. DBWE 11:360.

25. DBWE 4:77.

26. DBWE 11:356–69. Hereafter, "On the Theology Foundation." Rasmussen also focuses heavily on this document, but relies mostly on quotations without much commentary.

The Simplicity of Discernment

his attendance at the conference.[27] From the minimal student notes that survive, one can see that common themes existed between the seminar course and his Ciernohorské Kúpele address (e.g., the nature of God's concrete commandment).[28] Because we do not have a complete record of the seminar course, his words at Ciernohorské Kúpele become all the more valuable.

In the address Bonhoeffer argues that the church, as the present Christ, not only *can*, but *must* proclaim God's commandment and that this commandment must be concrete.[29] This concreteness means that God's commandment must be historical and must relate to the present reality of a particular situation. It is not enough to speak, for instance, of loving one's neighbor in a general and abstract manner: instead; the church must proclaim how, *precisely*, in a particular situation here and now one might love one's neighbor.[30] As he emphatically states: "A commandment must be concrete or it is not a commandment."[31] Thus, the task of the church is to boldly proclaim God's commandment while trusting in the promise of forgiveness; as he puts it, "the proclamation of the forgiveness of sins" makes valid "the proclamation of the commandment."[32]

Such a belief in forgiveness is necessary because the church can never enjoy absolute certainty when it comes to perceiving God's commandment, but must content itself with trusting in God and turning to God in prayer. This is why Ernst Feil is correct when he argues that the words from 2 Chronicles 20:12, "we do not know what to do, but our eyes are on you," become a leitmotif in Bonhoeffer's theology, particularly during the 1930s.[33] When Bonhoeffer preached on this favorite text in 1932 he spoke of the hiddenness of God's commandment and the need to look not to human programs and human knowledge, but to the crucified and risen Christ in

---

27. Compare his address "On the Theological Foundation" with the surviving fragments from his seminar course "Is There a Christian Ethic?," DBWE 11:356–69; and DBWE 11:333–41, esp. 338–41.

28. See DBWE 11:340–41.

29. Despite Bonhoeffer's call for the church to proclaim the concrete commandment, he will later lament in a 1932 letter to his friend Helmut Rößler the church's failure to do so; see DBWE 12:83.

30. DBWE 11:359–60.

31. Ibid., 360.

32. Ibid., 361.

33. Feil, "Gewissen und Entscheidung," 220.

order to perceive the commandment.[34] Put differently, God's commandment remains hidden insofar as human beings disobediently turn to other sources for moral guidance. At the same time, as Bonhoeffer's later formula from *Discipleship* states, "*only the believers obey,* and *only the obedient believe.*"[35] This implies that while one must look to Christ in order to act rightly, it is precisely by obeying God's commandments—despite the uncertainty one might have—that one comes to know God and God's divine commands.[36] He repeats this line of thinking again on the eve of beginning his *Ethics*, when he comments on Psalm 119:19: "Our distress is not that we do not know God's commandments but that we don't do them—and that as a result of such disobedience, we are gradually unable to recognize them"[37]

Because of the hiddenness of God's commandment, the moral life can be difficult. In a 1932 review of Karl Heim's *Glaube und Denken* Bonhoeffer argues, contra Heim, that one is not always blessed with "the accent of eternity" in one's actions, but must walk the path of obedience with "fear and trembling."[38] Moreover, he says in "Christ and Peace," yet another document written in 1932, that the left hand must not know what the right hand is doing in discipleship (Matthew 6:3-4); i.e., one can never have full knowledge of the good or evil of one's moral action, but must leave such judgment up to God.[39] But despite all this talk of uncertainty, he is not contradicting his belief in a concrete and specific commandment that guides human behavior in a given instance. The difficulty arises not from God's side, as if God's commandment were somehow insufficient, but from the human side.[40] When a person tries to perceive God's commandment,

---

34. DBWE 11:435, 438–39. Bonhoeffer marked and annotated 2 Chronicles 20:12 in his Luther Bible, indicating its importance (See DBWE 6:412n10). The text appears several times in 1932, not only in his address, "On the Theological Foundation," but also in a letter to Erwin Sutz (DBWE 11:121). He also mentions the text in a 1933 letter to Karl Barth (DBWE 13:24) and in his 1932–33 lecture on "New Publications in Systematic Theology," DBWE 12:213. Interestingly, he does not explicitly mention the text after this.

35. DBWE 4:63.

36. Ibid., 63–64.

37. DBWE 15:524.

38. DBWE 12:257.

39. Ibid., 259; see also the discussion in chapter 2 of the use of Matthew 6:3-4 in "God's Love."

40. Bartel employs this same distinction between divine and human perspectives to demonstrate how God's commandment can be clear and concrete and yet still require discernment. Unfortunately, she does not explore in any detail how Bonhoeffer tries to combine the two perspectives. See Bartel, "Rationality of Discernment," 103.

The Simplicity of Discernment

disobedience can get in the way (i.e., one looks to other sources of moral knowledge and tries to turn them into God's commandment) or one finds the commandment obscured because of the fallen created order. Because human beings are not God and have no transcendent vantage point, one can never presume with certainty that he or she has perceived God's commandment and acted rightly in response.

Despite some uncertainly, however, one is not completely in the dark when it comes to God's commandment. Bonhoeffer makes the intriguing argument in "On the Theological Foundation" that just as the sacraments make valid the preaching of forgiveness, reality makes valid the preaching of God's commandment. In his own words: "What the sacrament is for the proclamation of the gospel, the knowledge of concrete reality is for the proclamation of the commandment. *Reality is the sacrament of the commandment.*"[41] This passage compares the relationship between sacrament and gospel with the relationship between reality and commandment. Just as the sacramental life of the church provides an interpretive context for the preaching of the gospel, so also does "knowledge of concrete reality" provide an interpretive context for the proclamation of God's commandment. What he means to suggest is that God's commandment can only make sense for Christian ethics if a person understands it within the context of the way things really are in the world.[42] He wishes to anchor God's commandment in the concrete, historical experience of both the church and the individual Christian and by doing so bring together the *is* and *ought* of traditional ethics. For example, the sacrament of Christ's body and blood makes the forgiveness of sins an immediate and historical reality: something happening *right here and right now*. I can see and taste the bread, which is Christ's body, and this assists me in understanding the truth of the gospel, its immediate relevance for my situation, and how I ought to respond. In a similar way, by recognizing the reality of a given situation—for instance, the reality of my spouse lying beside me *here and now*—I gain an immediate sense of God's commandment against adultery.[43] Reality makes the commandment historical and concrete, and in so doing, also makes it more tangible and easier to follow.

A little later in the manuscript Bonhoeffer inquires into the source of God's commandment: that is, where does the church (or an individual, for

---

41. DBWE 11:361; Bonhoeffer's italics.
42. For another explanation of this passage, see Plant, "Sacrament," 80–81.
43. I am indebted to Oliver O'Donovan for providing this image.

that matter) come to know God's concrete commandment in order to proclaim it into the present situation? He acknowledges that this is "apparently . . . not self-evident."[44] He suggests two sources: Scripture (particularly the Sermon on the Mount) and the orders of creation (*Schöpfungsordnungen*).[45] It follows that any attempt to discern a course of action in accordance with God's will requires both close attention to the Bible and, as he already discussed, a keen awareness of the shape and structure of reality. However, Bonhoeffer is hesitant in speaking about Scripture and the created order for fear that someone might misunderstand the role of each. He says that while Scripture "could be" a source of knowing God's commandment and while one might "want to find" God's commandment within the orders of creation, neither Scripture nor the created order *as such* can reveal God's commandment.[46] In the case of Scripture, he is worried about people looking to biblical commandments as universal ethical norms and uncritically applying them to contemporary situations with no regard for the situation itself. Such a procedure is misguided, for Bonhoeffer, because God's commandment is not static, but living and active and coming to humanity ever anew. It is not the law of Scripture that one turns to in order to hear God's commandment, but the present Christ, who fulfills God's law and speaks God's commandment through the church into the contemporary situation. Thus, while Scripture is slowly becoming more significant for him as a source of moral guidance as he moves into the 1930s, one can still perceive hints of his Barcelona address in which he advocated a radical freedom from the letter of the law in Scripture.

In addition to his concerns about Scripture, he also argues that the orders of creation are not reliable because humanity lives in a fallen world and can no longer perceive God's will directly through the created order. However, the orders of creation (*Schöpfungsordnungen*) still retain some relative value if one sees them as orders of *preservation* (*Erhaltungsordnungen*). By shifting his language from the more traditional *Schöpfungsordnungen* to *Erhaltungsordnungen*, he means to emphasize the significance of the created order as the arena of God's acts of preservation, which draw the fallen creation toward the new creation accomplished in Christ. Thus, while one

---

44. DBWE 11:362.

45. Ibid.; cf. DBW 11:335.

46. DBWE 11:362. This point comes through more clearly in Bonhoeffer's German: "*Die erste Antwort* könnte sein: das *biblische Gesetz*, die *Bergpredigt* ist die absolute Norm für unser Handeln . . . Die *zweite Antwort* will das Gebot Gottes in der *Schöpfungsordnung* finden"; DBW 11:335; Bonhoeffer's italics.

The Simplicity of Discernment

cannot perceive God's revelation directly from the created order, and while any given order becomes invalid if it closes itself off from Christ, one might nevertheless draw upon the created order as a source of limited moral guidance insofar as it remains open to Christ. As we already saw above, Bonhoeffer says as much when he speaks of "reality" being "the sacrament of the commandment." At least in July 1932, Bonhoeffer appreciated the relative value of the reality of the created order to help guide moral decision and action, which means that he also acknowledged a space for moral reflection and deliberation in Christian life. While he believed that one must take seriously the Sermon on the Mount and respond obediently to what it says, he also knew that the Sermon does not supply a comprehensive list of specific commandments for every situation one might face. Thus, moral discernment is required in order to consider the authoritative voice of the present Christ speaking through Scripture and the created realm, and then to determine, in faith, how best to respond to God's commandment in a particular instance. This is similar to his position in his Barcelona text in 1929, although in 1932 the role of Scripture has increased, as has the emphasis on God's concrete and specific commandment.

Several months later, however, Bonhoeffer sounds a quite different tone. In a document entitled "Christ and Peace" he admits that Christ does not give specific instructions for "every possible complex political, economic, or other situation that may arise in human life," but nevertheless: "To the simple reader of the Sermon on the Mount, what it says is unmistakable."[47] The belief that a commandment such as "love your enemies" might be straightforward and easily acted upon is the opposite of what he said in "On the Theological Foundation," where he insisted that a commandment such as "love your enemies" was too general to be useful. Such a commandment required concretization; in particular, the church needed to draw on its knowledge of reality, which would help it proclaim the commandment in the most concrete form possible, thereby making it immediate and intelligible for Christians to obey.[48] In "Christ and Peace" we see the same emphasis on concreteness and immediacy, but now Bonhoeffer replaces his talk of the sacrament of reality with a new emphasis on simple obedience. He argues that the Christian disciple must embrace a simple faith that avoids reflection and knowledge of good and evil and embraces simple obedience, which "knows nothing of good and evil but lives

47. DBWE 12:259.
48. DBWE 11:360–61.

in discipleship to Christ and does its good work as a matter of course."[49] Here, Bonhoeffer's account appears to eliminate any reflective space for the moral agent and to insist that implicit obedience to God's commandment is all that is required for Christian discipleship. In order to fully appreciate his commitment to simple obedience and to determine whether simple obedience really does rules out all manner of moral reflection, as Bonhoeffer's description in "Christ and Peace" appears to suggest, we turn now to a closer examination of the theme as it develops in his writing, especially in his book *Discipleship*.

Simple Obedience to God's Commandment

Even before he began using the idea of simple obedience, Bonhoeffer had already spoken of the value of simplicity (*Einfalt*) from the time of his early sermons in the late 1920s and continuing into his final letters from prison in the 1940s.[50] However, beginning in 1932 in "Christ and Peace" and *Creation and Fall* and taking shape especially in his book *Discipleship*, he begins to formulate his understanding of simple obedience as the only appropriate response to God's concrete commandment. For him, an immediate and direct commandment from God leaves no room for vacillation. He says in *Creation and Fall* and a year later in his *Lectures on Christology* that God's commandment encounters the human person as divine speech; it is a word of address rather than a word as an idea.[51] Such an encounter with God's commandment places a person into a relationship of freedom with the Creator and requires a response: "The word as idea remains essentially within itself, but the word in the form of address is only possible as word between two persons, as speaking and response, responsibility."[52] And according to Bonhoeffer, one's response can take one of two forms: one either responds in obedience, hearing and accepting the commandment as both prohibition and also permission, *or* one responds in disobedience by

---

49. DBWE 12:259–60; DBW 17:117–18.

50. For examples of Bonhoeffer's early and late uses of the term "simple" (*einfältig, einfach*) and "simplicity" (*Einfalt, Einfachheit*), see DBWE 10:514, 576; DBW 10:497, 571; and DBWE 8:294, 427, 507; DBW 8:323, 478, 564–65. For brief comments on Bonhoeffer's use of these terms in his theology, see Green, "Editor's Introduction" (DBWE 10), 7–8 and de Gruchy's note in DBWE 8:294n7.

51. DBWE 3:40–41; DBWE 12:316–17.

52. DBWE 12:316.

The Simplicity of Discernment

asking the seemingly innocent question of the serpent: "Did God really say . . . ?"[53] As he describes it in his 1934 "Address to the Fanø Conference," it is either "the unconditional, blind obedience of action, or the hypocritical question of the Serpent [which is] the mortal enemy of obedience."[54] The first path suggests a relationship of unity with God, enjoyed by Adam before the fall, but also by those reconciled with God through Christ; the second path indicates a rupture between divine and human in which human reason presumes to question God's command and ask: is it really "for me"? This second approach ignores the concrete and particular nature of God's commandment and treats it as though it needs further clarification and interpretation. In so doing, this approach misunderstands the divine-human relationship by presuming to place the individual on a level with God in determining the actual meaning of a commandment. As we already saw in chapter 2, he articulates this same division between simple obedience and the temptation to ask "Did God really say . . . ?" in the prelude to his discussion of discerning God's will in "God's Love."

But perhaps his greatest expression of simple obedience comes in his book *Discipleship*, a text whose origins begin as early as 1932 and which encapsulates much of his thinking during the mid 1930s about what it means to follow Christ and keep his commandments, especially as expressed in the Sermon on the Mount. He describes God's commandment as something clear and concrete, something that applies to all (not only a spiritual elite), and something that confronts the human person and leaves him or her no room for equivocation. The story of the rich young man from Matthew 19:16–22 helps to illustrate this. He sees the young man's response, "which ones?," to Jesus' call to "keep the commandments" as a manifestation of the original temptation of the serpent: "Did God really say?" To ask such a question is to flee the path of "simple childlike obedience" and to decide that God's commandment needs "interpretation and explanation."[55] Rather than trust in God's ability to speak a clear and binding commandment, one turns instead to the inner conscience, which decides ethical issues for itself according to its own knowledge of good and evil.[56] He proceeds to draw out this contrast in various ways: he speaks of the "simple act" of the

---

53. DBWE 3:107–8.

54. DBWE 13:307. For another reflection on the temptation of Genesis 3:1, see Bonhoeffer's 1938 "Bible Study on Temptation," DBWE 15:391.

55. DBWE 4:71.

56. Ibid.

faithful disciple versus the "[d]ouble-minded thinking" of people who trust in their knowledge of good and evil; the "child of obedience" opposed to the "person of free conscience"; "God's reality" in contrast with "human possibility"; "faith" opposed to "doubt."[57] And the implication for moral discernment is clear: "The only answer to the predicament of ethical conflict is God's commandment itself, which is the demand to stop discussing and start obeying."[58] It is precisely ethical reflection that is the problem, or so it appears, because it stands in the way of simple obedience, which is the only true mode of discipleship.

In fact, Bonhoeffer devotes an entire chapter to the topic of simple obedience, indicating its importance as the only legitimate response to Christ's call of discipleship. He begins the chapter by warning that many things threaten to interrupt one's direct relationship of obedience to Christ, including one's reason, conscience, sense of responsibility, practice of piety, and even one's close attention to "the law and the principle of Scripture."[59] Added to these things is the human tendency to favor a figurative interpretation of Christ's words over a literal interpretation, which threatens to devalue the seriousness of Christ's call. He gives the example of the child whose father tells her to go to bed. The child reasons that the father's command is really intended to alleviate her tiredness, and since she can just as well alleviate her tiredness by going to play, it follows that going to play is the true meaning of the father's command to go to bed.[60] Contrary to this, simple obedience takes seriously the literal meaning of Christ's commandments and seeks to respond fully and immediately without any intervening moral reflection, which, as the story of the child illustrates, might reverse the commandment's true meaning.

But notice what Bonhoeffer says next in the passage: he argues that despite the faulty argumentation of the child, which runs counter to simple obedience by changing the true meaning of the father's commandment, there "is actually something quite right" in what the child says.[61] Though her conclusion about needing to stay up and play may have been wrong, the child correctly realizes that a commandment might have a deeper purpose apart from its literal meaning. While the father wanted the child to go to

57. Ibid.
58. Ibid., 72.
59. Ibid., 77.
60. Ibid., 79.
61. Ibid., 80.

The Simplicity of Discernment

bed in a literal sense, what the father might *really* have wanted, deep down, was to alleviate the child's tiredness out of love for the child. This "paradoxical understanding" of a commandment also applies to God's commandments.[62] Because the core purpose of God's commandment is calling one to faith, not the accomplishment of any particular action, a Christian might have cause to understand a commandment in a different way from its literal meaning. Or, put slightly differently, a Christian will realize that the very idea of implicit obedience to the "literal meaning" of a commandment is a rather abstract notion unless given content by the reality of a situation and by one's relationship with God.[63] For example, Jesus' command to the rich young man to sell all his possessions was ultimately intended to bring the man to faith and into community with Jesus, not to deprive him of everything he owned; thus, whether or not the man sold his possessions was not the primary issue as long as faith and communion were the ultimate result. Interestingly, we see here that Bonhoeffer picks up his discussion about the purpose of keeping God's commandments that he had raised, but not developed, in his early student explorations on the theology of John and Paul.[64]

Despite the possibility of a paradoxical interpretation of God's commandment, it remains dangerous. He cautions people not to jump too quickly from the "simplest possibility" in keeping a commandment to a "paradoxical understanding."[65] He explains:

> A paradoxical understanding of the commandments has a Christian right to it, but it must never lead to the annulment of a simple understanding of the commandments. Rather, it is justified and possible only for those who have already taken simple obedience seriously at some point in their lives, and so already stand in community with Jesus, in discipleship, in expectation of the end. Understanding Jesus' call paradoxically is the infinitely more difficult possibility. In human terms it is an impossible possibility, and because it is, it is always in extreme danger of being turned over

---

62. For a helpful introduction to the issue, see Tödt, "Paradoxical Obedience," 3–16.

63. Cf. O'Donovan's discussion of the limits of implicit obedience in O'Donovan, "Moral Authority of Scripture," 165–75.

64. In a 1944 reflection on 1 John 3:24 Bonhoeffer affirms once again that the purpose of keeping God's commandments "is that we abide in God and God abides in us," DBWE 16:629.

65. DBWE 4:80.

into its opposite and made into a comfortable excuse for fleeing from concrete obedience.[66]

Here he argues that one cannot ignore a simple, literal understanding of God's commandment and replace it with an alternative understanding. For those who have "taken simple obedience seriously" and "stand in community with Jesus," however, there exists freedom to embrace a paradoxical interpretation on some occasions. What he means by this is that if someone has responded to Christ and entered into relationship with him, one then enjoys a new perspective on reality, which provides the grounds to venture a paradoxical interpretation of God's commandment. While it might seem that this paradoxical understanding would run counter to a simple understanding, it is never separate from simple obedience. In fact, a paradoxical understanding exists only because of simple obedience and always in service to simple obedience. As mentioned in chapter 3, he will argue later in *Ethics* that free, responsible action might sometimes break the divine law in an extraordinary situation, but it always does so in order to ultimately affirm it once more.[67] In the same way, a paradoxical interpretation, while on the surface different from a simple interpretation, nevertheless has the exact same purpose as a simple interpretation: faith and communion with Christ.

His discussion of a paradoxical interpretation of a commandment appears to leave room for moral reflection; otherwise, one would have no way to reason that a particular situation might call for a response other than literal obedience. If we look elsewhere in *Discipleship*, we find further evidence to support such an assertion. For instance, we might consider his striking interpretation of Matthew 10:16 where Jesus tells his disciples to be "wise as serpents and innocent as doves." The text comes from a section of *Discipleship* not usually commented upon: Bonhoeffer's discussion of Matthew 10 entitled "The Messengers."[68] The innocence (*Einfalt*) he refers to in the passage points to the concept of simplicity and also connects with his discussion of simple obedience.[69] More interesting is his discussion of

---

66. Ibid., 80–81.

67. DBWE 6:274, 296–97.

68. DBWE 4:183–98. In fact, this section did not even make it into earlier abridged versions of *Discipleship*. See Kelly and Godsey, "Editors' Introduction," 29–30.

69. DBWE 4:192–94. The Matthew 10:16 text Bonhoeffer quotes from the Luther Bible speaks of the disciples being "klug wie die Schlangen und ohne Falsch wie die Tauben." While he uses Luther's "ohne Falsch" when directly quoting the verse, he quickly substitutes the term "Einfalt" when discussing the meaning of the verse, thus connecting it with his discussion of unity in "God's Love" and his other discussions of simplicity.

The Simplicity of Discernment

wisdom. For him, the wisdom (*Klugheit*) spoken of in this passage is a kind of "spiritual wisdom" (*geistliche Klugheit*) and not a "worldly cleverness" (*weltlicher Schlauheit*).[70] The second of these can have a slightly negative connotation in the German (shrewdness, slyness, craftiness) and, for Bonhoeffer, operates apart from Christ. This wisdom would be akin to the kind of moral reflection that looks only to a human knowledge of good and evil and attempts to evaluate situations on that basis. The former wisdom, however, is more positive (*Klugheit* meaning wisdom or prudence) and draws its efficacy from God's word, which illuminates situations and teaches one to recognize what is wise.[71] Bonhoeffer believes that Christ's disciples must combine both simplicity and wisdom in order to act rightly. He says:

> How tempting it is, therefore, to renounce all "wisdom" and only be as simple as doves, which, one-sided, is disobedience. Who tells us when we avoid suffering out of fear and when we seek it out of recklessness? Who shows us the hidden boundaries drawn here? It is the same disobedience, whether we use the commandment to be wise against innocence, or the other way around, whether we use innocence against wisdom . . . They [the disciples] will have to act wisely and simply at the same time.[72]

He argues that simplicity alone will not suffice in the life of discipleship. One must balance simplicity with a proper dose of wisdom: only in combining the two can the disciple act rightly. The same disobedience results whether one relies only on simplicity while renouncing all wisdom or depends only on wisdom while rejecting simplicity. The two must work together lest the disciple become overly reckless (due to lack of wisdom) or begin to act contrary to Christ's word (due to lack of simplicity). While Bonhoeffer does not fully explain how simplicity and wisdom are held together in the life of a disciple, he does assert that both are grounded in the word of Christ: it is the word that demands simple obedience and the word that will teach a person "to recognize what is wise."[73] Thus, one attains simplicity and wisdom only by standing in communion with Christ's word. In the language of *Gestaltung*, only as Christ draws one deeper and deeper into the process of conformation will one learn to hear Christ's word more clearly and respond accordingly.

70. DBWE 4:193; DBW 4:204.
71. DBWE 4:193–94.
72. Ibid., 193.
73. Ibid., 194.

In short, what we see here is an acknowledgment from Bonhoeffer, following Jesus' own words, that simplicity left unchecked can threaten the life of discipleship. In the context of Matthew 10 this means that too much simplicity on the part of the disciples could result in unnecessary danger or persecution; thus, they need to exercise wisdom along with their simplicity. However, in the larger context of *Discipleship*, this passage hints at the possibility that despite his emphasis on simple obedience throughout the text, he recognizes the dangers of a one-sided simplicity that leaves no space for any exercise of wisdom or moral reflection. Thus, the passage is most significant because it is an attempt by Bonhoeffer to grapple with the tension in Christian ethics between a simple, unreflective approach and a rational, reflective approach to God's will. Speaking of combining simplicity and wisdom is his way of acknowledging the paradoxical truth that while simple obedience rules out moral reflection, in one sense, it also creates the very grounds, through communion with Christ, to rehabilitate moral reflection as a valid and necessary part of Christian life.

But what *kind* of moral reflection does simple obedience allow? To begin to answer this we will consider one final reference that Bonhoeffer makes in *Discipleship* to the relative value of moral reflection. It occurs in his treatment of Matthew 6 where he addresses the hidden nature of Christian life.[74] Despite the extraordinary righteousness to which Christ calls his disciples, a righteousness that exceeds that of the Pharisees, Christians must nevertheless display a proper humility. Thus, while Christ calls one to be the "light of the world" (Matt 5:14), that is, the "visible community of faith," he also warns the disciple to "beware of practicing your righteousness before others" (Matt 6:1).[75] While discipleship maintains an extraordinary and visible character, it must resist the temptation of falling into a "thoughtless, unbroken, simple joy in what is visible."[76] And the remedy to avoid this temptation is surprising: Bonhoeffer says that "Jesus calls us to reflection [*Reflexion*]."[77] The purpose of this reflection is to help one discern when he or she is out of balance and leaning too far toward visibility at the expense of hiddenness. Thus, reflection plays a moderating role in a life of discipleship that is too caught up in the joy of extraordinary, visible obedience. However, he argues that this kind of reflection is only

---

74. Ibid., 146–168.
75. Compare ibid., 112–13, and ibid., 146.
76. Ibid., 148.
77. Ibid.

valid when it is completely *un*reflective. What he means by this confusing assertion is that Christian moral reflection, in distinction from other kinds of moral reflection, looks inward to consider the self and its resources, but finds instead the person of Christ who is "alive in the person."[78] One recalls here his discussion of self-examination in "God's Love," which describes a process of turning inward not to the self, but to Christ who has taken up the space formerly occupied by the knowledge of good and evil. Thus, this kind of reflection is "unreflective" insofar as it does not look upon the self's own relative goodness and presumed knowledge of good and evil; instead, this "unreflective" reflection looks to the person of Christ and Christ's word.

The foregoing examples sufficiently establish that despite Bonhoeffer's strong emphasis on simple obedience to Christ, which often seems to rule out any kind of moral reflection, he is nevertheless aware of its dangers and aware that some account of moral reflection is necessary, even during his work on *Discipleship*. Commentators have not often recognized this fact, assuming that his reservations about simple obedience occurred much later. Certainly, evidence for this exists in *Letters and Papers from Prison* where he acknowledges the dangers of his book *Discipleship*, but also his willingness to continue to stand by what he wrote.[79] As I have argued above, however, even in the midst of working on *Discipleship*, it seems that he was struggling with how to account for both simplicity and wisdom, recognizing that both carried possibilities for abuse, yet both also remained essential for Christian life.

In short, Bonhoeffer believed one must be simple *and* wise if one is to be Christ's disciple. On the one hand, blind obedience to Christ really is blind insofar as it ignores other possible sources of moral guidance and looks only to Christ with a single-minded focus. Here, simplicity is crucial because it draws one into close communion with Christ and provides one with an essential orientation to the moral life. On the other hand, blind obedience is not blind to how one's communion with Christ "develops not only a new way of thinking, willing, and doing things, but a new image, a new form."[80] Here, simple obedience, far from eliminating moral reflection, actually creates space for it insofar as the reality of Christ both shapes and focuses it.

78. Ibid., 152.
79. DBWE 8:486.
80. DBWE 4:284.

Becoming Simple and Wise

Meditative Reflection on God's Commandment

While Bonhoeffer explores the idea of an unreflective moral reflection in *Discipleship*, he does not yet have the language he wants to fully explain the kind of moral reflection that can co-exist with simplicity: this he finds through his unfinished commentary on Psalm 119, as I argued in chapter 4.[81] In many ways, his exegesis of Psalm 119 is a transitional work between *Discipleship* and *Ethics*; Brian Brock even argues that it is a central text for understanding Bonhoeffer's view of ethics.[82] Undoubtedly, Psalm 119 was an important text for Bonhoeffer, and one of his favorite psalms throughout his life.[83] He mentions the psalm in many places, including his 1932 address "On the Theological Foundation," discussed above, but it is only in 1939–40 that he begins to work seriously on his own exegesis.[84]

A primary theme of Psalm 119 is that of God's commandment and the human attempt to walk the path of discipleship by meditating on and following God's commandments. Thus, this psalm, more than many, is a commentary on the Christian moral life. Brock highlights the many different terms in the psalm that point to the Christian life as a path or a way: a teleological movement toward the final goal of communion with God.[85] The primary means of guidance and support for this journey of Christian discipleship are God's commandments, which Brock argues provide "a form within which humans may live."[86] The psalmist expresses a longing for these commandments on many occasions, because only through receiving God's instruction will he know how to proceed in life.

To obey God's commandments, however, one must first perceive God's commandments. Here, we see in Bonhoeffer's commentary the familiar tension between simple obedience and moral reflection. On the one hand, he hints at the way of simple obedience in his interpretation of verse 6 when he suggests that one's own "thoughts or experiences" are secondary to the direct and immediate command of God, which requires one only to

---

81. Regrettably, he only completed work on the first twenty-one verses; see, DBWE 15:496–528.

82. See Brock, "Bonhoeffer and the Bible," 7–29.

83. Bethge, *Bonhoeffer*, 412, 667.

84. For a list of references to Psalm 119 in Bonhoeffer's writings, which span his earliest student work to his letters from prison, see DBW 17:277–78.

85. Brock, "Bonhoeffer and the Bible," 11.

86. Ibid., 14.

The Simplicity of Discernment

listen and obey.[87] And yet, he goes on with his exposition of verse 6 in the following manner:

> Thus I can be certain that there is no situation in my life for which God's word would not give me the necessary advice. But serious attention, tireless asking, and learning are necessary to recognize [*vernehmen*] the right commandment and to recognize [*erkennen*] the inexhaustible kindness of God in all his commandments.[88]

He suggests that while God has a directly applicable commandment for each situation, perceiving that commandment requires close attention and study. This means both that one must turn to Scripture again and again, because it is here that one encounters God's commandments, and also that one must know *all* of God's commandments in order to discern which one among them has a special bearing on the situation at hand.[89] But how does one come to know God's commandments in such a way?

He begins to answers this when he considers verse 15. He argues that Christians must make time in their lives to meditate (*nachsinnen*) on God's word in Scripture.[90] Only through times of "silence and contemplation [*Besinnung*]" can one gain the necessary moral insight and guidance to walk the path of discipleship.[91] He explains what he means by this meditation and reflection as follows:

> God's word is not the sum of a few general sentences that could be in my mind at any time; rather it is God's daily new word addressed to me, expounded in its never-ending wealth of interpretation [*Auslegung*]. Meditation [*Meditation*], that is, prayerful consideration of the Scriptures [*betende Schriftbetrachtung*], and exegesis [*Auslegung*] are indispensable for the one who honestly seeks God's precepts, not his own thoughts. A theologian who does not practice both denies his office. But every Christian will be granted the time that he needs if he truly seeks it. Meditation [*Meditation*] means to take God's word prayerfully into my heart; exegesis [*Auslegung*] means to recognize [*erkennen*] and understand God's word in Scripture as God's word. The one does not

---

87. DBWE 15:507.
88. DBWE 15:508; cf. DBW 15:512–13.
89. Brock, "Bonhoeffer and the Bible," 16.
90. DBWE 15:517–18; cf. DBW 15:523–24. Bonhoeffer occasionally uses *Nachsinnen*, but mostly *Meditation* to refer to meditation in this passage; likewise, he employs two terms—*Nachdenken* and *Besinnung*—to speak of reflection.
91. DBWE 15:517; DBW 15:524.

> exist without the other. But both are reflection [*Besinnung*], which needs to be practiced on a daily basis.[92]

Bonhoeffer clearly states that daily reflection (*Besinnung*) is proper to Christian life. One cannot continue on the path of discipleship if one does not correctly perceive and understand God's commandments, and this requires times of silence and reflection. Through such times one comes to know God's commandments not as "moral maxims" one must follow, but as words that train one "to listen to God in ever new and historically unique occasions."[93]

In addition, this kind of reflection (*Besinnung*), which is also called meditation (*Meditation*), consists of two important elements: prayerful consideration of Scripture (*betende Schriftbetrachtung*) and exegesis or interpretation (*Auslegung*). Here we see an alternative vision of moral reflection from that which Bonhoeffer laments at the beginning of "God's Love" when he notes that "the knowledge of good and evil appears to be the goal of all ethical reflection [*Besinnung*]."[94] The important difference between these two alternatives is that the former seeks to treasure God's word in the heart while the latter seeks to gain knowledge of God's word in the intellect.[95] This is the same kind of distinction present in "God's Love" where Bonhoeffer speaks of hearing God's word in order to do God's word as opposed to hearing God's word in order to gain and possess knowledge of God's word.[96] Moreover, the meditative reflection he describes in his commentary on Psalm 119 begins with a presupposition of the authority of God's word. One does not seek to reflect upon God's word for the purpose of finding fault with it, improving it, or interpreting it in order to make intelligible what is supposedly unintelligible; instead, one seeks to ponder this word in one's heart and to discover how it illuminates the contours of a particular life situation. The other kind of reflection, alluded to in "God's Love," operates from the presupposition that God's word is only one possible source of moral knowledge among many other sources; thus, one looks to things such as one's own self-knowledge and ethical principle in order to supplement God's commandment.

---

92. Ibid.
93. Brock, "Bonhoeffer and the Bible," 17.
94. DBWE 6:299.
95. DBWE 15:513–14.
96. DBWE 6:328–29.

The Simplicity of Discernment

Such meditative reflection calls to mind Bonhoeffer's words from a 1936 letter to Rüdiger Schelicher.[97] He states quite unequivocally: "I believe that the Bible alone is the answer to all our questions, and that we merely need ask perpetually and with a bit of humility in order to get the answer from it."[98] When considering this passage, it is important not to divorce the second part of the statement from the first. Bonhoeffer believes that the Bible *does* hold the answer to one's questions, but only insofar as one takes time to actively question the Bible, meditate upon it, and consider, in humility, how one of God's various commandments might indeed provide the answer for how one can appropriately respond to a particular situation. The question is not whether the moral resources of God's word in Scripture are sufficient for the many complexities of Christian moral life, but whether one learns to incorporate the great resource of Scripture into one's moral thinking.

Furthermore, this kind of meditative moral reflection requires time; it is a discipline one cannot rush, but must faithfully practice each day. Moreover, it is a discipline dependent on prayer because only through prayer will God enlighten one's eyes and allow that person to see the world in terms of unity and to perceive correctly the commandments in all their depth, variety, and myriad applicability.[99] Brock argues that this emphasis on prayerful, scriptural meditation indicates the importance of scriptural exegesis for Bonhoeffer's account of the Christian moral life; I would add that this emphasis also makes clear once again the significant role of spiritual exercise in Bonhoeffer's understanding of discipleship.[100]

Finally, the passage quoted above, and indeed his entire commentary on Psalm 119, suggests that one can only understand God's commandments within a contextual relationship. Thus, it is only because God has drawn one into relationship that one can make sense of God's word. Bonhoeffer illustrates this beautifully near the beginning of his exegesis of verse 1. To understand what it means to be happy and blameless by walking according to God's law, one must first grasp the meaning of God's law. To define God's law, Bonhoeffer points the reader to a telling passage from Deuteronomy 6:20–25.[101] In this passage Moses instructs the Israelites that

---

97. DBWE 14:166–70.
98. Ibid., 167.
99. DBWE 15:520–21.
100. Brock, "Bonhoeffer and the Bible," 8, 23, 25.
101. DBWE 15:498–99.

the first thing they should do when their children ask about the meaning of God's law is to tell them the story of God delivering them out of Egypt. What Moses is saying is that whatever meaning God's law might have, one can only understand it within the context of the story of God's relationship with Israel. For Moses, and for Bonhoeffer, one grasps the meaning of God's commandments only within a contextual relationship. Bonhoeffer argues that no one knows the law who does not also know about the deliverance of Israel out of Egypt and the deliverance of humankind from the bondage of sin.[102] This reinforces yet again the importance of understanding reality—and the relationships, situations, and structures it encompasses—for moral discernment.

The Motif of God's Commandment in *Ethics*

Up to this point, I have described the importance of the theme of simplicity in Bonhoeffer's understanding of the Christian moral life (the first task of this chapter), and I have argued that even in the midst of discussing simple obedience, Bonhoeffer recognized the necessity for some type of moral reflection in Christian discipleship (the second task of the chapter). Moreover, the final words of the last section have already pointed toward the third task of the chapter: to demonstrate that one cannot divorce simple obedience from the reality of the world, which provides the act of simple obedience with an interpretive context. To best complete this third task, we turn now to Bonhoeffer's use of the God's commandment motif in his *Ethics* manuscript "The 'Ethical' and the 'Christian' as a Topic."[103]

Having previously identified both God's reality and God's will as the subject of Christian ethics, Bonhoeffer now claims in "Ethical and Christian" that God's commandment "is the only possible subject matter"

---

102. Ibid.

103. Although unmentioned in this text (hereafter, "Ethical and Christian") the influence of Karl Barth is clearly present. In a 1942 letter to Barth, Bonhoeffer indicates that he had the galley proofs of *Church Dogmatics* 2/2 in hand and was preparing "to work through at least the second part" (the section which treats Christian ethics under the heading: "The Command of God") prior to continuing work on his *Ethics*. See DBWE 16:276–77; cf. CD 2/2:509–781. Rasmussen, who has detailed the striking similarities between the final portion of Bonhoeffer's *Ethics* and the second section of *Church Dogmatics* 2/2, argues that while Bonhoeffer chiefly borrows the God's commandment motif from Barth, he commandeers it for his own purposes; thus it is *"genuine"* but not *"original"* to Bonhoeffer. See Rasmussen, "A Question of Method," 119–24.

The Simplicity of Discernment

because of its all-encompassing nature.[104] For him the notion of God's commandment embraces all aspects of the human experience, both the realm of everyday life and the realm comprised of extraordinary situations, which he calls the *ethical*. To fully understand his description of God's commandment, one must first grasp his idiosyncratic use of the term *ethical* as it relates to his vision of the Christian moral life.

As he argued earlier in "God's Love," continuity and freedom rather than conflict and uncertainty should characterize the Christian moral life. For Christian ethics to truly be *Christian* ethics, the moral agent must proceed from a point of unity and reconciliation with God. The human individual is not like Hercules at the crossroads, forced time and again to make a momentous and decisive decision for virtue or vice.[105] Individuals should not think that they must always "do something decisive, fulfill a higher purpose, meet an ultimate duty."[106] To understand the moral life as the task of endlessly negotiating a series of ethical conflicts and decisions is to violate the integrity of life and to join with the New Testament Pharisees in the "abnormal fanaticizing" and the "total moralizing" of life.[107] In short, human life sometimes requires serious moral thinking and careful decision, but it is often rather normal and routine: one makes decisions and moves forward without a constant preoccupation with ethical deliberation. Thus, one mostly exists in the realm of everyday life, but occasionally enters the realm of ethical life, which interrupts one's normal rhythm.

Following the wisdom of Ecclesiastes 3, Bonhoeffer argues that both the realm of everyday life and the ethical have their proper place.[108] This is because human life consists of many things, all of them appropriate at various times; for instance, "eating, drinking, sleeping, as well as conscious decision making and acting, working and resting, serving a purpose and just being without purpose, meeting obligations and following inclinations, striving and playing, abstaining and rejoicing."[109] For the most part, human individuals live within a structure marked by things such as community,

---

104. DBWE 6:378. For instances where God's reality and God's will emerge as the subject matter of Christian ethics, see ibid., 49, 313.

105. DBWE 6:385. For Barth's use of this image, see Barth, *Ethics*, 74, 75, 248, 249, 479.

106. DBWE 6:365.

107. Ibid., 366; cf. Ibid., 309–12.

108. Ibid., 365.

109. Ibid., 365–66.

family, and work. In this everyday realm the decisions one makes, consciously and unconsciously, and the actions one undertakes do not require in-depth analysis and do not involve decisive choices between good and evil; instead, morality is self-evident. However, because the order and structure of everyday life is subject to the inherent state of decay brought about by human sin, there are inevitable interruptions when morality is no longer self-evident, and the ethical breaks in and demands careful attention. Bonhoeffer describes such an occasion as a "boundary event [*Grenzereignis*]": that which occurs at a particular time and place and demands careful reflection and decisive action.[110] While Bonhoeffer does not mean to imply that the everyday realm is bereft of moral content, he does want to differentiate between the daily practice of living life in the penultimate realm and the practice of intense ethical deliberation that some situations demand; for instance, the ethical situation arising in his own time when the National Socialists took power and interrupted the normal state of affairs in Germany.

While the ethical becomes an important topic for reflection at particular times and places, however, it must be a limited phenomenon and recede back into its dormant state once the occasion for its arrival has passed.[111] If the ethical were to remain permanently within the realm of everyday life then life would become an obsessive exercise in fulfilling moral duty, which would in turn compromise the "richness of life" and restrict human freedom. Moreover, the ethical imperative (the "ought"), which confronts the human person in the ethical situation, would cease to be an ultimate word that challenges one from outside of everyday life and would become instead a moral system or method for life, the idea of which Bonhoeffer strongly opposes.[112] He argues that an ethic cannot mean a book of laws and rules or a "reference manual" for moral behavior; likewise, an ethicist cannot be an arbiter of the moral life or an ethical know-it-all who continually interrupts life with commentary about what to do or not to do.[113] If this were the case, then one *would* be like Hercules at the crossroads at each moment of life and would not have the freedom to live without constant disruption.

---

110. Ibid., 366. Earlier in *Ethics*, Bonhoeffer spoke of both the "extraordinary situation of ultimate necessity [*außerordentliche Situation letzter Notwendigkeiten*]" and "the borderline case [*Grenzfall*]"; see, ibid., 273; DBW 6:272–73.

111. DBWE 6:369.

112. Ibid., 368–69.

113. Ibid., 369–70.

Thus, while the ethical demand of the ought sets limits for the moral life, the "art of living" is motivated not by the prohibitions and commands that constitute the ought, but by what is natural and by "the richness of life's impulses."[114] Here, Bonhoeffer again shows his distaste of Kantianism as he understood it. For Bonhoeffer, the moral life is not motivated by an understanding of duty to moral principles, but by concrete relationships to others within a natural structure of freedom.

Through his description of the everyday and the ethical Bonhoeffer positions ethical discourse as a phenomenon that happens at particular times and places when everyday life experiences an interruption and morality is no longer self-evident. Such ethical discourse, therefore, is entirely concrete and historical rather than abstract and universal. The authorization for ethical discourse comes from "the situation at hand" with its particular complex of relationships determined by an "objective order of above and below."[115] This does not mean a sanctioning of official status, but recognition that one's office (*Amt*)—for example, as a master craftsman as opposed to an apprentice—creates the stability and trustworthiness necessary for ethical speech.[116] Bonhoeffer is not arguing in favor of a rigid social hierarchy, but indicating the importance of the structure of reality for determining ethical discourse. Most importantly, this concrete authorization derives not from the way things exist at any given time, which he calls "empirical positivism," or from a developed "system of authorities and orders," which he labels "metaphysical-religious positivism."[117] For him, only one thing can provide a foundation and authorization for ethical speech: God's commandment.

As mentioned already, he explains that God's commandment is the all-encompassing reality under which human beings live their lives. God's commandment is God's total and complete claim on human beings and therefore encompasses within it both the everyday realm and the ethical realm.[118] The theme of God's commandment allows him to join the two without falling into two-realm thinking. More importantly, he recognizes that both the ultimate and penultimate aspects of God's commandment are crucial: while God's commandment can address the ethical demand of the

---

114. Ibid., 370.
115. Ibid., 371, 372–73.
116. Ibid., 375.
117. Ibid., 376–77.
118. Ibid., 378.

ought and require simple obedience, its embedded position in everyday life grounds it in the reality of what is, thus giving the natural and historical world an added significance.

Moreover, viewing Christian ethics through the lens of God's commandment allows Bonhoeffer to emphasize the continuity and freedom of the moral life. The permission granted by God's commandment transforms Christian ethics from a duty-based system ruled by law to a teleological approach in which the moral life becomes a matter of journeying forward in freedom and looking to the future. While God's commandment does place limits on the moral life, these limits are meant not to restrict life, but to allow for growth and improvement. God's commandment is not in the business of interrupting the narrative of life, but in facilitating it; even when interruptions must occur, they too become part of life's overall flow. In short, one does not have to endure "innumerable new beginnings" or continual ethical conflicts in the moral life, but can experience life as a continual journey of discipleship, which begins from a point of reconciliation and moves deeper and deeper into communion with Christ and solidarity with the world.[119]

Insofar as God's commandment contains both the ethical and the everyday realm, one can describe it as having two forms. First, God's commandment takes on a "solemn form" in which it deals with prohibition ("you ought not to do this") and command ("you ought to do this").[120] In this form, the commandment addresses the boundary situations that, as already discussed, constitute the ethical. He suggests that one might label this form of the commandment as law and understand it as that which interrupts the normal course of life when it is needed and sets limits for human life together.[121] To use one of his examples, the commandment from Exodus 20:12 ("Honor your father and your mother") sometimes takes the solemn form of command (you should honor your parents) and prohibition (you should not rebel against your parents) both of which help to define a child's relationship to his or her parents by setting limits for appropriate and inappropriate behavior.[122]

However, God's commandment also takes on an everyday form that gives permission and freedom to live life as human beings. Here, God's

119. Ibid.; cf. DBWE 15:504.
120. DBWE 6:381.
121. Ibid., 366–69.
122. Ibid., 381.

The Simplicity of Discernment

commandment acts as daily guidance within one's everyday experience. The commandment in this form encounters a person not on the boundary, but in the center of his or her life; it provides continuity and allows one to make decisions and perform actions without questions of permission constantly arising. One is freed from the necessity of becoming a self-judge and allowed to act in confidence and freedom under God's commandment.[123] Thus, one might say that while the commandment in the form of the ethical has a negative content, setting limits for human life together, the commandment in the form of the everyday has a positive content, allowing one to get on with the living.[124] To go back to Bonhoeffer's example of the commandment to honor one's parents, the everyday form of the commandment does not constitute the "threatening and judging warning" of the solemn form (you shall not rebel against your parents) but addresses a child in his or her daily life and offers guidance in particular situations.[125] The fact that the commandment exists in two forms does not imply disunity; in fact, it simply reinforces the fact that God's one commandment encompasses all of life.[126]

Having described the shape of Christian ethics as an ethics of divine command, we are left to ponder how one perceives God's will in such an understanding. Bonhoeffer argues that God's commandment is always "utterly specific, clear, and concrete" speech to human beings: it is God's particular and personal address that leaves no room for "application and interpretation," but only for a response of obedience or disobedience.[127] He says later that it "liberates us for authentic life and for unreflective doing."[128] This line of thinking sounds very similar to his exposition of simple obedience in the 1930s, but just as then, so now he tempers his account of unreflective simplicity so that it is not completely one-sided. He implies that just because God's speech is particular and concrete does not mean that a person always knows exactly what to do. One is not given "special, direct divine inspiration" regarding how to act on every occasion and God does not, at every moment, "unambiguously mark a specific action, as willed by God, with the 'accent of eternity.'"[129] Here, he maintains his earlier position

---

123. Ibid., 385.
124. Ibid., 386.
125. Ibid., 381.
126. Ibid.
127. Ibid., 378–79, 381.
128. Ibid., 381.
129. Ibid., 379.

that while, from God's perspective, the commandment is clear, from the fallen human perspective, it might remain difficult to perceive. At the same time, however, one is not left to "grope around in the dark"; instead, God's commandment offers "unified direction and personal guidance, in the form of everyday seemingly small and insignificant words, sentences, hints, and aids."[130] Moreover, the primary way that such guidance becomes manifest in human experience is through concrete historical and social structures to which God has given form.[131]

Here is the bold shift in Bonhoeffer's argument, especially given his historical context that made any notion of orders of creation potentially dangerous. He carefully proposes that God's commandment becomes contemporary and assessable through particular, temporal realms of social life: the divine mandates of church, family, work, and government.[132] We have already seen at many points throughout the book his emphasis on reality, the ethical moment, and concrete situations; now, this strand of thinking reaches its culmination through his belief that the structure of the created realm *does* play an important role in the moral life and in Christian discernment.

It is interesting to compare Bonhoeffer's thinking in this regard with the thinking of Barth. One way Barth tries to explain how the concrete commandments in Scripture maintain contemporary relevance without becoming timeless, universal principles is to contend that humans today must become contemporaneous "in every sense [*ganz und gar*]" with the historical persons who heard the original commandments.[133] Presumably, becoming contemporaneous with the biblical text allows a person to hear the concrete commandments in their original context and realize how they apply to the contemporary context as well.[134] However, it is difficult to

---

130. Ibid., 385–86. This language points to the activity of the Holy Spirit.

131. Ibid., 380.

132. Ibid. Bonhoeffer usually refers to four divine mandates: 1) marriage and family (sometimes simply family), 2) work (sometimes called culture), 3) church, and 4) government. For Barth's later reservations regarding the doctrine of divine mandates, see CD 3/4:22.

133. CD 2/2:701.

134. Ibid. Barth also argues that the concrete commands in Scripture have the character of testimony before a court: testimony that holds a certain authoritative status and whose purpose is to influence one's own decisions and actions. This explanation rests on Barth's assumption that situations and commandments given to address those situations "then and there" are the same situations and commandments that are relevant "here and now." See ibid., 706. For a commentary and critique of Barth's argument, see O'Donovan,

know what Barth means by suggesting that one becomes contemporaneous "in every sense"; certainly one cannot become contemporaneous in a literal or historical sense. This is something that Bonhoeffer warns against in *Discipleship* when he argues: "simple obedience would be misunderstood hermeneutically if we were to act and follow as if we were contemporaries of the biblical disciples."[135] For him, it is not only Jesus' commandment to a disciple, but the disciple's response that constitutes God's word. Thus, one must maintain a hermeneutical distance from the text so that one can understand the entire proclamation of Scripture; as he puts it, a person must not "go behind the word of scripture to the actual events."[136]

In the end, despite Barth's influence on him, Bonhoeffer decides that the only response to the problem of how God's commandments become contemporary and assessable is through speaking of the divine mandates. The divine mandates do not reveal God's revelation directly, but insofar as each are "grounded in the revelation of Christ and the testimony of scripture," they function to concretize and structure one's reception of God's commandment.[137] As Moltmann asserts, Bonhoeffer's teaching on the mandates is his formulaic way of speaking about how God's commandment becomes concrete in the world today.[138] Through speaking of the mandates he wants to ground Christian ethics in historical and social reality and avoid the problem of subjectivism; that is, the critique that an ethics of divine command leads invariably to relativism because it lacks any kind of objective basis. At the same time, he wants to do this without losing sight of the supremacy of Christ, who alone makes real any social or historical order. When he speaks of the everyday realm of human life, the mandates become particularly important because they provide a context in which one can make decisions, interact with others, and go about daily life without a deep analysis of every decision and action. The mandates make morality self-evident in a way that allows a person to live within the freedom granted by God's commandment. The divine mandates do not render moral considerations obsolete, but, when functioning properly in relation to Christ and to each other, they remove the ethical conflict that would otherwise dominate human life, and simplify life by allowing one to make sense of

---

"Moral Authority of Scripture," 165–75.

135. DBWE 4:82.
136. Ibid.
137. DBWE 6:389.
138. Moltmann, "Wirklichkeit der Welt," 59.

God's commandment in practical ways. While these brief comments about the mandates only serve as an introduction, I will have much more to say in the following chapter, which deals fully with the natural, penultimate realm in which the Christian moral life proceeds.

Conclusion

I have argued in this chapter that the theme of simple obedience is, for Bonhoeffer, a crucial feature of the Christian moral life. At its core, simple obedience is not about obedience for its own sake, but obedience for the purpose of drawing one into closer communion with Christ. Simplicity names the original state of relations between God and Adam before the fall; it also names the state of affairs that exists between God and the redeemed human individual after the fall. Thus, simplicity helps one maintain a proper perspective on the divine/human relationship and also reminds one of the demands of Christian discipleship. In particular, a disciple should not seek to determine what is good or evil in a particular situation, but should focus instead on what is the will of God; a disciple must not try to evade God's commandments or ponder alternatives, but to learn to take God's commandments seriously and to respond to them directly. Without an emphasis on simplicity and simple obedience, many of these truths about human identity and Christian discipleship become obscured.

In such a simple relationship, it appears that one needs no recourse to moral reflection because the knowledge of God through Christ is immediately at hand, waiting for the human person to receive it in faith. However, it is precisely at this point that a paradox arises. Because simple obedience brings one into an immediate relationship with Christ, one experiences an entirely new orientation to the moral life. One now views the world, and particular situations that occur in one's experience, through a Christological lens. One's relationship with Christ provides a context for discerning God's will. Thus, in one sense, moral reflection is unnecessary because one no longer has to look to a presumed human knowledge of good and evil for guidance; however, in another sense, a meditative reflection, which focuses on the reality of Christ, becomes available to the disciple. Precisely by eliminating the need for one manner of moral reflection, simple obedience opens up space for another.

This second kind of reflection looks inward to consider the self and its motives, but finds that Christ has taken up the very same space

The Simplicity of Discernment

formerly held by the knowledge of good and evil. Such self-reflection is no longer self-centered, but becomes Christ-centered. Moreover, this kind of reflection approaches God's will with the presupposition that God's word is authoritative. Thus, it seeks to treasure God's word in the heart and to meditate upon it rather than possess God's word in the intellect and analyze it in order to find faults and inadequacies. In short, the disciple gains freedom through the simplicity of relationship with Christ to live fully as a human being, including using one's intellect and reason for the purposes of meditative reflection. Moreover, Bonhoeffer insists that to live in such a way also demands a keen awareness of reality structured according to the divine mandates. This is because it is through the divine mandates that God's commandment becomes concrete and historical in one's contemporary experience. Thus, without betraying the importance of a simple relationship with Christ, he suggests that Christian moral life cannot proceed outside of its natural, penultimate context. It is to this engagement with natural life and with natural human ability that we now turn.

6

The Penultimate Context of Discernment

Despite a strong emphasis in his theology on the importance of a simple, unreflective approach to God's will, Bonhoeffer nevertheless allows room for a meditative moral reflection, as described in the previous chapter. While discernment must strive for simplicity, which brings one into close communion with Christ, it must also involve appropriate reflection and deliberation that leads to responsible decision and action. As he asserted in "God's Love," moral discernment draws upon "the entire array of human abilities," meaning that attributes such as reason and conscience, despite sometimes being the objects of Bonhoeffer's sharp criticism, have a role to play in perceiving God's will.[1] To state this in a different way, moral discernment is not only a spiritual activity, encompassed by faith, but also a noetic activity, dependent on reason. Moral discernment not only proceeds out of one's justified existence and operates within an ecclesial context, but it also flows out of one's human nature and functions within the context of the natural world. While I have already investigated some of these themes in part, it is the task of this chapter to take them up more fully; thus, I will explore the role of human attributes such as reason and conscience in discernment and the role of the natural, penultimate world as the context for discernment.

Just as the motif of God's commandment helped to guide the exploration of simple obedience in the last chapter, the motif of natural life will help guide the investigation in the current chapter. Bonhoeffer takes up this theme in one of the largest sections of *Ethics*, a noteworthy portion of

1. DBWE 6:324.

his text because of its originality in moving against the stream of Protestant thought, which tended to devalue the natural world and natural human life. In the first section of this chapter I will investigate his theology of the natural, which recognizes the relative value of the created order for the moral life when viewed through a Christological lens. Next, I will discuss how he views the structure of the penultimate world in terms of divine mandates, a concept introduced in the last chapter. Here, I will trace the evolution of his thinking on the created order and its importance for his vision of Christian ethics and the task of moral discernment. Following this, I will explore moral discernment as a task embedded in the natural world. In particular, I will consider how the divine mandates guide discernment and how two natural human attributes, reason and conscience, aid discernment. Finally, at the end of the chapter, I address a question, already raised in chapter 2, that emerges from the preceding discussion: Given that natural human ability is a part of moral discernment and that discernment takes place in the natural world, is the kind of moral discernment Bonhoeffer articulates a distinctively *Christian* activity, or can others participate in it as well?

A Theology of the Natural

As we have already seen throughout the book, Bonhoeffer was not afraid to think theologically about the reality and structure of the natural world. At the same time, he was quick to reject a kind of natural theology that presumed to know God's will directly from the created world, which functioned as an autonomous source of authority.[2] Because of this, Jordan Ballor suggests that one might speak of Bonhoeffer having a negative natural theology in which the very concealment of Christ in creation points to God's revelation. Here, the natural world *does* play some role in one's knowledge of God, but only by pointing to places where Christ's presence is veiled.[3] Moreover, one could argue that Bonhoeffer's view of the natural world is similar to Alistair McGrath's proposal of a Christian natural theology that does not move from empirical observation to God's existence, but which presupposes a particular lens (Christ) through which one views the natural world and through which one can discern the transcendent within the

---

2. On Bonhoeffer's rejection of this kind of natural theology, see, for example, Green, *Theology of Sociality*, 203; de Gruchy, "Editor's Introduction," 11–12.

3. Ballor, "Christ in Creation," 1–22.

natural.⁴ McGrath contends that because nature, as such, is ambiguous, it is only through a hermeneutical framework that one can understand it as a source of knowledge about God.⁵ He writes: "The enterprise of natural theology is thus one of discernment, of seeing nature in a certain way, of viewing it through a particular and specific set of spectacles."⁶ Here, one sees similarities with Bonhoeffer, who also posits that the natural world has value precisely when one views it through a Christological lens. The difference is that in McGrath's work there is a disconnect between his stated Christological presuppositions and his ensuing methodological approach. Thus, while he argues at the beginning of his book that Christology is crucial for re-envisioning natural theology, he offers no sustained Christological discussion in the subsequent chapters. It is Bonhoeffer who better illustrates the main lines of McGrath's argument through his frequent Christological discussions throughout his corpus, many of which suggest that it is only through Christ that one can understand the true nature of reality.⁷

But despite similarities with McGrath's view of natural theology, perhaps the best approach to speaking about Bonhoeffer's view of the created realm might be to eschew the term "natural theology" entirely for the sake of clarity and to suggest, along with William Connor, that Bonhoeffer does not so much have a "natural theology" as he does a "theology of the natural."⁸ This theology of the natural begins not with the empirical reality of what exists, but with certain theological presuppositions about the supremacy of Christ and the mediating role of Christ. Given these presuppositions, one does not employ the natural world as a lens through which to perceive God; rather, one uses Christ as a lens through which to appreciate the natural world. The created order is not the source of theology, but something that one might understand theologically. Moreover, the created order is not a static repository of God's will, but becomes a relative source of knowing God's will because the incarnate Christ, the fullest expression of God's will, has given it form. That Christ has given it form means that a theology of the natural can view the natural world teleologically, as the penultimate realm that opens itself up to and prepares the way for the coming of Christ.

---

4. McGrath, *Open Secret*.
5. Ibid., 73, 116.
6. Ibid., 3.
7. For example, see DBWE 3:21–23; DBWE 4:93–96; DBWE 6:47–75.
8. Connor, "Natural Life of Man," 95.

Bonhoeffer develops his theology of the natural most thoroughly in his aptly named manuscript "Natural Life." His purpose in the manuscript is to rehabilitate the natural as a constructive concept for thinking about the Christian moral life; as he laments at the beginning of the text: "The concept of the natural has fallen into disrepute in Protestant ethics."[9] He argues that although the natural is a concept grounded in Scripture, Protestants often ignore or misuse it either by viewing it as completely sinful and unhelpful for theological thought, or by seeing it as an untainted realm, which maintains autonomous authority apart from Christ. He was especially fearful of this latter problem, which resulted in the kind of natural theology he opposed and easily led to indifference, helplessness, or even tacit support for the National Socialist government of the era.[10] Yet, the problem of Protestants simply ignoring the natural was also serious; without the concept, one could not "give clear guidance on the burning questions of natural life," thus leaving people "without answers or help in vital decisions."[11] One can see that despite his disapproval of the casuistic method in Catholic moral theology, he nevertheless envied its ability to draw on the concept of the natural in order to speak concretely about ethical issues.

Bonhoeffer's first step in rehabilitating the natural is to carefully define the concept by making two distinctions.[12] First, he argues that the natural world is not identical to what was originally created, a distinction that takes into account the reality of both creation and sin.[13] In the original created order, sin was absent and humanity enjoyed an unmediated relationship with God; in the postlapsarian world, sin is a reality and human beings receive a relative freedom that allows them to either open themselves to God's revelation in Christ or to close themselves to such revelation. Here, there is a second distinction within the natural world between what is truly natural and what is unnatural. Insofar as human individuals rightly use the relative freedom given by God, the natural remains directed toward Christ, open to Christ's coming, and retains its status as natural. If, however, human individuals misuse this relative freedom, the natural becomes unnatural, closes itself off from Christ, and risks its own destruction.[14]

9. DBWE 6:171.
10. Ibid., 171n3.
11. Ibid., 172.
12. Ibid., 173.
13. Ibid.
14. Ibid., 176–77

A noticeable by-product of this differentiation between the original created order and the natural world is the removal of his discussion from what would seem to be its natural doxological context: that of creation. One should not read into his distinction, however, a disregard for the doctrine of creation; instead, his purpose is to guard against what he felt was a high probability for misunderstanding. In particular, he did not want people to think that the original, created realm maintained independent value apart from Christ by virtue of its creation. For a similar reason, he also recast his conversation about the natural world away from the language of order (*Ordnung*), so as to distance his position from others such as Paul Althaus who sought "to place God's imprimatur" on the given order in German society.[15] The problem, as Bonhoeffer perceived it, was that *Ordnung* language could suggest to some that the government, despite whatever atrocities it committed, maintained an inherent authority by virtue of its status as an order of creation instituted by God. Thus, as we will see below, he deliberately settles on "divine mandates" to describe the structure of the created order, thereby eschewing both creation and order language completely.

It is Bonhoeffer's belief in the significance of the natural world for the Christian moral life that causes him to make such careful distinctions and to avoid problematic language. He stresses that natural life is not merely "a preliminary stage" a Christian passes through on the way to life with Christ.[16] On the contrary, because Christ has taken on human form and vindicated the natural order, natural life becomes the penultimate realm in which human life proceeds. The form of natural life, bestowed by God, is "that form of life preserved by God for the fallen world that is directed toward justification, salvation, and renewal through Christ."[17] While some choose to reject this form of life, and thereby embody the form of the unnatural, Bonhoeffer believes there is a "basic will" inherent in one's natural and preserved life that helps one to perceive and affirm the natural world.[18] Put differently, one's very life tends toward what is natural and away from what is unnatural, serving as a basic orientation for the moral life.

Bonhoeffer further describes the importance of the natural world for the Christian moral life by asserting that natural life is both an end in itself and a means to an end. The fact that life is an end in itself points toward the

15. Ericksen, *Theologians Under Hitler*, 116.
16. DBWE 6:174.
17. Ibid.
18. Ibid., 176.

created goodness of life and rejects the notion that life has value only insofar as it is useful for something else. At the same time, the fact that life is a means to an end points toward the participation of life in God's kingdom and guards against an understanding of life as its own absolute goal.[19] By insisting that natural life is both an end in itself *and* a means to an end he reaffirms that Christians are fully rooted in both the penultimate and the ultimate realm simultaneously. He says: "In Jesus Christ life as an end in itself expresses its createdness, and life as a means to an end expresses its participation in the kingdom of God";[20] thus, Christian life includes deep engagement through simple obedience with the ultimate reality of God's kingdom, but it also consists of full participation in the penultimate reality of the world, where one makes use of God's natural gifts on the journey of discipleship.

Moreover, Bonhoeffer claims that natural life includes inherent rights and duties, which correspond to his declaration that life is both an end in itself (rights) and a means to an end (duties).[21] The rights of natural life are given as a gift of God and always come prior to duties: "God gives before God demands."[22] These rights have no autonomous value before God, but insofar as God gives them to natural life, they become "the reflection of the glory of God the Creator in the midst of the fallen world."[23] The duties associated with natural life "spring from the rights themselves" and remain valid only if rights are taken seriously.[24] One cannot ascertain a moral duty without first recognizing and embracing one's inherent rights. His preference to begin with rights and then to speak of duties mirrors his entire approach to ethics, which focuses first of all on the reality of what is the case before moving to action in accordance with that reality. But this preference also points to the role of human rights as a guide in the Christian moral life. For instance, he argues that the most general right of bodily life, "suum cuique [to each his own]," guides human interaction by protecting the rights of an individual from unhealthy absorption into the priority of

19. Ibid., 178–79.

20. Ibid., 179.

21. Tödt points out that prior to the Second World War, Bonhoeffer's discussion of rights was "the only systematic Protestant attempt to conceive of human rights"; see Tödt, "Theological Ethics and Human Rights," 144.

22. DBWE 6:180.

23. Ibid.

24. Unfortunately, Bonhoeffer never finished his planned treatment of duties; see ibid., 181n37.

the community.²⁵ He also speaks of the right to bodily preservation of life and the right to bodily enjoyment. Both rights stem from the fact that being embodied is the divinely willed "form of human existence" and therefore "becomes an end in itself."²⁶ Moreover, he asserts the right of protection from arbitrary killing of innocent life, which leads him to a discussion of euthanasia.²⁷ In each case, an understanding of natural rights serves as a relative guide to moral deliberation.

This is not to suggest that Bonhoeffer is unaware of the limitations of natural rights. For example, there are times when natural rights come into conflict with one another and therefore become inadequate as a source of moral guidance. Nevertheless, he believes they still hold a relative value within the penultimate world, largely because the guarantor of these rights is "God, and through God life itself."²⁸ James Laney critiques this attempt to ground natural rights in God, arguing that doing so undermines Bonhoeffer's insistence that there is no "pressure of the penultimate from the ultimate for any ethical value."²⁹ This does not take into account, however, Bonhoeffer's reconciled view of reality, in which both God and world are brought together in Christ. Such an understanding precludes any account of the natural that has no connection to the ultimate; moreover, Bonhoeffer makes clear that it is not so much God or, as Heinz Eduard Tödt points out, the human individual who is the bearer of human rights, but natural life itself.³⁰ The penultimate *does* have its own value, but one can never conceive of such value apart from God in Christ having entered into the natural world.

A second critique of Bonhoeffer, however, concerns his seemingly inconsistent approach to the place of ethical principles in moral deliberation. While ethical principles appeared to play a role in moral deliberation in his 1929 Barcelona lecture on Christian ethics, as we saw in chapter 5, an aversion to ethical principles marked his theological trajectory throughout the 1930s and into the 1940s. However, despite his continual disparagement

---

25. Ibid., 183.

26. Ibid., 185–88.

27. Ibid., 190–96. He goes on to treat the problem of self-murder, the rights of marriage, contraception, and abortion, as well as other issues associated with freedom in bodily life: freedom from rape, slavery, torture, etc.; see ibid., 189–217.

28. Ibid., 184–85.

29. Laney, "Ethical Contextualism," 308.

30. Tödt, "Theological Ethics and Human Rights," 146.

of Christian ethics based on ethical principles, it is hard to argue that he is not following just such an approach when dealing with issues of natural life in 1941. For example, he believes one should oppose the Nazi program of euthanasia based on the principle that human life has an inherent right to preservation.[31] This is very different from saying that one should oppose euthanasia because of Christ's commandment to love the neighbor and care for the poor and oppressed, a line of reasoning one might have expected from Bonhoeffer.

Different scholars have various opinions regarding this apparent contradiction. Despite what seems to be obvious evidence to the contrary, Burtness argues that it is "not the case" that Bonhoeffer "having abandoned an ethic of principles, returns to such an ethic as soon as he gets to specific issues."[32] He explains his claim only by the vague assertion that the word "principle" appears more often in the English translation of *Ethics* than it does in the German original, thus misleading people into thinking Bonhoeffer is more concerned with ethical principles than he really is.[33] Rasmussen argues to the contrary that Bonhoeffer's mention of the "suum cuique" is the introduction of a philosophical principle imported from somewhere apart from Christ and is therefore out of place.[34] At the heart of Rasmussen's observation is a larger critique of Bonhoeffer's methodology: he questions how Bonhoeffer can use, in practice, an ethical method involving the casuistic application of ethical principles that he formally rules out in theory.[35] Connor, who wrote a dissertation on the theme of the natural in Bonhoeffer, also notes this apparent methodological inconsistency, but argues that principles can serve as "relative" or "secondary" norms, yet "have no claim to absolute principles or laws whose authority is binding in all cases."[36] Thus, Bonhoeffer "does not deny the validity of principles altogether" and understands that even principles can be "tools" to use for a time as long as they do not take on a "timeless validity."[37] In short, Bonhoeffer does not abandon his fundamental rejection of timeless ethical

---

31. See Bonhoeffer's discussion of euthanasia, ibid., 189–96.
32. Burtness, *Shaping the Future*, 107.
33. Ibid.
34. Rasmussen, *Reality and Resistance*, 161–62.
35. Ibid., 161.
36. Connor, "Natural Life of Man," 170.
37. Ibid., 129.

norms that one can apply indiscriminately to any situation regardless of the context. His ethic remains concrete and wholly Christological.

The most useful question to ask, however, may not be whether Bonhoeffer has methodological inconsistencies, which it seems that he does, but *why* such inconsistencies manifest themselves in his writing. Part of it has to do with the incomplete nature of his *Ethics*, which was left unfinished due to his arrest. According to Rasmussen, another part may involve Bonhoeffer's tendency to caricature certain positions when making methodological statements, which then leads to contradictions in his practical approach to concrete moral issues when the caricatures are revealed as such.[38] But above all, the inconsistencies point to the paradoxical tension between simple obedience and moral reflection at the heart of his theology. Bonhoeffer is often unable to capture the paradox in certain methodological statements, though the paradox reveals itself in his subsequent discussions of the moral life. Thus, for example, some methodological statements exclude reason and the knowledge of good and evil as aids to the moral life in order to preserve his belief in a single, ultimate reality of Christ as the starting point for Christian ethics and in the sufficiency of simple obedience for Christian life. However, embedded in those statements, though not fully evident, is the fact that one *does* make use of reason and one *is* aware of good and evil on the path of Christian discipleship. In fact, each has value precisely because Christ entered fully into the reality of the world, making possible a life of simple obedience. Thus, while methodological inconsistencies might exist, they serve as an important indication of Bonhoeffer's continual attempt to speak about the need to combine simplicity and wisdom in the Christian moral life.

It should already be apparent from several previous comments that this theology of the natural under discussion, which views the natural world through a Christological lens and sees it as a significant context and relative guide for Christian discipleship, is not a sudden development in *Ethics*.[39] For instance, we saw in the last chapter how Bonhoeffer, in his 1929 Barcelona lecture on Christian ethics, describes ethics as "a matter of earth and blood" and something that "can be found only within the bonds of history."[40] In that same text, he famously employs the image of the giant

---

38. Rasmussen, *Reality and Resistance*, 164.

39. For a good overview of the developing theme of worldliness in Bonhoeffer, see Lawrence, *Bonhoeffer*, 54–76.

40. DBWE 10:376.

Antaeus whose strength derives from his firm connection to the earth.[41] He argues further that those who "abandon the earth" will similarly lose their strength and their connection to God for "[t]he earth remains our mother just as God remains our father, and only those who remain true to the mother are placed by her into the father's arms."[42] We also saw in chapter 3 how Bonhoeffer speaks at the very end of *Creation and Fall* of the cross of Christ firmly planted "in the center of the world."[43] It is no mistake that it is precisely the fallen world, which is nonetheless "upheld and preserved" by God, which provides the foundation for the new "kingdom of life and of the resurrection" that the cross of Christ establishes.[44]

In addition to these early indications of the significance of the natural world, Bonhoeffer's theology of the natural also continues beyond *Ethics* into his writing from prison, where he pursues the theme through his explorations of worldliness (*Weltlichkeit*) or this-worldliness (*Diesseitigkeit*). For instance, in a 1944 letter from prison, he restates a question that he had asked continually, in one form or another, throughout his life: "[W]hat is Christianity, or who is Christ actually for us today?"[45] One of his primary answers to the question centers on the theme of worldliness, which is one of the dominant motifs of his prison theology. By invoking the idea of worldliness he does not mean "the shallow and banal this-worldliness of the enlightened, the bustling, the comfortable, or the lascivious"; instead, he wants to indicate the worldliness of the Christian who recognizes God in the midst of the world.[46] Drawing on his increased appreciation for the Old Testament, and its emphasis on the historical and concrete over and against the metaphysical, he argues that because the Word became flesh (John 1:14), "God is the beyond in the midst of our lives," fully embedded at the center of the world.[47] This means that engaging in the reality of the world is essential for Christian life. As he puts it: "What matters is not the beyond but this world, how it is created and preserved, is given laws, reconciled, and renewed."[48] One learns to see oneself rooted in the natural,

41. Ibid., 377.
42. Ibid., 378.
43. DBWE 3:146.
44. Ibid.
45. DBWE 8:362.
46. Ibid., 485.
47. Ibid., 406.
48. Ibid., 373.

penultimate world, and Christian life becomes an exercise of "living fully in the midst of life's tasks, questions, successes and failures, experiences, and perplexities."[49]

One implication of such an understanding is that Christians learn to hope in resurrection not as a means of escape from the world into the spiritual realm, but as a reorientation for how to view the world and live within it.[50] Only by seeing oneself "as belonging wholly to the world" can a person engage in the primary penultimate tasks of being human and being good.[51] These tasks do not mean being religious or pious in one's behavior, but being conformed to the humanity of Jesus, which allows a person to share in his sufferings, and by extension, the sufferings of the world.[52] A person travels this way of the cross through responsible action and through prayer, which are the foundation for "[a]ll Christian thinking, talking, and organizing."[53] As Christians look to the resurrection they also gain a sense of the eschatological time in which they live: a time where the ultimate gives meaning to the penultimate, but has not yet arrived in all its fullness. Thus, as Bonhoeffer reminds us, "[t]his-worldliness must not be abolished ahead of its time."[54] Put differently, one must patiently engage with the penultimate reality of the world, recognizing its relative value as a source of moral guidance and making full use of one's natural, human abilities in the journey of discipleship. One must embody the kind of wisdom in one's moral discernment that can act as a proper counterpoint to simplicity.

The Divine Mandates

One cannot fully understand Bonhoeffer's theology of the natural without an account of the structure and order of the natural world. As a young Lutheran theologian Bonhoeffer had used the traditional language of "orders of creation [*Schöpfungsordnungen*]" to speak of the structure of reality.[55] By 1932, however, the notion of autonomous created realms that exercised their own authority became problematic given the historical situation

49. Ibid., 486.
50. Ibid., 447.
51. Ibid., 364; DBWE 6:159.
52. DBWE 8:447, 480–81.
53. Ibid., 389.
54. Ibid., 447.
55. DBWE 1:33n21; cf. DBWE 10:368–75, where Bonhoeffer speaks of "God's orders."

in Germany. Because of this, Bonhoeffer chose to drop the language of *Schöpfungsordnungen* and to adopt a different term: *Erhaltungsordnungen* or orders of preservation.[56] As already noted in the previous chapter, one can see a shift from one term to the other in his 1932 address "On the Theological Foundation," when he suggests that it is not orders of creation (*Schöpfungsordnungen*), but orders of preservation (*Erhaltungsordnungen*) that play a role in revealing God's commandment, though only insofar as the orders remain open to Christ and receive their value from Christ.[57] The language of preservation appears again about one month later when he begins his lecture series on Genesis 1–3. In his commentary on Genesis 1:21, where God makes clothes for Adam and Eve, he argues that after the fall God does not abandon the world, but becomes its preserver.[58] God preserves the world through order (*Ordnung*), but the resulting orders "are not orders of creation but orders of preservation. They have no value in themselves; instead they find their end and meaning only through Christ."[59] In addition, while he does not use the precise formula "orders of preservation," he does continue speaking of God's acts of preservation in both *Discipleship* and *Ethics*.[60]

However, this language of "orders of preservation" eventually gives way in 1941 to Bonhoeffer's formulation of "divine mandates," which persists until the time of his death in 1945.[61] Given his incomplete exposition of the doctrine in *Ethics* and his continual rumination upon it in his prison correspondence, one can conclude that his thinking on the mandates was not fully formed.[62] Moreover, his decision to speak of the created realm in terms of divine mandates rather than an "order," "estate," or "office" was largely due to his fears that those latter terms, while useful in the past, had become problematic and could easily lead to misunderstandings about the natural world.[63] Thus, while his position is not an entirely new belief com-

56. For example, see DBWE 3:135, 139–40.

57. DBWE 11:362–64; DBW 11:335–37; cf. chapter 5.

58. He writes: "The Creator is now the preserver; the created world is now the fallen but *preserved world*," DBWE 3:139; Bonhoeffer's italics.

59. Ibid., 140.

60. DBWE 4:136, 259; DBWE 6:173, 176.

61. For Bonhoeffer's description of the divine mandates, see DBWE 16:518–21, 549–50; DBWE 6:68–74, 296, 380–81, 388–408; DBWE 8:267–69. For Barth's comments on Bonhoeffer's doctrine of the divine mandates, see CD 3/4:21–22.

62. DBWE 6:408; DBWE 8:267–69.

63. DBWE 6:389–90. Nevertheless, Dumas maintains that the mandates are unhelpful

pletely at odds with the Protestant tradition, it is nevertheless a distinct view employing carefully chosen language to emphasize particular features of the natural world and their importance for Christians.

As mentioned in the previous chapter, Bonhoeffer speaks of four divine mandates—marriage and family, work (or culture), government, and church—that structure reality and provide a context and boundary for one's daily life, and in particular, for one's moral action.[64] The authority of the mandates comes not from their positive content, but from their character as commands given by God (the word "mandate" derives from the Latin word *mandatum*, meaning "commandment").[65] As Bonhoeffer explains: "We speak of divine mandates rather than divine orders, because thereby their character as divinely imposed tasks [Auftrag], as opposed to determinate forms of being, becomes clearer."[66] Thus, the mandates have no autonomous authority in themselves because their significance does not derive from their "actual givenness in this or that concrete form" but from God's commission, which confers "divine authority on an earthly institution."[67] He also explains that only as God forms an earthly domain does it become authorized as a bearer of the divine commandment. Here, there are interesting parallels with the Christian formation spoken of in chapter 4. We observed in that chapter that, for Bonhoeffer, human individuals do not transcend their humanity, but become more fully human through the process of formation. In the same way, the earthly domain is not pulled out and made into a heavenly or spiritual reality; rather, through its formation, it becomes more true to its very being as a worldly structure.[68]

---

because they are too closely aligned to the Lutheran tradition of orders of creation. See Dumas, *Theologian of Reality*, 157.

64. DBWE 6:68, 296, 388. Bonhoeffer's list of mandates relates almost exactly to Luther's three estates, although the economic order (*status economicus*), which for Luther included both family and work, is now split apart, better reflecting a twentieth century context in which domestic life no longer corresponded so closely to work life. See Green, "Editor's Introduction" (DBWE 6), 19n73.

65. See DBWE 6:68–69n.75; DBWE 16:519n85.

66. DBWE 6:68–69.

67. Ibid., 69–70, 389.

68. Ibid., 389.

The Penultimate Context of Discernment

The Mandates as a Guide for Discernment

According to Bonhoeffer the divine mandates, when functioning properly, act as conduits for God's commandment, allowing it to take shape within history. Because of this, the mandates are deeply involved in human attempts to discern God's will. According to Bonhoeffer:

> God's commandment is not to be found anywhere and everywhere, not in theoretical speculation or private enlightenment, not in historical forces or compelling ideals, but only where it gives itself to us ... God's commandment is to be found not wherever there are historical forces, strong ideals, or convincing insights, but only where there are divine mandates [Mandate] which are grounded in the revelation of Christ.[69]

As he argued in "God's Love," moral discernment "will be encompassed and pervaded by the commandment," which means the task of discernment takes place within the structure provided by the divine mandates and looks to the divine mandates as the means through which God's commandment takes form.[70] Without an understanding of the reality of a particular historical situation, one is at a disadvantage when it comes to discerning the nature of God's commandment.

The usefulness of the divine mandates as an aid to moral discernment rests on their continual connection to Christ and on their interdependent relationship with one another.[71] The mandates, while each distinct, exist in a mutual relationship of being "with each other, beside each other, together with each other, and over against each other."[72] No single mandate has absolute authority over the others or the right to "identify itself alone with the commandment of God."[73] God's commandment is only revealed through any one mandate insofar as it stands in proper relation to the other three. This means a mandate can lose its status as a mandate just as the natural can become unnatural when it loses its orientation toward Christ. If a mandate becomes closed to Christ and disconnected from the reality of the divinely imposed task, it can cease to function as a dependable guide to the moral life. Thus, there is freedom to act contrary to a divine mandate if doing

---

69. Ibid., 388.
70. Ibid., 324.
71. Ibid., 69.
72. Ibid., 380–81.
73. Ibid., 380.

so keeps one in obedience to God. Because of this, the mandates might sometimes become subject *to* one's discernment rather than guides *for* one's discernment. Rainer Mayer illustrates both of these possibilities when he argues that an understanding of the proper relationship among the mandates informed Bonhoeffer's discernment about the illegitimacy of the concept of an absolute *Führer*.[74] On the one hand, understanding the balanced interrelationship of the mandates helped Bonhoeffer discern when one of them (in this case, the government) became disconnected from Christ. Here, the doctrine of the mandates helped to guide discernment. On the other hand, his determination that the mandate of government would fall out of balance and thereby lose its legitimacy if it allowed an absolute *Führer* is an example of a mandate becoming subject to discernment.

The mandates also assist one's moral discernment by inviting the kind of meditative reflection spoken of in the last chapter: that is, the type of moral reflection embodied by one who seeks to be both simple and wise. This is because Bonhoeffer insists that the mandates are not historical or sociological descriptions of the structure of reality; they are categories taken directly from Scripture.[75] He even hints that Luther's doctrine of the three estates is inadequate precisely because it does not connect closely enough to Scripture: the three estates "must be replaced by a *doctrine—created from the Bible—of the four divine mandates.*"[76] Brock picks up on this link with Scripture and argues that the mandates are clusters of scriptural emphasis with moral content that serve as a "heuristic" in guiding Christians along the way of discipleship by helping them discern "theologically relevant facts" that apply to their particular historical context.[77] He describes the mandates as "Bonhoeffer's pedagogical drawing together of what he believes are the important signposts of the way of *Nachfolge* . . . They are christologically keyed descriptions of the features of reality which allow us to encounter Christ."[78] This description links reality and Scripture by making creation "a location *within* the law."[79] Moreover, insofar as the mandates originate from Scripture, they open themselves to Christians as objects of meditative reflection. The same kind of meditative reflection that

---

74. Mayer, "Bonhoeffers Mandatenlehre," 66–69.
75. DBWE 16:549.
76. Ibid.; Bonhoeffer's italics.
77. Brock, "Bonhoeffer and the Bible," 23, 26.
78. Ibid., 24.
79. Ibid., 13.

ponders God's word in the heart and approaches God's word with presuppositions concerning its authority might also apply to the mandates. As one considers the reality of the world structured through the mandates, one begins to determine which aspects of the created order are morally relevant at each point of one's journey; in short, the mandates help a person remain attentive to the concrete situations he or she encounters and thereby enable the person to perceive how to respond to God's will and continue forward in discipleship.[80]

Finally, in an essay written from prison in 1943 entitled, "What Does It Mean to Tell the Truth?," Bonhoeffer gives perhaps his strongest indication that the success or failure of discerning God's will depends upon an accurate perception of reality structured by the divine mandates.[81] He does this through a discussion of truth telling. To speak the truth, for him, does not mean adhering to a strict, formal principle of truth, as Kant would suggest; instead, it means accurately perceiving one's historical and relational context and responding accordingly.[82] Put differently, truthfulness is not based on a principle, but on the concrete situation at hand.[83] This means, in turn, that "lying is the negation, denial, and deliberate and willful destruction of reality."[84] Lying names a situation where a word is uttered "without regard for the person to whom it is said," thereby detaching itself from what is real.[85] Sometimes such "lying" can appear to be "truth," as in the famous example of the murderer at the door who asks if the one he pursues with an intent to kill is hiding inside the house. For Bonhoeffer, answering "yes" to the murderer's question is "true" in a formal sense, but decidedly untrue in a much deeper sense. In fact, answering "no" would almost certainly be more truthful, given the reality of the situation and the nature of the relationship between the people in question.

Telling the truth in this manner is a learned activity and depends upon "accurate perception and . . . serious consideration of the real circumstances" of a situation.[86] It also depends upon one's learning how to see

---

80. Ibid., 23–24.

81. For a close reading and analysis of Bonhoeffer's essay on truth telling, see Burtness, *Shaping the Future*, 126–63.

82. DBWE 16:602–4.

83. Ibid., 602–3.

84. Ibid., 607.

85. Ibid., 604.

86. Ibid., 603.

reality through a Christological lens. Here, the divine mandates come into play because they provide the kind of structure needed for one to make sense of reality. Bonhoeffer argues, for example, that the context of family determines the truth required between a father and his child, and how this differs from the truth required between a governing authority and those subject to the authority.[87] Thus, the mandates are guides for one's moral thinking because they provide a contextual grounding for one's reception of God's commandment.

The Role of Reason in Discernment

The fact that moral discernment occurs within the context of the natural, penultimate world means that natural human ability performs a crucial role in perceiving and acting upon God's will. Two particularly relevant attributes of natural life for a discussion of moral discernment are human reason and conscience.[88] However, both attributes receive sharp criticism from Bonhoeffer at various points of his writings, which we have already seen in chapter 2 in the case of conscience.[89] Nevertheless, each remains significant for the moral life. In fact, Connor argues that because of Bonhoeffer's description of the natural, reason and conscience both retain their validity as "ethical authorities."[90] Indeed, in his discussion of discerning God's will in "God's Love," Bonhoeffer speaks of the importance of intellect, cognitive ability, and self-examination, which points toward a place for both reason (intellect, cognitive ability) and conscience (self-examination).[91] The following offers a brief account of these natural attributes in order to illustrate how the simplicity of moral discernment is not a one-sided phenomenon.

Focusing first on reason, one sees from his very early work a mistrust and skepticism regarding reason's role in the Christian life. For instance, in *Act and Being* he argues that reason is dangerous because it tends to turn inward upon itself and to relate everything to itself.[92] By doing this it presumes to operate from a transcendent and objective vantage point,

---

87. Ibid., 602.

88. For an insightful study of both reason and conscience in Bonhoeffer's theology, see Connor, "Natural Life of Man."

89. See chapter 2; DBWE 6:307–8.

90. Ibid., 102.

91. See DBWE 6:321, 323–24, 325–26.

92. DBWE 2:45.

which knows no outside limits other than those that are self imposed.[93] In his *Lectures on Christology* he speaks of "horrified, dethroned human reason" that wants to classify and systematize Christ, but finds that it cannot do so.[94] In *Discipleship*, reason is one of the things that gets in the way of simple obedience to God's commandment.[95] In *Ethics*, he laments the fact that even "reasonable people" ultimately fail in the task of morality and that "the ethical is not essentially a formal principle of reason, but a concrete relationship based on a command."[96]

In voicing these various criticisms Bonhoeffer is aiming at several things: reason's presumption of objectivity and transcendence, reason's supposed pathway to divine knowledge independent of God's revelation, reason's self-imposed boundaries, which do not recognize the claim of God and others, and reason's belief that it can untangle even the most difficult moral dilemmas through the careful application of ethical principles.[97] In all of these aspects reason fails as a guide to God's revelation and to the Christian moral life. This is not to say, however, that Bonhoeffer is anti-rational, despite his rhetoric.[98] In fact, he indicates both implicitly and explicitly in many of his writings that one should not condemn natural human reason altogether. For instance, even in *Act and Being*, where he critiques human reason, he mentions reason being "brought into obedience to Christ"; in his *Lectures on Christology*, where he also criticizes human reason, he presupposes a useful role for human reason through his very act of articulating both a positive and negative Christology.[99] Thus, even in his earlier period Bonhoeffer hints at what he will develop more fully later: the relative value of reason in the Christian moral life.

Both the negative and positive aspects of reason appear in his historical reflection about the triumph of reason in the Enlightenment.[100] There were negative developments to this triumph, especially reason's grasp for

93. Ibid., 45–46.
94. DBWE 12:302.
95. DBWE 4:77.
96. DBWE 6:78, 374.
97. Connor argues that Bonhoeffer's sharpest critique of reason is aimed at its role "as the purveyor of an unrealistic, theoretical ethics of general principles"; see Connor, "Natural Life of Man," 126–27.
98. Connor suggests that Bonhoeffer is not anti-rational, but anti-speculative; ibid., 48.
99. DBWE 2:45; DBWE 12:331–60.
100. See his *Ethics* manuscript "Heritage and Decay," DBWE 6:103–33.

autonomy and its loss of connection to faith. On the other hand, the positive aspect was that reason's achievement "created an atmosphere of truthfulness, light, and clarity" and fostered "[i]ntellectual honesty in all things, including questions of faith."[101] He continues with the following insight:

> Contempt for the age of rationalism is a suspicious sign of a deficient desire for truthfulness. Just because intellectual honesty does not have the last word on things and rational clarity often comes at the cost of the depth of reality, we are not absolved from our inner duty to make honest and clean use of ratio. We can no longer go back to the time before Lessing and Lichtenberg.[102]

This statement is significant because even as Bonhoeffer affirms the value of reason and argues that one must make "honest and clean use of ratio," he cautions that "rational clarity often comes at the cost of the depth of reality." Reason alone is not enough to achieve the depth of moral insight needed to act according to God's will. At the same time, reason remains essential for one cannot "go back" to a more anti-rationalistic period before the Enlightenment. To put this theologically, one cannot "go back" to the innocence of Eden where reason was unnecessary because of the direct, immediate, and untainted relationship of unity between God and humanity. What is needed now is a combination of reason and faith, or as Bonhoeffer puts it on other occasions, wisdom and simplicity.

Whatever value reason does hold for the Christian moral life is due to his understanding of *Christuswirklichkeit*, already discussed in chapter 3.[103] In "Christ, Reality, and Good" he writes:

> [T]he world, the natural, the profane, and reason are seen as included in God from the beginning. All this does not exist "in and for itself." It has its reality nowhere else than in the reality of God in Christ... Just as the reality of God has entered the reality of the world in Christ, what is Christian cannot be had otherwise than in what is worldly, the "supernatural" only in the natural, the holy only in the profane, the revelational only in the rational.[104]

---

101. Ibid., 115.

102. Ibid., 115-16. The references are to Gotthold Ephraim Lessing, an Enlightenment "dramatist, philosopher, and critic," and Georg Christoph Lichtenberg, "a physicist and satirist at the University of Göttingen"; see ibid., 116n58.

103. For a discussion of the link between Bonhoeffer's understanding of reality in *Ethics* and his more positive assessment of reason, see Tietz, "Uses and Limits of Philosophy," 31-45.

104. DBWE 6:59.

The Penultimate Context of Discernment

This is a radical statement, especially given some of his earlier comments about reason. Not only is reason given value because it is included within the ultimate reality of Christ, but the rational can now serve as a source of revelation. This is because "Christ is the center and power of the Bible, of the church, of theology, but also of humanity, reason, justice, and culture."[105] Thus, for one who perceives *Christuswirklichkeit*, not only one's faith but also one's reason takes part in responding to Christ. We see this in his discussion of the natural where he points out a specific function of reason. While one recognizes the reality of the redeemed form of the natural world through faith, reason perceives the content of the natural world within that redeemed form and allows one to consciously function within it.[106] In short, Bonhoeffer does not completely reject human reason, but recognizes its relative value in moral reflection. While he is aware that an unhealthy reliance on reason can lead one astray and that reason cannot, in the end, lead one to God, he is also aware that simplicity without the wise use of reason ultimately fails in the task of moral discernment.

The Role of Conscience in Discernment

Turning to conscience, one can see a similar dynamic at work: despite his many negative depictions, conscience still holds relative value for Christian moral reflection.[107] From his early work through to his later ethical writings, Bonhoeffer makes consistent statements linking the conscience with fallen humanity, with the knowledge of good and evil, with a turning inward toward the self, and with a desire to preserve unity within the self.[108] The conscience is not a dependable moral guide because it is not the voice of God, but rather one's own attempt to reflect on the self and pass judgment. Green describes the tension in Bonhoeffer's account of conscience:

> Negatively, conscience is the self-accusation which arises from violated sociality. Positively, conscience is also one's self-exhortation to live up to his "better self," that is, to relate freely to others in love and service . . . The dilemma of conscience in Bonhoeffer's

---

105. Ibid., 341.
106. Ibid., 184.
107. For two insightful discussions of Bonhoeffer's view of the conscience, see Tödt, "Practice of Conscience," 151–68; Mokrosch, "Gewissensverständnis Dietrich Bonhoeffers," 59–92.
108. For example, see DBWE 2:138–45, 155–57; DBWE 3:128–30; DBWE 6:307-9.

phenomenology, however, is that it is a self-serving instrument. It is "the ultimate grasp of a person for himself, the confirmation and justification of his autocratic solitude." As *self*-accusation and *self*-exhortation, it is a powerful means of self-assertion and self-justification.[109]

As we saw in chapter 2 one can find support for Green's analysis in Bonhoeffer's critique of conscience in "God's Love." Here, Bonhoeffer contends that the conscience seeks unity with the self at the expense of true unity with God and others. The moral implication of this is that the self's own knowledge of good and evil becomes the ethical criterion for judgment and action: "All knowing is now based on self-knowledge."[110] One consults the conscience at every moment of ethical conflict, and this often proves overwhelming. One risks the temptation to settle for "an assuaged conscience instead of a good conscience."[111] The danger is that one might base decisions and actions solely on the feelings associated with the conscience rather than on the nature of reality and the demands of a particular situation.

However, as early as *Act and Being* Bonhoeffer suggests that the conscience does have a positive function for Christians. According to Green, Bonhoeffer overcomes the problem of conscience by arguing that "Christian conscience is transformed conscience, in which self-reflection is embraced by Christ, so that people see themselves only as forgiven by Christ."[112] Here, we find an implicit distinction between a fallen conscience and a Christian conscience; later, in *Ethics*, Bonhoeffer makes this more explicit by distinguishing between the "natural conscience" and "the conscience that has been set free in Jesus Christ."[113] In both cases the conscience remains a call to unity within the self and also a turning inward toward self-reflection, which can influence moral decision and action. The difference, however, lies in the identity of the "unifying center" of one's existence.[114] As he explains: "In the natural human being, the call of conscience is the attempt of the ego who knows good and evil to justify itself to God, to others, and to itself, and to be able to sustain this self-justification."[115] This stands in

---

109. Green, *Theology of Sociality*, 115.
110. DBWE 6:308.
111. Ibid., 79.
112. Green, *Theology of Sociality*, 97.
113. DBWE 6:278.
114. Ibid.
115. Ibid., 277.

contrast to the freed conscience "[w]here Christ... has become the unifying center of my existence."[116] Here, conscience is still a call to unity within the self, but one realizes this unity through Jesus Christ rather than one's autonomous ego.[117]

Several implications arise from Bonhoeffer's distinction. Most importantly, the freed conscience can engage in a kind of self-reflection that is not destructively egocentric, but focused on Christ within, making it a more promising activity for Christian moral reflection and action. Moreover, the freed conscience makes possible responsible action, which includes taking on the guilt of another. The conscience is no longer bound to the law, but yields to the ultimate authority of Christ, which makes possible a temporary transgression of the law in order to act responsibly in a particular situation.[118] Bonhoeffer does warn, however, that the free act of responsibility, whereby one willingly takes on the guilt of another, is reserved for extraordinary times and not to be done lightly. He asserts that one should never "act against one's own conscience. All Christian ethics agrees on this point."[119] Thus, the freed conscience remains a call to unity with the self and helps determine the limit of guilt that a particular individual can bear.[120] While this "ability to bear the weight of making responsible decisions can and should grow," Bonhoeffer suggests, there is a "concrete limit" for how much responsibility or guilt each individual can handle.[121] Finally, the freed conscience continues to confront the individual with the law to love God and neighbor. While this "law of life" is not the final authority for Christians and holds no autonomous status in the moral life, it nevertheless remains useful as a guide in the same way that the divine mandates act as a guide for everyday life within the penultimate world.[122]

---

116. Ibid., 278.

117. Ibid. Bonhoeffer also indicates the danger of trying to ground the conscience outside the self when he makes the stark and chilling contrast between those who said "'my conscience is A.H. [Adolf Hitler]'" and those who affirmed that "Jesus Christ has become my conscience"; Ibid.

118. Ibid., 278–83.

119. Ibid., 276.

120. Ibid., 281–82.

121. Ibid., 281.

122. Ibid., 282.

The Inclusivity and Exclusivity of Discernment

In chapter 2 we saw the clear distinction made by Bonhoeffer in "God's Love" between those in unity with God and those in disunity with God. The former group participates in the kind of Christian discernment Bonhoeffer describes using the language of *Prüfung*, which looks away from the self and toward Christ for its moral guidance. The latter group engages in a different kind of moral reflection and judgment that originates in one's own knowledge of good and evil.[123] Thus, according to Bonhoeffer's account, discerning God's will is an exclusive practice in which only Christians can participate. However, there are times in "God's Love," as noted in chapter 2, where the distinction between unity and disunity is less stark than it might appear at first. Moreover, because Bonhoeffer chooses to ground his account of moral discernment in the natural world, as we have seen in the preceding sections of this chapter, one begins to wonder if Bonhoeffer's notion of moral discernment is more inclusive than it first appears.

Most intriguing in this regard are his comments in "Church and World," a text written just after "God's Love," in which he suggests a more inclusive approach to the issue of who can and cannot act in accordance with reality and thereby discern and do the will of God.[124] In this manuscript he claims that certain values, like reason, law, and autonomy, which formerly fought against Christianity, are now, in the current situation, countering the irrationality and lawlessness of the Nazi regime. In so doing, these values find themselves "in very close proximity to the Christian domain" and their defenders "have much in common with Christians."[125] At the root of this inclusive account is his view of reality in which Christ is the center of everything, including things like "humanity, reason, justice, and culture."[126] He suggests that it might be a quite "unconscious knowledge" that leads these values and their defenders back to their origin in Christ, especially during times of great distress.[127]

To illustrate this view further he develops a distinction between both the inclusivity and exclusivity of Christ's claim. Each aspect of the claim is grounded in Scripture and exists together with the other in a dialectical

---

123. See the discussion in chapter 2.
124. DBWE 6:339–51.
125. Ibid., 340.
126. Ibid., 341.
127. Ibid., 341–42.

tension. On the one hand, Christ says, "'[w]hoever is not against us is for us'" (Mark 9:40), pointing to the inclusive nature of God's kingdom. Here, those who suffer for a just cause are suffering for the sake of Christ even though it is not in direct confession of his name. This stands in stark contrast to those who do confess Christ's name, but are unwilling to suffer for justice.[128] In *Discipleship*, Bonhoeffer argues that "Jesus calls his disciples blessed, not only when they directly confess his name, but also when they suffer for a just cause"; now, in *Ethics*, this blessing seems to extend even to those who are not Christian.[129] On the other hand, Christ also says "'[w]hoever is not for me is against me'" (Matt. 12:30).[130] Here, the exclusive nature of Christ's call stands out. Bonhoeffer argues that this exclusivity is especially needed during times of pressure from "anti-Christian powers" when the church must focus on the essential aspects of its faith and offer a clear and firm confession of this faith to the world.[131]

While the difference between these two statements of Christ might seem "irreconcilable," Bonhoeffer argues that this is not the case: one can and must hold the two together.[132] He argues that the extreme exclusivity of Christ's claim eventually becomes inclusive in the same way that extreme obedience to Christ actually results in the fullest experience of freedom. In the case of the Confessing Church, this meant that as the church focused more closely on the essential aspects of its faith (for instance, the reality of Christ's lordship) it cared less and less about peripheral issues, especially those which sought to "erect boundaries" between people.[133] This led to "an inner freedom and openness" to those outside the church who sought to act in accordance with the same reality to which those in the church sought to respond.[134] He summarizes his thinking in the following paragraph:

> Both sayings necessarily belong together, one as the exclusive claim [Ausschließlichkeitsanspruch], and the other as the all-encompassing claim [Ganzheitsanspruch], of Jesus Christ. The more exclusive, the more free and open. Isolated from each other, however, the exclusive claim leads to fanaticism and sectarianism,

---

128. Ibid., 342, 346.
129. DBWE 4:109.
130. DBWE 6:343.
131. Ibid.
132. Ibid., 343–44.
133. Ibid., 343.
134. Ibid.

> the all-encompassing claim to the secularization and capitulation of the church. The more exclusively we recognize and confess Christ as our Lord, the more will be disclosed to us the breadth of Christ's lordship.[135]

Thus, one must hold together both the inclusive and exclusive nature of Christ's call lest serious dangers result from overemphasizing either one or the other. This, in turn, forces one to rethink common conceptions about Jesus' relationship to different groups of people, such as the sinners and outcasts or the good and righteous Pharisees spoken of in Scripture. The question is: do only the sinners and outcasts teach people about God's kingdom or do people learn something from the Pharisees as well, a group commonly excluded from the kingdom?

Here, Bonhoeffer argues two different things. First, he contends that during normal and stable times it is often people like the tax collector or the sinner who illustrate the meaning of the gospel and call people to Christ.[136] Second, however, he asserts that during times of chaos it is possible that a righteous person (*ein Gerechter*) who struggles for justice, truth, and righteousness might actually provide a clearer example of what the gospel demands.[137] Thus, it is the very same Pharisee whom Bonhoeffer critiques in "God's Love" who now receives affirmation, thus blurring the line between exclusivity and inclusivity.[138] Moreover, it is interesting to note that in "God's Love" he uses the verb *prüfen* to speak in a negative way of the Pharisees' examining and judging others about their life decisions; in "Church and World" he employs *Selbst-prüfung* in a more positive manner as an example of the kind of "goodness" that a "good" and righteous person (such as the Pharisee) might embody.[139]

In some ways, Bonhoeffer's "Church and World" manuscript acts as a counter balance to the sharp distinctions drawn in "God's Love." He paints a more inclusive picture of who can act rightly in accordance with reality. The impetus for such thinking was at least in part his very own experience in the resistance against National Socialism. While increasingly disappointed

---

135. Ibid., 344.

136. Ibid., 347. Bonhoeffer references Matt 21:31 about the tax collectors and prostitutes going first into God's kingdom.

137. Ibid.

138. Ibid. For a discussion of the link between his language of "ein Gerechter" and the Jewish leaders in the New Testament, see ibid., 347n37.

139. See ibid., 310; DBW 6:312 and DBWE 6:349; DBW 6:352.

by fellow Christians who were not addressing the social evils in Germany, he also experienced a strong solidarity with those outside the church fighting alongside him for justice.[140] Even so, his move toward inclusivity did not entail relinquishing his strong belief in the ultimate supremacy and mediating role of Christ. To put this differently, he consistently maintains throughout his writing a strong Christological ethic over and against a purely natural ethic.[141] In the end, we know that as late as 1944 he remained preoccupied by questions of inclusivity and exclusivity.[142] What we cannot say for certain is what direction his thinking may have taken and what theological resolution, if any, he might have found. The question regarding the inclusive nature of moral discernment, as Bonhoeffer describes it in "God's Love," must therefore remain open.

Conclusion

We have seen in this chapter that the task of moral discernment is a human activity, deeply rooted in the reality of the natural, penultimate world. This aspect of discernment provides the necessary balance to Bonhoeffer's description of simple obedience explored in the previous chapter. His focus on the ethical moment, the sacrament of reality, and the divine mandates in his various discussions of Christian ethics from his time in Barcelona to his time in prison show that his moral vision demanded space for the created order as a source of moral knowledge. He did not see such a proposal at odds with his understanding of simple obedience; rather, the two held together on Christological grounds. He believed that any account of concrete ethics must look to the natural world, reconstituted in Christ, in order to provide Christians with concrete guidance on their journey of discipleship. Thus, he exhibited a theology of the natural, which understood the world as a significant penultimate context for human life and recognized the importance of natural gifts such as reason and conscience for moral discernment. This theology of the natural led him to embrace what one

---

140. See Bethge, *Bonhoeffer*, 857.

141. Bonhoeffer's thinking on this issue is somewhat akin to Karl Rahner's notion of "anonymous Christianity," although the parallels are not exact. For an excellent summary of Rahner's understanding of anonymous Christianity, see Kilby, *Introduction to Karl Rahner*, 30–37.

142. See, for instance, Bonhoeffer's references to the notion of "unconscious Christianity" in his prison writings, DBWE 8:489, 491.

might call a Christological-natural ethic that prevented moral discernment from deteriorating into a matter of intuition that failed to recognize the place of the penultimate within the ultimate.

This attempt to ground his vision of Christian ethics in the natural world serves as a defense against critiques from the viewpoint of subjectivism. One could claim that an account of ethics centered on the question, "What is the will of God?," is inherently faulty because there is no objective basis, as such, for pursuing such an inquiry. But by arguing that God's will, revealed through God's commandment, does not simply appear in a moment of inspiration, but is mediated in some way through the structure of reality, Bonhoeffer offers a firm basis for moral discernment. Gaining moral insight is not only a matter of embracing one's simple relationship with God through Christ, but also a matter of living fully in the reality of the world, the place where Christ continually takes form among his people. In short, the central argument from "God's Love" appears once again in his treatment of natural life: the complex task of discerning God's will requires simple faith and self-reflection on the person of Christ who replaces the knowledge of good and evil within the individual. However, such discernment also demands the best of human ability to perceive the shape of situations and relationships, to draw upon the knowledge of Christ, and to respond accordingly within the context of the natural world.

7

Conclusion

The Centrality of Discernment

DURING THE COURSE OF this book I have sought to establish two things: first, that the activity of moral discernment is of central importance for Bonhoeffer and helps to unify his ethical vision; second, that his understanding of discernment attempts to reconcile both simplicity and wisdom into one unified and coherent account. As stated several times in the previous chapters, the primary question for Christian ethics, according to Bonhoeffer, is the question: what is the will of God? Only through perceiving and acting upon God's will can the Christian remain in unity with God through Christ and proceed along the path of discipleship. Because he believed one could not know God's will in advance or assume that God's will corresponded to the way things currently existed, the task of moral discernment was essential. This became most clear in chapter 2 through the investigation of "God's Love," where he spoke of discerning God's will and self-examination. The fact that this manuscript could have been the preface to the entire *Ethics* suggests an added importance for the topic of discernment, as if Bonhoeffer intended the idea of discernment to provide the structure for his moral thinking in the remaining manuscripts. But even if "God's Love" were somehow proven not to be the intended preface, the centrality of discernment in *Ethics* and in Bonhoeffer's overall vision of the moral life would still be obvious. One can demonstrate this in two ways.

First, we see the theme of moral discernment appear again and again in his various approaches to Christian ethics using different motifs. For example, we saw that when he approached Christian ethics through the motif of *Christuswirklichkeit*, or Christ-reality, moral action hinged on an accurate perception of reality. Similarly, when he spoke of ethics as formation, the entire discussion presupposed a process of moral discernment that combined both simplicity and wisdom. One could say similar things about the motif of God's commandment or natural life: on all these occasions, the characteristics of simplicity and wisdom are present and the Christian must embrace each in order to discern and respond to God's will. At every turn, the task of discernment is crucial and serves as a unifying theme for the various approaches that Bonhoeffer makes to Christian ethics.

Moreover, while it is difficult to give a single label to his "understanding" or "theory" of Christian ethics, discernment provides the necessary language to speak of his ethical vision.[1] For him, Christian ethics is about the journey of discipleship, which involves listening to God's voice, perceiving Christ's presence in the world, and then responding accordingly. There is no program, method, or guiding principle to help determine the course of the Christian moral life; instead, one can only describe it as an ongoing process of discernment, seeking ever anew to do the good by responding to the reality of Christ in the world. Such a process is dynamic and creative and guided both by faith and by the shape and structure of reality. Such a process invites participation in the church, where one grows through spiritual exercise and relationship with others, and in the world, where one learns to have wisdom by seeing the world as both judged and redeemed.

Second, we find that throughout *Ethics*, and indeed throughout much of his writing that deals in some way with the Christian moral life, the idea of discernment, as an act that combines both simplicity and wisdom, structures his ethical expressions. He is constantly working within the tension represented by simplicity and wisdom and the continual interplay between the two stimulates his thinking and leads to many of his most creative formulations, such as the conceptual distinction between ultimate and penultimate. At times, he will emphasize one over the other: for instance, in *Discipleship* the theme of simplicity is primary. However, the opposite theme is always lying in the background, emerging now and then as a

---

1. Scholars have variously described Bonhoeffer's view of ethics, to name just a few examples, as deontological (Robin Lovin), teleological (James Burtness), situational (Fritz de Lange), contextual (Nancy Duff), and relational (Larry Rasmussen). While one could defend each of these designations to varying degrees, none of them adequately captures Bonhoeffer's overall vision. See Lovin, *Christian Faith*, 140; Burtness, *Shaping the Future*, 16; de Lange, *Waiting for the Word*, 114; Duff, "Dietrich Bonhoeffer's Theological Ethic," 270–73; Rasmussen, *Reality and Resistance*, 158–61.

Conclusion

reminder that the moral life must always operate within the space determined by both simplicity *and* wisdom. His moral thinking is a continual movement inward toward the simplicity of relationship with God, which names one's justified and sanctified life transformed by the form of Christ, and then outward toward the reality of the world, reconstituted by Christ, which names the necessary context for one's moral life. Of course, both of these movements are wholly Christological. Without this central space for Christology, Bonhoeffer's conception of discernment falls apart, as does his entire vision of Christian ethics. Thus, everything always comes back to Christ as its primary ground.

Perhaps the best image to capture this truth is his image of polyphony from *Letters and Papers from Prison*.[2] This is a musical term that refers to a complex composition consisting of many independent parts, yet held together by a central melody: the *cantus firmus*. He uses this image to speak of the multi-faceted nature of Christian life: it is directed toward many different loves and has many different points of reference, each of which has its own value and integrity insofar as it relates back to the *cantus firmus* of Christ. Dahill captures this beautifully when she writes:

> For Bonhoeffer, the image of polyphony evokes our participation in Christ whose resurrection draws us into the heart of the world, and whose own being in us is that *cantus firmus* in relation to whom our lives' own "counterpoint has a firm support and can't come adrift or get out of tune, while yet remaining a distinct whole in its own right."[3]

Because Christ exists as the *cantus firmus* of life, one remains grounded in Christ even as one engages deeply with the world. Moreover, Bonhoeffer argues: "Where the cantus firmus is clear and distinct, a counterpoint can develop as mightily as it wants."[4] This means, paradoxically, that the stronger one's connection to Christ in simple faith, the more deeply one can draw upon the natural world and natural human ability in the task of moral discernment.

---

2. DBWE 8:393–94, 397, 405.
3. Dahill, "Probing the Will of God," 47; cf. DBWE 8:394.
4. DBWE 8:394.

Becoming Simple and Wise

Reimagining Bonhoeffer

What vision of Bonhoeffer emerges from this study? Above all, it is the vision of a man whose mind is always at work, exploring new ideas, reworking old formulations, and boldly challenging the status quo. This is what makes him an interesting subject to study: one is always waiting for the next shift or development in his thinking or the next occasion where early ideas suddenly reappear, sometimes in a different form. More specifically, the Bonhoeffer that emerges is one who struggled throughout his life with the tension between a simple, unreflective approach to God's will and a rational, reflective approach. It was not only late in life, during his time in prison, that he expressed some hesitancy with the idea of simple obedience.[5] As demonstrated in chapter 5, this hesitancy was present even in the 1930s when he wrote *Discipleship*, the very text in which simple obedience finds its greatest expression. Thus, one must be cautious when attempting to make general characterizations of Bonhoeffer's different "periods" of thinking; it is far better to realize that throughout all the periods, despite the prominence of some themes over others at different times, one can usually find a dual concern for both simplicity and wisdom, which provides the starting point for the different formulations he offers.

In addition to this, the Bonhoeffer who emerges is also one who is not as negative about the natural world as some might assume, even though, at times, he might give that impression in his writings. Certainly, his Christological understanding of reality and his conception of the relationship between the ultimate and penultimate open the door for a positive account of the world; indeed, his writing in *Letters and Papers from Prison* bears this out. Still, his connection to Barth and his tendency sometimes to offer sharp criticisms of the world (e.g., in *Discipleship* or "God's Love") leaves readers wondering about the true place of the natural world within his vision of the moral life. But, as explored in chapter 6, the problem was never whether he desired a place for the natural world, but how he could adequately express that desire within his historical context. He finally arrived at his formulations of "the natural" and the "divine mandates," which gave him the language to illustrate the significance of the natural world, redeemed and reconstituted in Christ, as a context for Christian life.

Finally, the Bonhoeffer who emerges is not only a deep and creative thinker, but also a devoted Christian who knew the challenges of trying to

---

5. See ibid., 486.

Conclusion

discern God's will. The same man who produced rigorous academic and theological material was also the man who believed God could speak to him quite clearly through an encounter with a daily Bible reading. The same man who saw the immense value in setting aside time for his own academic work is also the man who found spiritual exercises such as prayer and Bible reading to be indispensable. It is no mistake that the spiritual practice of scriptural meditation influenced his thinking about the kind of moral reflection that could co-exist with the simplicity of discipleship. He was a practical theologian, and as such, drew upon his experience to inform his theology even as he allowed his theology to shape his experience. What might, in the end, seem an incongruous relationship, however, is merely an honest description of a real human individual who truly embodied aspects of both the simple faith and the rational, moral reflection he spoke of in his writings. This does not mean that Bonhoeffer was always correct in his own discernment; in fact, he would have admitted as much. For him, the act of moral discernment was an inevitably human act, but ultimately an act of faith. One has faith in God's mercy and judgment. One maintains hope in God's ultimate vindication, which has already begun in Christ. And one trusts that the greatest danger for Christian life is not to discern wrongly, but to avoid the activity altogether. To move forward on the path of discipleship one must seek to discern God's call in freedom, listening and responding to God's voice at each step of the moral journey.

Bibliography

Abromeit, Hans-Jürgen. *Das Geheimnis Christi. Dietrich Bonhoeffer erfahrungsbezogene Christologie*. Neukirchen-Vluyn: Neukirchener, 1991.

Adams, Robert Merrihew. *Finite and Infinite Goods: A Framework for Ethics*. New York: Oxford University Press, 1999.

Altenähr, Albert. *Dietrich Bonhoeffer—Lehrer des Gebets: Grundlagen für eine Theologie des Gebets bei Dietrich Bonhoeffer*. Würzburg: Echter, 1976.

Augustine. *Confessions*. Translated by R. S. Pine-Coffin. New York: Penguin Classics, 1961.

Ballor, Jordan J. "Christ in Creation: Bonhoeffer's Orders of Preservation and Natural Theology." *The Journal of Religion* 86 (2006) 1–22.

Barnett, Victoria. *For the Soul of the People: Protestant Protest Against Hitler*. New York: Oxford University Press, 1992.

Bartel, Michelle J. "The Rationality of Discernment in Christian Ethics." PhD diss., Princeton Theological Seminary, 1998.

Barth, Karl. *Church Dogmatics: The Doctrine of God*. Vol. 2/2. Edited by G. W. Bromiley and T. F. Torrance. Translated by G. W. Bromiley et al. Edinburgh: T. & T. Clark, 1957.

———. *Church Dogmatics: The Doctrine of Reconciliation*. Vol. 4/2. Edited by G. W. Bromiley and T. F. Torrance. Translated by G. W. Bromiley. Edinburgh: T. & T. Clark, 1958.

———. *Ethics*. Edited by Dietrich Braun. Translated by Geoffrey W. Bromiley. Edinburgh: T. & T. Clark, 1981.

Bergman, Marvin. "Moral Decision Making in the Light of Kohlberg and Bonhoeffer: A Comparison." *Religious Education* 69 (1974) 227–43.

———. "Teaching Ethics and Moral Decision-Making in Light of Dietrich Bonhoeffer." In *A Bonhoeffer Legacy: Essays in Understanding*, edited by A. J. Klassen, 367–80. Grand Rapids: Eerdmans, 1981.

Bethge, Eberhard. *Dietrich Bonhoeffer: A Biography*. Revised and edited by Victoria J. Barnett. Translated by Eric Mosbacher et al. Rev. ed. Minneapolis: Fortress, 2000.

Bethge, Eberhard, ed. *Die Mündige Welt*. 4 vols. Munich: Kaiser, 1956–1963.

Blackburn, Vivienne. *Dietrich Bonhoeffer and Simone Weil: A Study in Christian Responsiveness*. Oxford: Lang, 2004.

Bibliography

Bonhoeffer, Dietrich. *Act and Being: Transcendental Philosophy and Ontology in Systematic Theology*. Edited by Wayne Whitson Floyd, Jr. Translated by Martin Rumscheidt. DBWE 2. Minneapolis: Fortress, 1996.

———. *Akt und Sein: Transzendentalphilosophie und Ontologie in der systematischen Theologie*. Edited by Hans-Richard Reuter. DBW 2. Munich: Kaiser, 1988.

———. *Barcelona, Berlin, Amerika: 1928-1931*. Edited by Reinhart Staats et al. DBW 10. Gütersloh: Kaiser, 2005.

———. *Barcelona, Berlin, New York: 1928-1931*. Edited by Clifford J. Green. Translated by Douglas W. Stott. DBWE 10. Minneapolis: Fortress, 2008.

———. *Berlin: 1932-1933*. Edited by Carsten Nicolaisen and Ernst-Albert Scharffenorth. DBW 12. Gütersloh: Kaiser, 1997.

———. *Berlin: 1932-1933*. Edited by Larry Rasmussen. Translated by Isabel Best et al. DBWE 12. Minneapolis: Fortress, 2009.

———. *Conspiracy and Imprisonment: 1940-1945*. Edited by Mark S. Brocker. Translated by Lisa E. Dahill. DBWE 16. Minneapolis: Fortress, 2006.

———. *Creation and Fall: A Theological Exposition of Genesis 1-3*. Edited by John W. de Gruchy. Translated by Douglas Stephen Bax. DBWE 3. Minneapolis: Fortress, 1997.

———. *Discipleship*. Edited by Geffrey B. Kelly and John D. Godsey. Translated by Barbara Green and Reinhard Krauss. DBWE 4. Minneapolis: Fortress, 2001.

———. *Ecumenical, Academic, and Pastoral Work: 1931-1932*. Edited by Michael Lukens. Translated by Nicolas Humphreys et al. DBWE 11. Minneapolis: Fortress, 2012.

———. *Ethics*. Edited by Clifford J. Green. Translated by Reinhard Krauss et al. DBWE 6. Minneapolis: Fortress, 2005.

———. *Ethik*. Edited by Ilse Tödt et al. DBW 6. Gütersloh: Kaiser, 1998.

———. *Fiction from Tegel Prison*. Edited by Clifford J. Green. Translated by Nancy Lukens. DBWE 7. Minneapolis: Fortress, 2000.

———. *Fragmente aus Tegel*. Edited by Renate Bethge and Ilse Tödt. DBW 7. Gütersloh: Kaiser, 1994.

———. *Gemeinsames Leben* und *Das Gebetbuch der Bibel*. Edited by Gerhard Ludwig Müller and Albrecht Schönherr. DBW 5. Munich: Kaiser, 1987.

———. *Illegale Theologen-Ausbildung: Finkenwalde: 1935-1937*. Edited by Otto Dudzus et al. DBW 14. Gütersloh: Kaiser, 1996.

———. *Illegale Theologen-Ausbildung: Sammelvikariate: 1937-1940*. Edited by Dirk Schulz. DBW 15. Gütersloh: Kaiser, 1998.

———. *Jugend und Studium: 1918-1927*. Edited by Hans Pfeifer et al. DBW 9. Munich: Kaiser, 1986.

———. *Konspiration und Haft: 1940-1945*. Edited by Jørgen Glenthøj et al. DBW 16. Gütersloh: Kaiser, 1996.

———. *Letters and Papers from Prison*. Edited by John W. de Gruchy. Translated by Isabel Best et al. DBWE 8. Minneapolis: Fortress, 2010.

———. *Life Together* and *Prayerbook of the Bible*. Edited by Geffrey B. Kelly. Translated by Daniel W. Bloesch and James H. Burtness. DBWE 5. Minneapolis: Fortress, 2005.

———. *London: 1933-1935*. Edited by Hans Goedeking et al. DBW 13. Gütersloh: Kaiser, 1994.

———. *London: 1933-1935*. Edited by Keith W. Clements. Translated by Isabel Best. DBWE 13. Minneapolis: Fortress, 2007.

———. *Nachfolge*. Edited by Martin Kuske and Ilse Tödt. DBW 4. Munich: Kaiser, 1989.

Bibliography

———. *Ökumene, Universität, Pfarramt: 1931–1932*. Edited by Eberhard Amelung and Christoph Strohm. DBW 11. Gütersloh: Kaiser, 1994.

———. *Register und Ergänzungen*. Edited by Herbert Anzinger et al. DBW 17. Gütersloh: Kaiser, 1999.

———. *Sanctorum Communio: A Theological Study of the Sociology of the Church*. Edited by Clifford J. Green. Translated by Reinhard Krauss and Nancy Lukens. DBWE 1. Minneapolis: Fortress, 1998.

———. *Sanctorum Communio: Eine dogmatische Untersuchung zur Soziologie der Kirche*. Edited by Joachim von Soosten. DBW 1. Munich: Kaiser, 1986.

———. *Schöpfung und Fall: Theologische Auslegung von Genesis 1–3*. Edited by Martin Rüter and Ilse Tödt. DBW 3. Munich: Kaiser, 1989.

———. *Theological Education at Finkenwalde: 1935–1937*. Edited by H. Gaylon Barker and Stephen Plant. Translated by Douglas W. Stott. DBWE 14. Minneapolis: Fortress, 2013.

———. *Theological Education Underground: 1937–1940*. Edited by Victoria J. Barnett. Translated by Victoria J. Barnett et al. DBWE 15. Minneapolis: Fortress, 2012.

———. *Widerstand und Ergebung: Briefe und Aufzeichnungen aus der Haft*. Edited by Christian Gremmels et al. DBW 8. Gütersloh: Kaiser, 1998.

———. *The Young Bonhoeffer: 1918–1927*. Edited by Paul Duane Matheny et al. Translated by Mary C. Nebelsick and Douglas W. Stott. DBWE 9. Minneapolis: Fortress, 2003.

———. *Zettelnotizen für eine "Ethik."* Edited by Ilse Tödt. Gütersloh: Kaiser, 1993.

Bosanquet, Mary. *The Life and Death of Dietrich Bonhoeffer*. London: Hodder & Stoughton, 1968.

Brock, Brian. "Bonhoeffer and the Bible in Christian Ethics: Psalm 119, The Mandates, and Ethics as a 'Way.'" *Studies in Christian Ethics* 18 (2005) 7–29.

Burtness, James. *Shaping the Future: The Ethics of Dietrich Bonhoeffer*. Minneapolis: Fortress, 1985.

Carter, Guy Christopher, et al., eds. *Bonhoeffer's Ethics: Old Europe and New Frontiers*. Kampen, Netherlands: Kok Pharos, 1991.

"Celebrating the *Dietrich Bonhoeffer Works English Edition*." *Newsletter, International Bonhoeffer Society, English Language Section*, 99 (Summer 2010) 1.

Connor, William F. "The Natural Life of Man and its Laws: Conscience and Reason in the Theology of Dietrich Bonhoeffer." PhD diss., Vanderbilt University, 1973.

Conway, John S. *The Nazi Persecution of the Churches, 1933–45*. London: Weidenfeld and Nicolson, 1968.

Craig, Gordon Alexander. *Germany, 1866–1945*. Oxford: Oxford University Press, 1981.

Dahill, Lisa. "Particularity, Incarnation, and Discernment: Bonhoeffer's 'Christmas Spirituality.'" *Studies in Christian-Jewish Relations* 2 (2007) 68–76.

———. "Probing the Will of God: Bonhoeffer and Discernment." *Dialog: A Journal of Theology* 41 (2002) 42–47.

———. *Reading from the Underside of Selfhood: Bonhoeffer and Spiritual Formation*. Eugene, OR: Pickwick, 2009.

Day, Thomas. *Bonhoeffer on Christian Community and Common Sense*. New York: Mellen, 1982.

De Gruchy, John W. *Dietrich Bonhoeffer: Witness to Jesus Christ*. London: Collins, 1987.

———. "Editor's Introduction to the English Edition." In *Creation and Fall: A Theological Exposition of Genesis 1–3*, by Dietrich Bonhoeffer, 1–17. Edited by John W. de Gruchy. Translated by Douglas Stephen Bax. Minneapolis: Fortress, 1997.

Bibliography

———. "The Reception of Bonhoeffer's Theology." In *The Cambridge Companion to Dietrich Bonhoeffer*, edited by John W. de Gruchy, 93–109. Cambridge: Cambridge University Press, 1999.

Dietrich Bonhoeffer Sources, The. Columbia University Libraries: The Burke Library at Union Theological Seminary. http://library.columbia.edu/locations/burke/archives/bonhoeffer/sources.html (accessed February 9, 2015).

Dumas, André. *Dietrich Bonhoeffer: Theologian of Reality*. Translated by Robert McAfee Brown. London: SCM, 1971.

Ericksen, Robert P. *Theologians Under Hitler: Gerhard Kittel, Paul Althaus and Emmanuel Hirsch*. New Haven: Yale University Press, 1985.

Feil, Ernst. "Gewissen und Entscheidung. Der Beitrag Dietrich Bonhoeffers." In *Glaube als Widerstandskraft*, edited by Gotthard von Fuchs, 215–45. Frankfurt am Main: Knecht, 1986.

———. *The Theology of Dietrich Bonhoeffer*. Translated by Martin Rumscheidt. Minneapolis: Fortress, 1985.

Feil, Ernst, ed. *Internationale Bibliographie zu Dietrich Bonhoeffer*. Gütersloh: Kaiser, 1998.

Floyd, Wayne Whitson, Jr. "Bonhoeffer's Literary Legacy." In *The Cambridge Companion to Dietrich Bonhoeffer*, edited by John W. de Gruchy, 71–92. Cambridge: Cambridge University Press, 1999.

Ford, David. "Bonhoeffer, Holiness and Ethics." In *Holiness: Past and Present*, edited by Stephen C. Barton, 361–80. London: T. & T. Clark, 2003.

Frick, Peter, ed. *Bonhoeffer's Intellectual Formation: Theology and Philosophy in His Thought*. Tübingen: Mohr/Siebeck, 2008.

Friesen, Leroy Gene. "A Comparative Analysis of the Ethical Methodologies Employed by Dietrich Bonhoeffer in his 'Ethics' Fragments." PhD diss., University of Iowa, 1972.

Godsey, John. "Bonhoeffer's Doctrine of Love." In *New Studies in Bonhoeffer's Ethics*, edited by William J. Peck, 189–234. Lewiston, NY: E. Mellen, 1987.

———. *The Theology of Dietrich Bonhoeffer*. Philadelphia: Westminster, 1960.

Green, Clifford J. "Beyond Fundamentalism, Nationalism, Religion, and Secularism: Bonhoeffer's Quest for Authentic Christianity." Lecture, Tenth International Bonhoeffer Congress, Prague, Czech Republic, July 26, 2008.

———. *Bonhoeffer: A Theology of Sociality*. Rev. ed. Grand Rapids: Eerdmans, 1999.

———. "Editor's Introduction to the English Edition." In *Barcelona, Berlin, New York: 1928–1931*, by Dietrich Bonhoeffer, 1–50. Edited by Clifford J. Green. Translated by Douglas W. Stott. Minneapolis: Fortress, 2008.

———. "Editor's Introduction to the English Edition." In *Ethics*, by Dietrich Bonhoeffer, 1–44. Edited by Clifford J. Green. Translated by Reinhard Krauss et al. Minneapolis: Fortress, 2005.

———. "The Translation of Bonhoeffer's *Ethics*: A Response to Jennifer Moberly." *Studies in Christian Ethics* 23 (2010) 316–20.

Green, Clifford J. et al., eds. *Dietrich Bonhoeffer Jahrbuch 2: 2005/2006*. Gütersloh: Kaiser, 2005.

———. *Dietrich Bonhoeffer Jahrbuch 3: 2007/2008*. Gütersloh: Kaiser, 2008.

———. *Dietrich Bonhoeffer Jahrbuch 4: 2009/2010*. Gütersloh: Kaiser, 2010.

Gremmels, Christian, and Hans Pfeifer, eds. *Dietrich Bonhoeffer Jahrbuch: 2003*. Gütersloh: Kaiser, 2003.

Bibliography

Gustafson, James. "Moral Discernment in the Christian Life." In *Norm and Context in Christian Ethics*, edited by Gene Outka and Paul Ramsey, 17–36. New York: Scribner's, 1968.

Harvey, Barry. "Augustine and Thomas Aquinas in the Theology of Dietrich Bonhoeffer." In *Bonhoeffer's Intellectual Formation: Theology and Philosophy in His Thought*, edited by Peter Frick, 11–30. Tübingen: Mohr/Siebeck, 2008.

Haynes, Stephen R. *The Bonhoeffer Phenomenon*. Minneapolis: Augsburg Fortress, 2004.

Huber, Wolfgang. "Bonhoeffer and Modernity." In *Theology and the Practice of Responsibility: Essays on Dietrich Bonhoeffer*, edited by Wayne Whitson Floyd, Jr. and Charles Marsh, 5–19. Valley Forge, PA: Trinity, 1994.

Huber, Wolfgang, ed. *Ethik im Ernstfall. Dietrich Bonhoeffers Stellung zu den Juden und ihre Aktualität*. Munich: Kaiser, 1982.

Kelly, Geffrey B., and John D. Godsey. "Editors' Introduction to the English Edition." In *Discipleship*, edited by Geffrey B. Kelly and John D. Godsey, translated by Barbara Green and Reinhard Krauss, 77–88. Minneapolis: Fortress, 2001.

Kelly, Geffrey B., and F. Burton Nelson. *The Cost of Moral Leadership: The Spirituality of Dietrich Bonhoeffer*. Grand Rapids: Eerdmans, 2003.

Kilby, Karen. *The SPCK Introduction to Karl Rahner*. Rev. ed. London: SPCK, 2007.

Kittel, Gerhard, ed. *Theological Dictionary of the New Testament*. Vol 2. Edited and translated by Geoffrey W. Bromiley. Grand Rapids: Eerdmans, 1964.

Laney, J. T. "An Examination of Bonhoeffer's Ethical Contextualism." In *A Bonhoeffer Legacy: Essays in Understanding*, edited by A.J. Klassen, 194–213. Grand Rapids: Eerdmans, 1981.

Lawrence, Joel. *Bonhoeffer: A Guide for the Perplexed*. London: T. & T. Clark, 2010.

Liguš, Ján. "Ultimate, Penultimate and Their Impact." In *Bonhoeffer's Ethics: Old Europe and New Frontiers*, edited by Guy Christopher Carter et al., 59–77. Kampen, Netherlands: Kok Pharos, 1991.

Luther, Martin. *Lectures on Galatians 1535: Chapters 1–4*. Edited by Jaroslav Pelikan and Walter A. Hansen. Translated by Jaroslav Pelikan. Luther's Works 26. St. Louis: Concordia, 1963

———. "A Simple Way to Pray." In *Devotional Writings II*, edited by Gustav K. Wiencke and Helmut T. Lehmann, translated by Carl J. Schindler, 193–211. Luther's Works 43. Philadelphia: Fortress, 1968.

Manoussakis, John Panteleimon. "'At the Recurrent End of the Uneding': Bonhoeffer's Eschatology of the Pentultimate." In *Bonhoeffer and Continental Thought*, edited by Brian Gregor and Jens Zimmermann, 226–44. Bloomington: Indiana University Press, 2009.

Marsh, Charles. *Strange Glory: A Life of Dietrich Bonhoeffer*. New York: Knopf, 2014.

Mayer, Rainer. "Die Bedeutung von Bonhoeffers Mandatenlehre für eine moderne politische Ethik." In *Dietrich Bonhoeffer heute. Die Aktualität seines Lebens und Werk*, edited by Rainer Mayer and Peter Zimmerling, 58–80. Giessen, Germany: Brunnen, 1992.

McGrath, Alister E. *The Open Secret: A New Vision for Natural Theology*. Malden, MA: Blackwell, 2008.

Moberly, Jennifer. "'Felicity to the Original Text'? The Translation of Bonhoeffer's *Ethics*." *Studies in Christian Ethics* 22 (2009) 226–56.

Mokrosch, Reinhold. "Das Gewissensverständnis Dietrich Bonhoeffers. Reformatorische Herkunft und politische Funktion." In *Bonhoeffer und Luther. Zur Sozialgestalt des*

Bibliography

Luthertums in der Moderne, edited by Christian Gremmels, 59-92. Munich: Kaiser, 1983.

Moltmann, Jürgen. "Die Wirklichkeit der Welt und Gottes Konkretes Gebot nach Detirch Bonhoeffer." In *Die Mündige Welt III*, edited by Eberhard Bethge, 42-67. Munich: Kaiser, 1960.

Müller, Gerhard Ludwig, and Albrecht Schönherr. "Editors' Afterword to the German Edition." In *Life Together* and *Prayerbook of the Bible*, edited by Geffrey B. Kelly, translated by Daniel W. Bloesch and James H. Burtness, 119-40. Minneapolis: Fortress, 2005.

Müller, Hanfried. *Von der Kirche zur Welt: ein Beitrag zu der Beziehung des Wortes Gottes auf die societas in Dietrich Bonhoeffers theologischer Entwicklung*. Leipzig: Koehler & Amelang, 1961.

Muers, Rachel. *Keeping God's Silence: Towards a Theological Ethics of Communication*. Oxford: Blackwell, 2004.

Nation, Mark Thiessen, et al. *Bonhoeffer the Assassin? Challenging the Myth, Recovering His Call to Peacemaking*. Grand Rapids: Baker Academic, 2013.

Northcott, Michael. "'Who Am I?' Human Identity and the Spiritual Disciplines in the Witness of Dietrich Bonhoeffer." In *Who Am I? Bonhoeffer's Theology through His Poetry*, edited by Bernd Wannenwetsch, 11-29. London: T. & T. Clark, 2009.

O'Donovan, Oliver. "The Moral Authority of Scripture." In *Scripture's Doctrine and Theology's Bible: How the New Testament Shapes Christian Dogmatics*, edited by Markus Bockmuehl and Alan Torrance, 165-75. Grand Rapids: Baker Academic, 2008.

Ott, Heinrich. *Reality and Faith: The Theological Legacy of Dietrich Bonhoeffer*. Translated by Alex A. Morrison. Philadelphia: Fortress, 1972.

Pangritz, Andreas. "Dietrich Bonhoeffer: 'Within, not Outside, the Barthian Movement.'" In *Bonhoeffer's Intellectual Formation: Theology and Philosophy in His Thought*, edited by Peter Frick, 245-82. Tübingen: Mohr/Siebeck, 2008.

———. *Karl Barth in the Theology of Dietrich Bonhoeffer*. Grand Rapids: Eerdmans, 2000.

———. "Theological Motives in Dietrich Bonhoeffer's Decision to Participate in Political Resistance." In *Reflections on Bonhoeffer: Essays in Honor of F. Burton Nelson*, edited by Geffrey B. Kelly and C. John Weborg, 32-49. Chicago: Covenant, 1999.

———. "Who is Jesus Christ, for us, today?" In *The Cambridge Companion to Dietrich Bonhoeffer*, edited by John W. de Gruchy, 134-53. Cambridge: Cambridge University Press, 1999.

Peck, William J., ed. *New Studies in Bonhoeffer's Ethics*. Lewiston, NY: Mellen, 1987.

Pelikan, Herbert Rainer. *Die Frömmigkeit Dietrich Bonhoeffers: Dokumentation, Grundlinien, Entwicklung*. Vienna: Herder, 1982.

Pelikan, Jaroslav. "Bonhoeffer's Christologie of 1933." In *The Place of Bonhoeffer*, edited by Martin E. Marty, 145-64. London: SCM, 1963.

Pfeifer, Hans. "An Aesthetic Voyage: Dietrich Bonhoeffer's Gradual Approach towards Full Reality and Eberhard Bethge's Contribution to It." *Journal of Theology for Southern Africa* 127 (2007) 63-81.

———. "Learning Faith and Ethical Commitment in the Context of Spiritual Training Groups: Consequences of Dietrich Bonhoeffer's Post Doctoral Year in New York City, 1930-31." In *Dietrich Bonhoeffer Jahrbuch 3*, edited by Clifford J. Green et al., 251-79. Gütersloh: Gütersloher, 2008.

Pfeifer, Hans, ed. *Frieden—das unumgängliche Wagnis*. Munich: Kaiser, 1982.

Bibliography

Philips, John. *Christ for Us in the Theology of Dietrich Bonhoeffer.* New York: Harper, 1967.
Plant, Stephen. *Bonhoeffer.* London: Continuum, 2004.
———. "The Sacrament of Ethical Reality: Dietrich Bonhoeffer on Ethics for Christian Citizens." *Studies in Christian Ethics* 18 (2005) 71–87.
Pugh, Jeffrey C. *Religionless Christianity: Dietrich Bonhoeffer in Troubled Times.* London: T. & T. Clark, 2008.
Rasmussen, Larry. *Dietrich Bonhoeffer: Reality and Resistance.* Rev. ed. Nashville: Abingdon, 2005.
———. "A Question of Method." In *New Studies in Bonhoeffer's Ethics,* edited by William J. Peck, 103–38. Lewiston, NY: Mellen, 1987.
Reuter, Hans-Richard. "Editor's Afterword to the German Edition." In *Act and Being: Transcendental Philosophy and Ontology in Systematic Theology,* edited by Wayne Whitson Floyd, Jr., translated by Martin Rumscheidt, 162–83. Minneapolis: Fortress, 1996.
Robinson, John A. T. *Honest to God.* London: SCM, 1963.
Rüter, Martin, and Ilse Tödt, "Editors' Afterword to the German Edition." In *Creation and Fall: A Theological Exposition of Genesis 1–3,* edited by John W. de Gruchy, translated by Douglas Stephen Bax, 1–22. Minneapolis: Fortress, 1997.
Rumscheidt, Martin. "The Significance of Adolf von Harnack and Reinhold Seeberg for Dietrich Bonhoeffer." In *Bonhoeffer's Intellectual Formation: Theology and Philosophy in His Thought,* edited by Peter Frick, 201–24. Tübingen: Mohr/Siebeck, 2008.
Schliesser, Christine. *Everyone Who Acts Responsibly Becomes Guilty: Bonhoeffer's Concept of Accepting Guilt.* Louisville: Westminster John Knox, 2008.
Schlingensiepen, Ferdinand. *Dietrich Bonhoeffer, 1906–1945: Martyr, Thinker, Man of Resistance.* Translated by Isabel Best. London: T. & T. Clark, 2010.
Tietz, Christiane. "Bonhoeffer on the Uses and Limits of Philosophy." In *Bonhoeffer and Continental Thought,* edited by Brian Gregor and Jens Zimmermann, 31–45. Bloomington: Indiana University Press, 2009.
Tödt, Heinz Eduard. "Dietrich Bonhoeffer's Practice of Conscience and Ethical Theory of Conscience." In *Authentic Faith: Bonhoeffer's Theological Ethics in Context,* edited by Ernst-Albert Scharffenorth and Glen Harold Stassen, translated by David Stassen and Ilse Tödt, 151–68. Grand Rapids: Eerdmans, 2007.
———. "Dietrich Bonhoeffer's Theological Ethics and Human Rights." In *Authentic Faith: Bonhoeffer's Theological Ethics in Context,* edited by Ernst-Albert Scharffenorth and Glen Harold Stassen, translated by David Stassen and Ilse Tödt, 142–50. Grand Rapids: Eerdmans, 2007.
Tödt, Ilse. "Appendix 2: Preparing the German Edition of *Ethics.*" In *Ethics,* by Dietrich Bonhoeffer, edited by Clifford J. Green, translated by Reinhard Krauss et al., 467–76. Minneapolis: Fortress, 2005.
———. "Paradoxical Obedience: Dietrich Bonhoeffer's Theological Ethics 1933–1945." *Lutheran Theological Journal* 35 (2001) 3–16.
Tödt, Ilse, et al. "Editors' Afterword to the German Edition." In *Ethics,* by Dietrich Bonhoeffer, edited by Clifford J. Green, translated by Reinhard Krauss et al., 3–55. Minneapolis: Fortress, 2005.
Wannenwetsch, Bernd, "The Fourfold Pattern of Christian Moral Reasoning According to the New Testament." In *Scripture's Doctrine and Theology's Bible: How the New Testament Shapes Christian Dogmatics,* edited by Markus Bockmuehl and Alan Torrance, 177–90. Grand Rapids: Baker Academic, 2008.

Bibliography

———. "The Whole Christ and the Whole Human Being: Dietrich Bonhoeffer's Inspiration for the 'Christology and Ethics' Discourse." In *Christology and Ethics*, edited by F. LeRon Shults and Brent Waters, 75–98. Grand Rapids: Eerdmans, 2010.

Webster, John. *Word and Church: Essays in Christian Dogmatics*. Edinburgh: T. & T. Clark, 2001.

Zimmermann, Jens. "Suffering with the World: The Continuing Relevance of Dietrich Bonhoeffer's Theology." In *Dietrich Bonhoeffer Jahrbuch 3*, edited by Clifford J. Green et al., 311–38. Gütersloh: Gütersloher, 2008.

Index

Abwehr, 12
Act and Being (DBWE 2), 5, 21, 36, 62, 90, 170, 171, 174
Adam, 22, 24, 92, 102, 133, 152, 165
   humans existing in, 21, 36, 43, 56, 98, 99
aufheben, 23, 35

Barth, Karl, 4, 5n10, 16n60, 22n9, 87, 128n34, 144n103, 145n105, 150–51, 165n61, 184
"Basic Questions of a Christian Ethic," 122–25
Bethge, Eberhard, 4n8, 5, 6, 7, 11, 16, 17, 70, 115n202, 118
Bible, 6, 7, 10, 63, 81n18, 94, 109, 111, 113, 115–16, 124, 125, 126, 130, 131, 134, 141, 142, 143, 150, 151, 157, 168, 176, 185
   Luther Bible, 38, 41n98, 93n81, 128n34, 136n69
   meditation on the, 7, 109, 111, 112, 114, 141, 143, 185
Bonhoeffer, Dietrich
   biography, 3–12
   vision of Christian ethics. *See* Christian ethics, Bonhoeffer's vision of

cantus firmus, 15, 57, 183
casuistry, 29, 32, 41, 46 51, 54, 84–85, 157, 161
Catholic moral theology, 46, 85, 157
"Christ and Peace," 128, 131–32
Christ, Jesus, 5, 6, 20–21, 29–35, 44, 45, 47–49, 50, 51, 52, 53, 54, 56–57, 58–60, 61–69, 72, 74, 76, 82–83, 99, 102, 106, 110, 113, 118, 122–23, 125, 133–38, 151, 159, 164, 174–75, 177–78
   bringing together simplicity and wisdom, 44, 49, 54, 56–57, 65–66, 76
   call to discipleship. *See* Discipleship, Jesus' call to
   as origin, essence, and goal, 62, 106
   and the Pharisees, 20–21, 28–35, 44, 50–51, 56, 178
   two natures of, 2, 18, 58–60, 65, 73
   See also Christology; form of Christ
Christ-reality, 18, 60–69, 82, 100, 162, 172–73, 182
"Christ, Reality, and Good," 17n68, 17n69, 61, 63, 65, 68, 172
Christian ethics, 14, 17, 20, 46, 60n17, 62, 66–68, 74, 80, 96, 129, 138, 155, 157, 175

Index

Christian ethics (continued)
  Bonhoeffer's vision of, 2, 17, 19, 21–38, 63, 66–68, 79–85, 114, 118, 121, 123–25, 129, 140, 144–52, 159, 160–63, 179–80, 181–83
  as formation, 77–78, 82–85, 88, 99, 118
  methodological approach to, 2, 13, 17, 45, 91, 121, 160–62, 182
Christology
  Bonhoeffer's understanding of, 56–76, 86, 91, 92, 171
  and discernment, 43, 53, 54, 183
  and natural theology, 156
  relieving the tension between simplicity and moral reflection, 18, 52
Christuswirklichkeit. *See* Christ-reality
"Church and World," 176–79
commandment, 1, 4, 5, 7, 13, 25, 28, 30, 42, 50, 53, 57, 67, 74–75, 81, 82, 83, 89, 95, 100, 101, 120–37, 140–54, 165–67, 170–71, 180
  concrete, 26, 39, 42, 52, 120, 126–33, 150–51, 153
  paradoxical interpretation of, 134–36
  solemn and everyday form, 148–49
community, 7, 14, 60, 89, 99, 100, 105, 138, 145, 160
  Christ in the form of, 59, 76, 86, 90, 91
  with Jesus, 135–36
Confessing Church, 3, 8–9, 111, 177
confession
  of faith, 177
  mutual, 111, 116
  of sins, 7, 27, 101, 109
conformation to Christ, 2, 15, 18–19, 43, 45, 47, 54, 58, 76, 77–78, 85, 88, 91–92, 96–107, 112, 116, 118–19, 125, 137, 164. *See also* formation, Christian; form of Christ
conscience, 11, 19, 27–28, 29, 31n56, 32, 79–80, 133–34, 154–55
  redeemed, 27–28, 175
  role in discernment, 28, 170, 173–75, 179

cor curvum in se, 25, 62
creation, 22, 61, 62–64, 67, 68, 86, 89, 91–98, 99, 106, 129–31, 155–58, 168–69
  See also natural world; natural life; orders of creation; *Creation and Fall*
Creation and Fall (DBWE 3), 8, 22, 62, 78, 86, 91–98, 100, 109, 120, 132, 163

Dahill, Lisa, 3, 14, 15, 47, 68, 90, 116, 183
discernment, 1–2, 16–17, 20–21, 28, 32, 35, 37, 38–49, 51–53, 54–55, 57, 58, 60n17, 67–68, 73–74, 76, 77–78, 80–85, 88, 90, 104–7, 107–9, 114, 116–19, 121, 124, 128n40, 130, 131, 134,138, 141, 144, 150, 154–55, 156, 164, 167–68, 169, 170–73, 179–80, 181–83, 185
  in Bonhoeffer's life. *See* Bonhoeffer, Dietrich, biography
  of God's will, 1–2, 13, 15–16, 18, 20–21, 28, 30–32, 37, 38–49, 51–52, 54–55, 56–57, 75, 77–78, 83, 116–19, 123–24, 130, 133, 138, 149, 152–53, 154, 167, 169, 170–73, 176, 180. 181–82, 184–85
  exclusivity of, 34–35, 176–79
  inclusivity of, 34–35, 176–79
  scholarly work on, 12–15
  See also prüfen (Prüfung); Christology, and discernment; love, as a guide for discernment; mandates, divine, as guides to discernment
discipleship, 4, 7, 15, 37, 45, 53, 98, 99, 100–101, 105, 109–111, 117, 126, 128, 132, 134, 135, 137–38, 140–43, 144, 148, 152, 159, 162, 164, 168–69, 181–82, 185
  Jesus' call to, 64, 88, 121, 134
Discipleship (DBWE 4), 8, 17, 18, 30n49, 31n58, 36, 41n98, 63, 64, 65, 75, 76, 83, 84, 86, 91, 98, 99, 100, 101n124, 102, 103, 105, 106, 110,

Index

111, 117, 121, 122, 126, 128, 132–39, 140, 151, 165, 171, 177, 184
disunity, 24, 27, 30, 34, 46, 49, 60, 64, 97, 122, 149
   with God, 20, 21, 22, 27–29, 32, 33, 34, 44, 46, 50, 97, 120, 176
   in the moral life, 30, 34, 52, 55, 68, 98, 99n111
divine command ethics. *See* "The 'Ethical' and the 'Christian' as a Topic"
doing the word, 21, 26, 30–31, 49–50, 110, 117
Dumas, André, 56n1, 67, 86–87, 92, 165n63

Einfalt. See simplicity
Erhaltungsordnungen. See orders of preservation
"The 'Ethical' and the 'Christian' as a Topic," 144–52
ethical formalism, 84–85
ethical principles (norms), 1, 29, 30, 32, 41, 48, 54, 61, 66, 79, 81, 82, 84, 89, 124–25, 130, 142, 147, 150, 160–62, 169, 171, 182
ethical theory, 78–82, 118–19, 121, 182
Ethics (DBWE 6), 1, 3, 4n7, 12, 13, 16–18, 20, 24, 36, 38, 39, 40, 42n105, 48, 53–54, 57, 61, 64–65, 69, 74, 75–76, 85, 86, 91, 97–98, 100–101, 102, 105, 106, 107, 113, 115, 120, 121, 123, 125, 128, 136, 140, 144, 146n110, 154, 161, 162, 163, 165, 171, 174, 177, 181, 182
"Ethics as Formation," 75, 78–88, 91, 103, 105
exercitium. See spiritual exercise

fall, the, 22, 24, 123, 133, 152, 165
Finkenwalde, 8, 45n119, 108, 113n188, 115n202
form of Christ, 1, 43, 56, 57, 59, 76, 77–78, 84, 85–91, 92, 98–99, 101–107, 112, 118–19, 158, 180, 183
   as incarnate, crucified, and risen, 62, 76, 83, 85, 87, 88, 91, 99, 101–107

   as Word, sacrament, and church-community, 59, 76, 86, 88–91
   See also formation, Christian; conformation to Christ
formation, Christian 14, 27, 43, 53, 76, 77–78, 82–84, 87–107, 110–11, 115, 118–19, 139, 166
   in *Creation and Fall,* 91–98
   See also conformation to Christ; form of Christ
freedom, 24, 25n22, 31, 34, 37, 42, 46, 54, 57, 79, 86n40, 92, 94, 95–96, 104, 110, 115, 117, 125, 130, 132, 136, 145, 146–49, 151, 157, 160n27, 167, 177, 185
   and obedience, 24, 57
   and simplicity, 31, 44, 56, 153

Gebot Gottes. See commandment
German Idealism, 25, 62, 88n57
Gestalt Christi. See form of Christ
Gestaltung. See formation
Gleichgestaltung. See conformation to Christ
"God's Love and the Disintegration of the World," 4n7, 16–18, 20–55, 56, 61, 68, 73, 74, 77, 81, 83, 88, 96, 97, 105, 116, 128n39, 133, 136n69, 139, 142, 145, 154, 167, 170, 174, 176, 178–80, 181, 184
God's Will, 10, 27, 30–31, 34, 35, 37, 50, 51–53, 61, 64, 67, 69, 75, 81, 89, 108, 112, 121, 123–24, 145n104, 155–56
   discernment of. *See* discernment, of God's will.
Green, Clifford, 12n39, 16, 36n75, 101n120, 103n132, 173–74

hearing the word, 1, 5, 21, 49–51, 53, 54, 74, 78, 82, 109, 110, 112, 114, 117, 130, 132, 137, 142, 150
Hegel, G. W. F., 16n60, 23, 87
"History and Good," 44, 48, 53n152, 83
Holy Spirit, 32, 42–43, 66, 67, 83, 93, 97, 99, 107, 113, 115n199, 150n130

Index

human nature, 102–4, 119, 154
   of Christ, 59
   fallen, 102
   the image of God (Christ) in, 22, 83, 92, 94, 97, 100, 102, 106

immediacy
   Christological, 63–64, 81
   of God's word, 7, 131
is and ought, 28, 66, 85, 129
"Is There a Christian Ethic?," 126–27

judgment, 42, 44, 49, 149, 173, 182
   Christian judgment, 31–32, 47, 51, 54. 105
   God's judgment, 10, 44, 49, 71, 81, 102, 104–5, 128, 185
   via the knowledge of good and evil, 23, 25–26, 28, 50–51, 54, 174, 176
   of the Pharisees, 29–30, 33, 47, 50–51, 178
justification, 34, 45, 69–72, 73, 97, 99, 102, 154, 158, 174, 183

Kant, Immanuel, 16n60, 169
Kantian ethics, 46, 84
Kantianism, 147
kingdom of God, 72, 159
knowledge of good and evil, 20, 22–23, 25–26, 28, 30–35, 44, 46, 47–49, 51, 54, 56, 83, 123, 131, 134, 137, 139, 142, 152–53, 162, 173–74, 180

law, 29, 32, 34, 35, 50, 75, 95, 115, 130, 134, 146, 148, 161, 163, 168, 175, 176,
   of God, 50, 52, 57, 130, 136, 143–44
Lectures on Christology, 57, 58–60, 62, 86, 113n190, 132, 171
Letters and Papers from Prison (DBWE 8), 12, 81n18, 139, 184
Life Together (DBWE 5), 8, 63n38, 111, 113
love, 52–53, 81, 116, 122, 123, 183
   of God, 21, 24, 52–53, 102, 103, 124
   as a guide for discernment, 14, 43
   toward others, 42, 72, 112, 124, 127, 131, 161, 173, 175
Luther, Martin, 6n14, 16n60, 25, 34, 38, 48, 62, 83n25, 87, 93, 114, 168,
Lutheran tradition, 46, 166n63

mandates, divine, 124n15, 150–53, 155, 158, 164–70, 175, 179, 184,
   as guides to discernment, 167–70
McGrath, Alistair, 155–56
meditation, 113, 116, 117, 142
   on the Bible. *See* Bible, meditation on the
meditative reflection, 2, 114, 121, 140–44, 152–53, 168
Mitte, 62–64
moral deliberation, 2, 13n47, 31, 35, 37, 41, 52, 57, 119, 125, 131, 145–46, 154, 160. *See also* moral reflection
moral reflection, 11, 13, 18, 19, 20–21, 22–23, 26, 28, 31n56, 32–33, 35–38, 43, 44, 46, 47, 49–53, 54–55, 56–57, 58, 60, 65–66, 69, 73, 74–76, 78, 84, 107, 113, 119, 120–21, 126, 131–32, 134, 136–39, 140–44, 146, 152–53, 154, 162, 168, 173–75, 176, 184–85
   and simplicity. *See* simplicity, and moral reflection
   See also moral deliberation

natural life, 19, 96, 147, 153, 154, 157–64, 170, 180, 182. *See also* creation; natural world
natural theology, 155–57
natural world, 19, 62, 65, 82, 84, 97, 104, 119, 121, 125, 148, 152, 154–64, 165–66, 167, 170, 172, 173, 176, 179–80. 183, 184. *See also* creation; natural life

"On the Theological Foundation of the Work of the World Alliance," 127n27, 128n34, 129, 131, 140, 165
orders of creation, 1, 68, 130, 150, 158, 164–66

Index

orders of preservation, 130–31, 165
"the ought," 146–48

peace, 5, 8, 9, 12, 125–26
penultimate world, 2, 110–11, 121, 146, 152, 153, 154–55, 156, 158, 163–64, 170, 175, 179. *See also* ultimate and penultimate
Pharisees, 20–21, 28–35, 46, 47, 50–51, 56, 68n61, 81, 96, 97, 138, 145, 178
prayer, 7, 60, 101n124, 108, 109, 110, 111, 112, 114–16, 117–18, 127, 141–43, 164, 185
prüfen (Prüfung), 13, 16, 20, 29, 38–41, 44, 45n117, 49, 176, 178. *See also* discernment

reality, 15, 24, 37, 42, 44, 45, 46, 53, 70–75, 79, 80–82, 83, 85, 86, 87–88, 99, 101, 103n132, 104, 106–107, 112, 116–17, 118, 125, 127, 129–31, 135, 136, 139, 145n104, 147, 148, 150, 151, 153, 156–57, 159, 160, 167, 168–70, 172–73, 174, 176–77, 182
  acting in accordance with, 104, 130, 159, 176–78
  Christological understanding of, 2, 40, 57, 60–69, 80–82, 184
  and possibility, 29n42, 134
  structure of, 84, 86, 92, 106, 130, 147, 150, 153, 155, 164, 166, 167–70, 180, 182
  of the world, 2, 46–47, 55, 71, 75, 82, 84, 90, 98, 100, 104, 121, 144, 155, 156–57, 159, 162, 163, 164, 179–80, 183
  See also Christ-reality
reason, 2, 19, 29, 32, 42, 45, 51, 58–59, 60, 63, 75, 79–80, 82, 119, 133, 134, 136, 153, 154, 155, 162, 176, 179
  in discernment, 162, 170–73
  as a source of revelation, 172–73
reconciliation, 22, 24, 27, 28, 30–32, 34, 44n114, 46, 51, 52, 53, 59–60, 63, 65–66, 67–68, 69, 76, 85, 86, 105, 133, 145, 148, 160, 163, 181. *See also* unity
religious enthusiasm, 46, 55
responsibility, 21, 80, 104, 132, 134, 175
resurrection 33n63, 48, 71, 87, 88, 92, 96, 102, 106, 163–64, 183
rights
  and duties, 159–160
  natural, 125, 160

sacrament, 116, 129, 131
  of reality, 129, 131, 179
sanctification, 45, 99–101, 110, 117, 183
Sanctorum Communio (DBWE 1), 5, 21, 36, 62, 90, 96
Schöpfungsordnungen. See orders of creation
Scripture. *See* Bible
Selbstprüfung. See Self-examination
Self-examination (self-reflection), 2, 16, 20, 21, 28, 32, 38, 39, 40, 44, 47–49, 51, 54–55, 56, 83, 116–17, 139, 152–53, 170, 163–75, 180, 181
Sermon on the Mount, 5, 6–7, 50, 101n120, 110n168, 123, 125, 126, 130, 131, 133
shame, 27
simple faith, 2, 35, 37, 42, 46, 75, 119, 120, 131, 180, 183, 185. *See also* simple obedience; simplicity
simple obedience, 2, 11, 13, 14n47, 19, 23, 35, 37–38, 51, 52, 57, 65–66, 74–75, 81, 113, 114, 119, 120–26, 131–32, 132–39, 140, 144, 148, 151, 152, 154, 159, 162, 171, 179, 184
  and moral deliberation, 31, 35, 37
  and moral reflection, 13, 14n47, 52, 65–66, 74–75, 120, 126, 138–39, 140, 144, 152–53, 162
  tension with moral reflection. *See* simplicity, tension with moral reflection
  See also simplicity; simple faith

Index

simplicity, 2, 18–19, 21, 23, 25, 28, 30–31, 34, 35–37, 41, 43, 44, 49–53, 54, 56, 57, 58, 60, 65, 69, 73–76, 77–78, 81, 82, 85, 106–7, 114n195, 118–19, 120–121, 126, 132 136–39, 140, 149, 152–53, 154, 162, 164, 170, 172, 173, 181–85
   of discernment, 120–153
   and moral reflection, 2, 18, 21, 23, 28, 35–36, 43, 49–53, 54, 56, 57, 58, 60, 65, 69, 73–76, 140, 185
   tension with moral reflection, 2, 13, 18, 20–21, 23, 28, 33, 35–37, 47, 49, 54, 56, 74, 119, 121, 140, 162, 182, 184
   and wisdom ("simple and wise"), 37, 58, 73, 75–76, 77–78, 81, 82, 85, 106–107, 118–19, 137–39, 162, 168, 172, 182–84
simul justus et peccator, 34
spiritual exercise (spiritual practice), 2, 4, 7, 15, 19, 77, 78, 91, 101 107–19, 143, 182, 185
Stellvertreter, 86
subjectivism, 31, 55, 121, 151

temptation, 30, 34, 75, 113, 174
   of the serpent, 24, 26, 42, 133, 138

theological anthropology, 18, 20, 21–28, 36n75, 91
ultimate and penultimate, 18, 57, 60, 69–75, 105, 119, 147, 159–60, 180, 182, 184. *See also* penultimate world
"Ultimate and Penultimate Things," 69–75, 105
unity, 51, 73, 87, 97, 98, 99n111, 101, 102, 122, 136n69, 143, 176
   between simplicity and wisdom/moral reflection, 18, 85, 107, 118
   with God (Christ), 20–21, 22–24, 27, 28–30, 31, 32, 34, 35, 44, 46, 49, 50, 52, 69, 74, 75, 81, 82, 92, 122, 133, 145, 172, 176, 181
   with the self, 27, 28, 31, 173–75
   See also disunity

vicarious representative action, 104, 115n200

"What Does It Mean to Tell the Truth?," 169–70
wisdom, 2, 73–74, 75, 77, 78, 81–82, 85, 106, 107, 115, 118–19, 137–38, 139, 162, 164, 172, 182–83, 184
worldliness, 55, 65, 162n39, 163–64

www.ingramcontent.com/pod-product-compliance
Lightning Source LLC
Chambersburg PA
CBHW070325230426
43663CB00011B/2219